My Heroes
Have Always Been Indians

Cora J. Voyageur, Ph.D.
Department of Sociology
University of Calgary

DETSELIG
ENTERPRISES LTD

Detselig Enterprises Ltd.
Calgary, Alberta

My Heroes Have Always Been Indians
© 2010 Cora J. Voyageur

Library and Archives Canada Cataloging in Publication
Voyageur, Cora Jane, 1956-

Includes bibliographical references.
ISBN 978-1-55059-387-7
    1. Indians of North America – Alberta – Biography.
2. Métis – Alberta – Biography. 3. Alberta – Biography.
I. Title

E78.A34V68 2010   971.23004'9700922   C2010-901782-X

Detselig Enterprises Ltd.   www.temerondetselig.com
210, 1220 Kensington Rd NW   temeron@telusplanet.net
Calgary, Alberta, Canada   DETSELIG   Phone: 403-283-0900
T2N 3P5   ENTERPRISES LTD   Fax: 403-283-6947

We acknowledge the support of the Government of Canada through
the Canada Books Program for our publishing program.

We also acknowledge the support of the Alberta Foundation for the
Arts for our publishing program.   Alberta Foundation for the Arts

Cover photo of Maggie Black Kettle by Terry Lusty
Cover design by James Dangerous

ISBN 978-1-55059-387-7   Printed in Canada

Preface

The germ of this project was born out of two events. The first was a discussion I had with Clayton Blood. Clayton is a man who had been my boss over five summers when I worked for the Indian Management Assistance Program (IMAP) as a graduate student and someone I respect greatly. At an Assembly of First Nations Annual General Assembly in Vancouver, Clayton approached me to write something about Aboriginal people in Alberta. He stated that most people did not know the contributions of that Aboriginal people have made to our province. I agreed and stored that suggestion in my memory bank.

My conversation with a few Aboriginal university friends revealed that the little we learned about Aboriginal people in school has stuck with me over the years. We learned about Switzerland, New Zealand and Africa. We also learned about the French and English in Canada but did not learn about our own Aboriginal people. Aboriginal people had been left out of Canada's history until recently.

Aboriginal people have been occupying this land that we know as Alberta since the ice receded during the ice age. The archeological record estimates this to be twelve thousand years. Not only have Aboriginal people lived in this area for a very long time but they have also contributed to its betterment. This fact sometimes seems lost by our focus on pioneers, European and eastern Canadian settlers, and the spirit of the frontier.

Our Alberta history tells the newcomer stories of the Norwegians, the Icelanders, the Ukrainians, the French, the British and others. Their hardships and their contributions to our province are bases of many films, museum exhibits and books. Tributes to their pasts are valid and are welcomed in our multi-cultural society. In fact, we have government departments and foundations, such as the Alberta Historical Resources Foundation, whose mandate it is to document this history and provide funding for these historically-based projects. However, Indigenous people have also helped make this a great province. They contributed greatly to the betterment of mainstream and Indigenous societies alike.

I would like to thank those who funded my project. They include: Alberta Aboriginal Affairs and Northern Development who stepped in to allow me to complete my project, Heritage Canada, and the Heritage Community Foundation.

Acknowledgments

This project was completed by the hard work of a great number of people. I would like to thank Clayton Blood of the Blood First Nation in southern Alberta for suggesting the idea for this book several years ago. The idea remained with me.

I would like to thank all the people who called, mailed, and emailed nominees to me. The nominees were drawn from all across the province and from all walks of life. I was inspired to research and write about each of these individuals.

Thank you to Terry Lusty for allowing me to use his photos. Thanks also to my summer students who worked on this project during the summer of 2003. These include: Marlaine Metchewais, Delilah Young, Brenda Prince, Patricia Colosimo, Drew Calliou and Carly Morton. Also, a few of my students from the University of Calgary agreed to edit their term papers into profiles on Aboriginal people. The University of Toronto Press was also generous to allow these profiles to be reprinted.

Thank you also to all the writers who stepped up to the plate to help bring this book together to try to meet the ever-looming deadline. The writers include: Lea Tunstall, Michelle Voyageur, Brian Calliou, Casie McGonegal, Joan Ryan, Margaret Burgess, David Christiansen, Teresa Fergason, Drew Calliou, Vivienne Biesel, Tina Dion, Yvonne Jobin, Yvonne Pratt, Jocelyn Orbeiter, Marlene Metchewais, and Carly Morton. Thank you to Lea Anderson for helping me with the typing. Thanks to Walter Hildebrandt and George Melnyk for his great publishing advice.

Thank you to the funders of this project. Without this support this project would not have been completed. They include Valerie Kaufman at Canadian Heritage, Adriana Davies at the Community Heritage Foundation, and Dorothy Schreiber and Trish Bartko at Aboriginal Affairs and Northern Development of the Alberta Provincial Government.

When the crunch came to complete this manuscript, I enlisted the help of my family and this book became a family project. Luckily

I have a family of great writers. Special thanks to my husband Brian Calliou for his support and his keen eye for editing. Thank you to my children Carly and Drew for always pitching in to do the little jobs that helped finish this project.

Members of the Aboriginal community in Alberta were very supportive of me and of this project throughout the process. I appreciated the moral support and the encouragement. I am eternally grateful to all of you. I could not have done it on my own.

Cora J. Voyageur

Contents

Photo Credits

Note from the Author

My family was part of that steady stream of First Nations people migrating from the reserves to the cities in the 1960s. As an Aboriginal child growing up in mainstream society I noticed a lack of people who looked like me in any of the printed materials or in the electronic media. Aboriginal people were the antagonists in Louis Lamour's western paperbacks. Academic books were not a part of my world back then. Few Aboriginals were featured in the magazine articles or in the newspaper headlines. We faired a little better in the electronic media with the likes of Jay Silverheels (the Lone Ranger's sidekick, Tonto) and Injun Joe on the Forest Rangers on television. On the big screen, Chief Dan George made a splash in the movie, *Little Big Man*. This lack of presence carried over into the school curriculum and textbooks where I learned how the French and English formed Canada but learned nothing about the Aboriginal peoples' participation. Aboriginal people were noticeably absent from mainstream society.

The recognition of Aboriginal people and their contributions to the creation of Canada and of Alberta is essential to the functioning of a modern multi-cultural society. Aboriginal people are members of an active, vibrant and rich cultural community that have a long-standing relationship with the land and who have made significant contributions to the growth of this province.

This book highlights the Aboriginal presence in Alberta and the diverse contributions that Alberta's Aboriginal people have made to our province since its creation in 1905. It has two parts. The first part provides a brief history of Alberta and a synopsis of the Aboriginal people who live there. The second part is one hundred biographical profiles of Aboriginal Albertans. This portion of the book was a grassroots endeavor since the individuals featured had their names submitted for inclusion in this project by members of Alberta's Aboriginal communities.

I solicited for nominees from across Alberta's Aboriginal community and received submissions from First Nations administrators, Aboriginal political representative groups, Metis communities, Metis organizations, Alberta Native Friendship Centres, Aboriginal newspapers, and other media outlets. Individual community members also submitted names, photos, and short biographies of individuals they felt have made a contribution to the development of Alberta. I solicited about forty nominations in this way. I gleaned the information to write the profile.

People highlighted in section two come from all walks of life and were active in a variety of sectors of Alberta society including: the arts, literature, commerce, community development, cultural identity, economic development, education, environment, health, justice, law, leadership, military service, politics, sports, traditional knowledge, volunteerism, and women's issues.

The profiled individuals fall into two separate, but sometimes overlapping categories of Aboriginal Albertans. The first group are individuals who are recipients of national, provincial, municipal, or local awards. This "official" recognition can include, but is not limited to, recipients of the Order of Canada, military, citizenship, community service or volunteerism awards. The second group of profiled individuals are less well-known by the general public. However, these individuals have contributed greatly to our Alberta society but have not been formally recognized. They are people who work tirelessly in their communities and have yet to receive acknowledgment. These nominees were singled out for a long overdue recognition by members of the Aboriginal community.

The writing style used in this book is geared more to the general public than it is to the academic reader. However, the profiles do contain citations and reference material in books, academic articles, magazines, and newspapers. Some profiled individuals are more famous than others. Because of this notoriety there is more published information available about them than lesser-known individuals. Those lesser known in mainstream society are prominent and well-appreciated as active and caring citizens in the Aboriginal community.

As the primary writer and editor of this project, I had the task of deciding who would be included in the book. It was not an easy task because I wanted to balance many factors: First Nation versus Metis, treaty areas, and historical versus contemporary individuals. It is important to note that this selection of profiles includes some people who were born outside Alberta, and in a few cases, born outside of Canada. My rationale for including these individual is that they are long-time Albertans, they made their mark on this province, and they view themselves as Albertans.

Lastly, for the sake of practicality, there needed to be enough information gathered about an individual through interviews or printed materials to write an approximately five-hundred-word profile. Some nominated individuals simply did not have enough available data.

This project is meant to enhance knowledge and challenge previous, and at times erroneous, notions about Aboriginal people and their contributions to our society. I hope this publication will be a source of pride for Aboriginal people. I also hope it will work to combat the prejudice and discrimination suffered by Aboriginal peoples at the hands of the uninformed. Thank you to all who participated. It should be noted that there are many other people who could have been or should have been included in this project.

Introduction

Aboriginal people inhabited the land that we now know as Alberta long before Alberta was a province and Canada was a country. Our province celebrated its one hundredth birthday on September 1, 2005. The Province of Alberta was named after the daughter of Queen Victoria, HRH Princess Louise Caroline Alberta. Until then, it had been part of the Northwest Territory as was the Province of Saskatchewan.

As a First Nations person raised in Alberta, I find that the general public knows little about us. The media's portrayal of us consists of a steady diet of conflict and sensationalism.

This project is close to my heart. In it I hope to raise the profile of Aboriginal people and highlight the many positive contributions they have made to our Alberta society since its creation in 1905. This book highlights the many and diverse contributions Alberta's Aboriginal people have made to our great province since its creation in 1905. It has two parts. The first provides a brief history of Alberta and a brief synopsis of the Aboriginal people who inhabit Alberta. The second part will be the one hundred biographical profiles of select Aboriginal Albertans.

People included in this section are involved in arts, literature, commerce, community development, cultural identity, economic development, education, environment, health, justice, law, leadership, military service, politics, sports, traditional knowledge, volunteerism, women's issues, and other areas. There are one hundred profiles included in this book.

The profiled individuals fall into two separate, but sometimes overlapping, groups of Aboriginal Albertans. The first group are individuals who have been recognized and who have received national, provincial, municipal, or local awards. This "official" recognition can include, but is not limited to, recipients of the Order of Canada, military, citizenship, community service or volunteerism Awards. For example, some or these people have a National Aboriginal Achievement Award or the Order of Canada. The members of the second group are individuals who have contributed greatly to our

Alberta society but who have not been formally recognized. They are people who work tirelessly in their communities and have yet to receive acknowledgement. I want to draw attention to these people to show how they contribute in positive ways to Alberta.

The writing style used through most of this book is academic. This means that the profiles are written in an academic style, using endnotes and citing sources such as books, academic articles, magazines, newspapers, among others. Because of the notoriety of some of the profiled individuals there is some published information available about them. However, some of the individuals are not the topic of written work. They are people who are well-known and well-appreciated as active and caring citizens known to the local community. As a result, these profiles are not written in an academic style and are based on interviews conducted with the individual or from information provided by family or friends.

This project as a truly grassroots endeavor. Information and the the individuals chosen were gathered in a number of ways. Nominations were solicited throughout Alberta from First Nations administrators, Aboriginal political representative groups, Metis communities, Metis organizations, Alberta Native Friendship Centres, Aboriginal newspapers, and other media outlets. Community members submitted names, photos, and short biographies of individuals they felt have made a contribution to the development of Alberta. About forty nominations were solicited in this way. The profiles were written from this information.

After this avenue was exhaused a proactive approach to seeking out nominations was used. Over the next three summers student researchers were hired to comb through newspapers, magazines, the Internet and archives. Research materials were gathered from the University of Calgary library system, the Digitization Project at the University of Calgary, the Glenbow Archives, The University of Alberta library system, the University of Alberta's Book and Records Depository, the Alberta Sports Hall of Fame, the Windspeaker Archives and the Alberta Sweetgrass archives and a variety of publications including the Alberta Historical Review.

Hopefully this research is widely received in both the academic and non-academic communities. In the non-academic community it is anticipated that this publication would appeal to school students of all ages (including post-secondary), members of the public interested in Aboriginal peoples, and those interested in Alberta history.

There are many people who could have been or should have been included in this project. However, it was decided to profile one hundred people to celebrate the one hundredth birthday of the province. I wanted to select a variety of people to showcase the talent in the Aboriginal community.

In writing and selecting the profiles for inclusion in this book, a delicate balance was needed among a number of factors. I wanted to be inclusive of both First Nations and Metis individuals and the profiles are split between the two groups. I also wanted to represent each of the three main treaty areas: Treaty 8, Treaty 7 and Treaty 6. In addition, Profiles of both historical and contemporary individuals needed to be shown. The historical profiles are those of people who are deceased or those still living who have made history in one way or another. It is important to note that this selection of profiles includes some people who were born outside Alberta, and in a few cases, born outside of Canada. The rationale for including these individuals is that they are long-time Albertans, they made their mark on this province, and they view themselves as Albertans.

Lastly, for the sake of practicality, there needed to be enough information gathered about an individual through interviews or printed materials to write an approximately five-hundred-word profile. Some nominated individuals simply did not have enough data.

This project is meant to enhance knowledge and challenge previous, and at times erroneous, notions about Aboriginal people and their contributions to our Alberta society. Hopefully this publication will be a source of pride for Aboriginal people and it will work to combat the prejudice and discrimination suffered by Aboriginal peoples at the hands of the uninformed. Thanks, to all who participated.

Part One: Aboriginal Peoples of Alberta: Then and Now

Aboriginal people are descendents of the first inhabitants of this province. Many theories have been developed about how the first inhabitants of Alberta arrived here. However, the most prominent one states that people from northeast Asia walked across a land bridge called the Bering Strait Land Bridge.[1] The exact time that people came to the New World is uncertain but the archeological record on northern Yukon shows evidence dating back eighteen thousand years.[2]

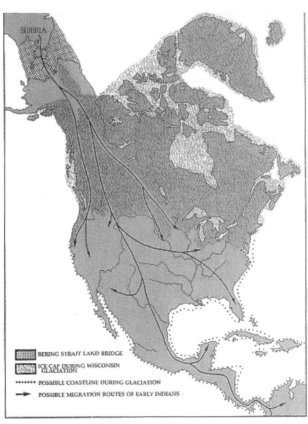

BERING STRAIT LAND BRIDGE

ICE CAP DURING WISCONSIN GLACIATION

•••••• POSSIBLE COASTLINE DURING GLACIATION

→ POSSIBLE MIGRATION ROUTES OF EARLY INDIANS

As the ice receded during the last ice age, the ancestors of indigenous people of Alberta lived on this land. Even the locations of present day Edmonton and Calgary were inhabited in pre-historic times.[3] Further, recent road construction along the Trans-Canada highway near Banff garnered artifacts dating back ten thousand years.[4] According to archeologist Jack Brink, ancient Alberta hunters and gatherers developed complex and ingenious technologies that allowed them to live and survive in a severe and harsh environment for thousands of years.[5] The Indigenous people of Alberta would continue living in this area for millennia.

The first reference to Alberta in the historical record was entered into Henry Kelsey's journal at York Factory in 1715. Kelsey wrote of a Cree trader named Swan who came from an area that would become northern Alberta: "he brought a sample of that gum or pitch that flows out of the banks of that river."[6] The gum or pitch Kelsey described was tar sand while the river was the Athabasca.

Aboriginal people were vital to the creation of Canada and the creation of Alberta. In the early days of European settlement on the land that would become Canada, Aboriginal manpower, technology, and ingenuity was vital for survival. Aboriginal people aided in early exploration such as Alexander Mackenzie's trek to the Pacific where Aboriginals served sundry roles such as guides, cooks, and provisioners, what Sylvia Van Kirk called "social brokers."[7] For example, historical records show that Aboriginal women travelling on the expedition made six hundred pairs of moccasins during this trip.[8] However, over the next centuries, Aboriginal people would become viewed as extraneous to the economy and subsequently marginalized.

Before the conditions surrounding Aboriginal life in Alberta are described what is meant by Aboriginal needs to be described. A definition of Aboriginal people as outlined in the Constitution Act, 1982 land treaties, the foundational basis of relations between First Nations of Alberta and settler society, are described. Then a description will be made of some of the current social and economic characteristics of Aboriginal people living in Alberta. First, a definition of Aboriginal people in Canada is needed.

Definition of Aboriginal People

There were trade relations and there were political relations. There were also conflicts. Some First Nations were traditional enemies such as the two Alberta bands that lived in relatively close proximity to each other. Historian Olive Dickason comments that "the Cree and the Blackfoot considered each other their worst foe."[9] They warred against each other and there were conflicts between the First Nations people in Alberta just as there were wars between nations in Europe.

Aboriginal people of Canada have more than fifty separate languages including Ojibway, Cree, Blackfoot, Saulteaux, Chipewyan, and others. These languages are as different from each other as French and Italian. First Nations cultures are geographically scattered throughout Canada and have unique historical experiences that shaped their present day culture.[10] Besides the First Nations cultural differences, there are the Metis with at least two distinct cultures, as we shall see below, and the Inuit. The most significant distinctions, however, are the legally imposed definitions.

Legal Definitions of Aboriginal Peoples in Canada

Three separate pieces of legislation determine the legal categorization of Aboriginal peoples in Canada: the Constitution Act, 1867 (the British North America Act); the Indian Act; and the Constitution Act, 1982.

A. The Constitution Act, 1867 (The British North America Act)

At Confederation, the British North America Act, 1867 (BNA) gave exclusive powers over "Indians and Lands Reserved for Indians" under section 91(24) to the federal government. Indians under the Constitutional definition is broader than the Indian Act definition. The Supreme Court of Canada in Re: Eskimo held that Indians under s. 91(24) includes the Eskimo (Inuit). Some have argued that this should also include the Metis.[11] However, the federal government has decided to exercise their jurisdiction in as narrow a fashion as possible. The federal government amended the Indian Act to state in its definition that Indian does not include Eskimo. The federal government has not exercised jurisdiction over the Metis. Under this authority, Parliament enacted a series of laws that became the Indian Act and exercised its jurisdiction over those defined as "Indians."

B. The Indian Act

The Indian Act has been, and still is, Canada's major instrument exercising its jurisdiction over and for dealing with its Aboriginal population – a population racially and legally different than other residents of the country. While recently the Act has become somewhat of an embarrassment to the federal government, it has come to be seen as a source of ethnic salvation and cultural survival by some First Nations people. The Indian Act is a product of an historical obligation to protect and, at the same time, "civilize" Indian people.[12] It pre-dates Confederation and has its roots in British Imperialism and is consistent with their treatment of indigenous peoples in its colonies.[13] The Indian Act has its origin in the British North America Act where "Indians" were categorized as persons deserving special attention under a federal mandate. Although one could interpret this mandate as discretionary, Canada interpreted it as impelling and exercised its mandate by narrowly defining who would or could be an "Indian." The evolution of the Indian Act has witnessed increasing federal power within the realm of Indian Affairs.

Most First Nations people have mixed emotions about the Indian Act although some have consistently criticized it for its constraints.[14] They resent the authority it exerts over their daily lives, yet see it as an important device for protecting their special rights. These "rights," supposedly enshrined in the Act, are variously perceived. Formulations vary according to region, tribe, personal experiences and local folklore. The Indian Act contains statements of freedom to maintain land; freedom of trespass from whites; freedom from some types of taxation; the ability to determine band membership; and other limited powers. Due to its restrictive rules, some demand the abolishment of the Indian Act. However, others fear its abolition will mean a loss of Indian Act rights and prefer to see its continuance rather than risk having no statutory protection.

The Indian Act also caused many First Nations women and their children to lose membership and status rights pursuant to section 12(I)(b). This section illustrates the male bias in the earlier Indian Act. It pertained specifically to a woman losing her status by marrying a non-Indian man, while it had no effect on Indian men marrying non-Indian women. In fact, non-Indian women became Indian upon marrying an Indian man until 1985.

Section 1 of the Bill of Rights guaranteed equality to all under the law regardless of race or sex. Two First Nations women, Jeanette Lavell and Yvonne Bedard, argued that under the Indian Act they were discriminated against on the basis of sex, which contravened the Bill of Rights. The case was heard before the Supreme Court of Canada, which affirmed a lower court's decision upholding the validity of section 12(l)(b), which deprived Lavell and Bedard of their Indian status. The decision stated that the Bill of Rights meant equality only in the administration and enforcement of the law. The actual substance of the law could discriminate between men and women as long as the law was applied by its administrator in an even-handed way.[15] The Court held that the Bill of Rights was merely a federal statute and could not supersede another federal statute (the Indian Act). It was not until the passage of the Charter of Rights and Freedoms, as entrenched in the Constitution Act, 1982, that a discriminatory federal statute could be superseded. That is, a statute infringed a constitutionally protected right would be invalid.

Section 12(1)(b) was repealed in 1985 by the Bill C-31 amendment to the Indian Act after the federal government was embarrassed in the international arena.[16] Sandra Lovelace, a Maliseet woman who lost her Indian status by marrying a non-Indian man, took her case to the United Nations Human Rights Tribunal that found Canada in breach of the International Covenant on Civil and Political Rights and in breach of its own Charter of Rights and Freedoms. Again, this ruling caused great embarrassment to the Canadian government but it took four years for the legislation to change.[17] Since 1985, the Indian Act no longer allows for people to lose or gain status through marriage.

C. The Constitution Act, 1982

The Constitution Act, 1982, which amended our earlier Constitution by adding a Charter of Rights and Freedoms, contains a definition of "Aboriginal peoples" that includes most Aboriginal groups in Canada, but does not include non-Status Indians.[18] The 1982 amendments to the Constitution contained explicit clauses referring to Canada's Aboriginal peoples. Section 35(1) provided that the "existing Aboriginal and treaty rights are hereby recognized and affirmed." Section 3 5(2) defines the Aboriginal peoples of Canada as the "Indian, Inuit and Metis peoples of Canada."[19] Since this is not an exclusive definition, non-Status Indians could be included, but as yet Parliament has not amended the Constitution to include them.

It was only after intensive lobbying by the various Aboriginal groups in Canada that s.35 was included in the Constitution.[20] With the entrenchment of s.35(1), an Aboriginal group or any person who can prove the existence of traditional practices or ties to specific territories can have their Aboriginal rights or title constitutionally protected. However, Aboriginal rights are not absolute and government legislation or action can be valid if it meets a strict test of infringement.

The Constitution Act, 1982 only identifies three: Indian, Metis and Inuit. Many have found that the myriad of names applied to Aboriginal people have caused enormous confusion and misunderstanding. Clarification of this matter is required. There is however, the more specific legal definition of Aboriginal people in the Constitution mentioned here.

Indian (First Nation)

The term "Indian" was more widely used in the past than it is today. This is a result, in part, to its pejorative connotation. This is especially true of those who point to its association with Columbus's case of mistaken identity. However, it does have a rather specific definition in Canadian law, that is the one given in the Indian Act s.2(l) which states: "'Indian' means a person who pursuant to this Act is registered as an Indian or is entitled to be registered as an Indian."[21] In this context, the term has a legal connotation since it specifies a type of Aboriginal people with special legal rights. One can therefore interchange the terms "registered," "legal," and "status" when referring to those with special ties to the federal government pursuant to the Indian Act. The legal status "Indian" confers special rights in Canadian law. As a result, those with this special status under the Indian Act are unwilling to dispense with it regardless of its negative connotation in some circles. This is especially true for people affiliated with the national organization representing "status" Indian chiefs – the Assembly of First Nations (formerly called the National Indian Brotherhood) – and its provincial affiliates.

The historical development of the Indian Act illustrates its racial and patriarchal nature. The new Dominion government's Indian Act of 1868 set out a definition of "Indian" as:

All persons of Indian Blood, reputed to belong to the particular tribe and their descendents;

All persons residing among such Indians, whose parents were or are descended on either side from Indians;

All women lawfully married to any [such Indians] and the children issue of such marriages, and their descendents.[22]

However, in 1869, the federal government began to say who was entitled to Indian status. As mentioned earlier, this legislation was particularly harmful to Indian women, more specifically, Indian women marrying anyone other than Indian men, since they would cease to be Indian as did any children from that marriage.[23] The imposed definition of Indian was very much a patriarchal idea with the elements of the definition focusing on a male person of Indian blood.[24]

a. Treaty vs Non-Treaty Indians

To further muddy the waters, there is a bifurcation of the term "Indian." This is the distinction between "Treaty" and "non-Treaty Indians." Treaty Indians are those who (or whose ancestors) entered into treaties with the Crown. The non-Treaty Indian designation refers to those who did not sign a treaty for some reason or another. However, non-Treaty Indians still have Indian status. For example, much of British Columbia (with the exception of the northwest region which is covered by Treaty 8, the lands covered by the Nisga'a and TsawwassenTreaties and parts of Vancouver Island) is not covered by treaty agreements, yet the majority of British Columbia Indians have Indian status because the federal government recognizes them under the Indian Act.

As a result of the imposition of the legal category of "Indian" the Canadian state had difficulty drawing clear lines on who was or was not an "Indian." This uncertainty resulted in the exclusion of some Aboriginal groups and the creation of a non-Status class of Indians. A person could become a non-Status Indian in a number of ways. Perhaps the most common way for a person to lose or give up their Indian status was through the enfranchisement process. The following is a brief explanation.

b. Enfranchisement

The "Indian Problem," as viewed by government officials, could be managed partly by eliminating the "Indianness" of First Nations people. The elimination of the culture of the First Nations was to occur through the removal of children from the cultures and subjecting them to education and religious training in European customs and values.[25] Separate legal Indian status was conceived as a stop-gap measure by white legislators, who expected that Indians would gradually abandon their native identity in order to enjoy the privilege of full Canadian citizenship – a state to which all would and should aspire.[26]

When Indians met the minimal requirements for citizenship – literacy, education, and "acceptable" moral character – they were allowed the rights of full citizenship through voluntary enfranchisement pursuant to sections of the Indian Act. They would be allowed to vote, purchase alcohol, and obtain land under the homestead system, and would no longer have to live under the aegis of the repressive Indian Act or have to tiptoe around the government's resident reserve babysitter – the Indian Agent. Enfranchisement was viewed by whites as a reward if the First Nations person obtained a university degree, joined the military, or became a minister. But it could also be seen as punishment, especially by those First Nations strongly attached to their culture. When one considers the psychological and social effects of whole groups of First Nations persons being forcibly separated from their communities and cultures enfranchisement was truly a punishment. They had brown skin in a society that valued whiteness. Discrimination was rampant at a time when Social Darwinism saw First Nations as inferior. Enfranchisement could also be used as a tool for punishment if the First Nations person was caught in possession of alcohol or raised the ire of the Indian agent who had the discretion to strike anybody, for any reason, from the band list. However, as discussed before, the majority of forcibly enfranchised "Indians" were First Nations women who married non-Indian men, and their children.

The Metis

The Metis were excluded from being "Indians" under the Indian Act. They are descendants of mixed marriages and the term is often used to include almost all people of mixed Indian and non-Indian ancestry. The Metis have their own distinctive history and culture.

Different groups of people called themselves "Metis." Historian John E. Foster argues that confusion surrounds the term Metis and that they emerged from two separate fur-trade systems.[27] The first, the Great Lakes trading system, led to the creation of the "Metis" identity, while the second, the Hudson's Bay system, its "Home Guard" provisioners, produced mixed-blood individuals who did not carry the "Metis" identity.[28] Still, others found diverse Metis groups having particular historical experiences with nebulous self-identification and living in complex class-based societal structures.[29]

Generally, the Metis have a strong sense of their own Aboriginal identit that is separate from their "Indian" and European roots. They make distinctions between two types of Metis: the descendants of Red River settlers and the "nomadic" Metis.[30]

Inuit

The Inuit are an Aboriginal people in northern Canada, who live predominantly above the tree line in the Northwest Territories, and in northern Quebec and Labrador. The word means "people" in the Inuit language – Inuktitut. The singular of Inuit is Inuk. They are listed in the Constitution Act, 1982 as one of the peoples in the definition of Aboriginal peoples. Pursuant to the 1939 Supreme Court of Canada case Re: Eskimo, Inuit effectively fall under federal jurisdiction as s.9 1(24) Indians.[31] However, Parliament has expressly defined "Indians" in the Indian Act as not including Eskimos (Inuit). They are distinct from "Indians" both legally and culturally. They are not administered under the Indian Act. Despite these legal definitions that give some clarification to who is or is not an "Indian," there is still uncertainty.

Treaties

The basis for most relationships between First Nations people in Canada and government is Treaty. A treaty is a negotiated agreement between two nations. Both First Nations people of Canada and the Europeans have long histories of treaty making. Treaties were made between distinct First Nations living throughout North America prior to contact with Europeans. Diplomatic protocols and agreements were made between these groups to settle conflicts and assist trade.[32] Europeans also had a long history of treaty making which helped them settle territorial disputes, form military alliances, and develop trade.

Treaty-making between the First Nations and the newcomers began soon after contact. The first treaties were Peace and Friendship Treaties made at a time of continuous warfare between France and England. These treaties sought to assure the neutrality or the assistance of the Indians. The first recorded Treaty between First Nations and the Europeans was in 1725.[33] Treaties between the Crown and various First Nation groups in Canada implied the recognition of an Aboriginal title to the territory occupied by the Indians concerned.[34] The government of Canada entered treaty because they feared Indian wars and wanted to ensure the peaceful settlement of the Northwest Territory.[35] The intent of treaty, at least in the Crown's mind, was to extinguish Indian title and clear any obstructions to Crown title.[36] First Nations contend that the purpose of the treaty was to establish nation-to-nation relations and live peacefully together as well as to share the land with the newcomers.

The treaty-making process was depicted as an "exchange of commodities" by the government. There was a sense that the Indians were compensated for their relinquishment. The fact that options were given to the Indians and the Metis and that compensation was also given helped to assure Canadians that they had treated their Indians better and more equitably than the Americans had treated theirs.[37] It was believed by Canadians that the land issue was settled and that the land surrendered by the Indians was now available to them.

Alberta Treaties

The source of much of Canada's wealth, and in particular Alberta's wealth, is its natural resources. These natural resources come from the land surrendered by the Indians under Treaty with the Crown. All Alberta's land is covered by one of five numbered treaties – those being Treaties 4, 6, 7, 8 and 10. Further to this point, many natural resources are actually extracted from First Nation land. An Indian and Northern Affairs Canada inventory[38] states that approximately 30 per cent of Canada's 2 267 Indian reserves have either good or moderate resource extraction potential. In fact, of the 564 permits, leases and agreements issued by Indian Affairs and Northern Development, 406 (72 per cent) were issued to the private sector; 79 (14 per cent) were given to provincial governments; and 34 (6 per cent) were allotted to municipalities.[39]

There are currently forty-six First Nation communities in Alberta. They are covered under the main three treaties covering Alberta.

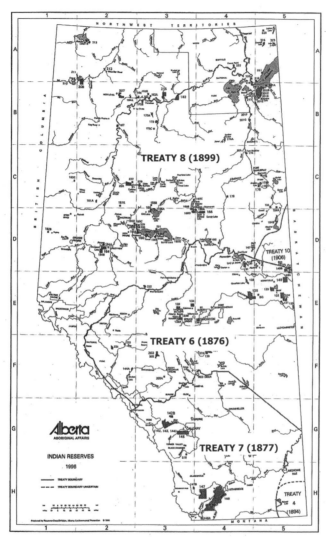

These are Treaties 6, 7 and 8, while small portions of the province are included in both Treaty 4 and Treaty 10. The land in Treaties 6 and 7 were part of what was called the "fertile belt" and was viewed as prime farmland. It was seen as being more suitable for settlers since it was in the southern part of the province. It was crucial for the government to settle the southern parts of Alberta because there was a fear that the American government would try to annex this land if it were left vacant.

Treaty 6

There are sixteen First Nations covered under Treaty 6. Treaty 6 was signed at Fort Carleton and Fort Pitt in 1876. It covers central Saskatchewan and central Alberta. The Alberta First Nations covered under Treaty 6 are: Alexander, Alexis, Beaver Lake, Cold Lake, Enoch Cree Nation, Ermineskin, Frog Lake, Heart Lake, Kehewin, Louis Bull, Montana, O'Chiese, Paul, Saddle Lake, Samson, Sunchild and Whitefish Lake (Goodfish Lake).[40]

Treaty 6 was negotiated by commissioners Alexander Morris, James McKay, and William Christie, and was signed at Fort Pitt, Fort Carleton, and Battle River in Saskatchewan.[41]

Prior to the signing of Treaty 6, the Indians of the area were concerned because they had heard that their land had been sold. In fact, a land transfer had taken place. The government of Canada had purchased Rupert's Land (all lands with rivers and tributaries that flow into Hudson's Bay) from the Hudson's Bay Company in 1870. The geological survey had been active in the west for many years and the Indians of the region were becoming increasingly agitated. They were also worried about food shortages because the buffalo stocks had depleted and the encroachment of white settlers on their land.

Food shortages had been a major concern of the signatories of Treaty 6. The disappearance of the buffalo had a profound effect on them. The buffalo herds that numbered in the millions only decades before had dwindled.

In Treaty 6 the Government of Canada made a number of promises to the Indians to get them to sign. These mutually agreed-upon terms included a specified amount of land (one square mile of land for every family of five); farming assistance; payments, annuities, and special benefits; hunting, trapping, and fishing rights; educational benefits; health benefits. The government also agreed that Indians, non-Indians, and the Government of Canada had a mutual agreement to live in peace and to have goodwill in dealings with each other.[42]

Treaty 7

Treaty 7 was negotiated at Blackfoot Crossing and at Fort McLeod in 1877. It covers Alberta south of the Red Deer River. The First Nations covered under Treaty 7 are: Blood, Pikani, Siksika, Stoney (Bearspaw, Chiniki, and Wesley) and Tsuu T'ina.[43] It was negotiated by commissioners David Laird and James McLeod, and was signed at Blackfoot Crossing near Gleichen, Alberta.[44]

In Treaty 7 the Government of Canada made a number of promises to the Indians to encourage their participation in the treaty process.[45] These promises were similar to those made in Treaty 6. These mutually agreed-upon terms included a specified amount of land (one square mile of land for every family of five); farming assistance; payments, annuities, and special benefits; hunting, trapping, and fishing rights; and educational benefits.[46] The government also agreed that Indians, non-Indians, and the Government of Canada had a mutual agreement to live in peace and to have goodwill in dealings with each other.[47]

Treaty 8

There are twenty-three First Nations covered under Treaty 8. Treaty 8 was signed at various points in Alberta and the Northwest Territory. The Alberta First Nations covered under Treaty 8 are: Athabasca Chipewyan, Beaver, Bigstone Cree, Chipewyan Prairie, Dene Tha', Driftpile, Duncan's, Fort McKay, Fort McMurray, Horse Lake, Kapowe'no, Little Red River, Loon River, Lubicon Lake, Mikisew Cree, Sawridge, Sturgeon Lake, Sucker Creek, Swan River, Tallcree, Whitefish Lake, and Woodland Cree.[52]

Treaty 8 covers northwestern Saskatchewan, Alberta, northeastern British Columbia, and the Northwest Territories. By signing Treaty 8, the Indians of this region gave up 324 000 square miles of land – an area about three-quarters the size of the province of Ontario.[48] The last numbered treaty in Alberta prior to 1899 was Treaty 7, which was signed in southern Alberta some twenty-two years earlier in 1877. According to researcher Dennis Madill, Treaty 8 was a long time in the making:

> Since the 1870s there had been pleas from missionaries, fur traders and Indians for a treaty in the Athabasca-Mackenzie region, but the federal government disclaimed any responsibility for these Indians, despite the hardships they suffered, and remained committed to that policy of not proceeding for settlement.[49]

As historian David Leonard says of the Treaty 8 region: "The perceived need for a settlement had been mounting for some time. Mineral resources along the lower Athabasca River seemed ripe for tapping, while the Peace River Country appeared to be on the verge of large-scale agricultural settlement"[50] The Klondike gold rush brought as many as forty thousand individuals through the Treaty 8 area on their way to the Yukon.[51] The Treaty and Scrip Commissions visited many areas in northern Alberta and the Northwest Territories during the summers of 1899 and 1900.

In Treaty 8 the Government of Canada made a number of promises to the Indians to encourage them to sign. These mutually agreed-upon terms included a specified amount of land (one square mile of land for every family of five); farming assistance; payments, annuities, and special benefits; hunting, trapping, and fishing rights; educational benefits; health benefits. The government also agreed that Indians, non-Indians, and the Government of Canada had a mutual agreement to live in peace and to have goodwill in dealings with each other.[53]

Scrip

The government decided to deal with the rights to land of the Indians and Metis at the same time. Historians Joe and Patricia Sawchuk and Teresa Fergason state, "one of the most important aspects of Metis history and tradition is scrip."[54]

Scrip was a certificate given to those individuals who did not sign a treaty as Indians and agree to live under the Indian Act. Metis claims to the land were handled by the government issuing Scrip Certificates. The Scrip Certificate gave the bearer 240 acres of land or money scrip worth $240. Most Metis in Treaty 8 chose money scrip.[55] In 1899, when the average man earned a dollar a day, $240 was a tremendous amount of money.

In most cases the land scrip was quickly purchased by land speculators who followed the Treaty and Scrip Commission in northern Alberta.

Historical geographer Frank Tough has conducted extensive research on the scrip process. The MatriX Project has uncovered fraud in the scrip process and the illegal sale and registration of Metis land by non-Aboriginal people. For example, one situation had a Metis woman from northern Saskatchewan being issued scrip one day around Prince Albert and presenting herself the next day at a Calgary land titles office wanting to sell her scrip to a non-Aboriginal.[56] Remember this is the end of the nineteenth century and people did not move as freely and as easily as they do today.

Aboriginal People in Alberta, 2010

Today, Aboriginal people can be found in all parts of the province. They live in the ranchlands of the South, parkland of central Alberta, and the boreal forest of the North. They live in urban, rural, and remote areas. They live in the foothills of the Rocky Mountains and on the Saskatchewan/Alberta border.

The forty-six First Nations reserves in Alberta have 121 reserves scattered throughout the province. Some of these reserves are on the outskirts of major Alberta cities such as the Tsuu T'ina First Nation which borders Calgary and the Enoch Cree Nation situated on the western outskirts of Edmonton. Most reserves are in rural areas while some are remote. Remote reserves must be accessed by airplane or by boat. Despite these reserve lands, set aside as a result of treaty negotiations between the Crown and the First Nations people, there are still a number of outstanding land claims in Alberta such as the Lubicon Lake land claim.

The Metis also live in urban, rural and remote regions of the province. The Metis of Alberta are unique in Canada because they have a land base of approximately 1.25 million acres.[57] The eight remaining Metis settlements include: Fishing Lake, Elizabeth Colony, Caslan, Kikino, Paddle Prairie, Gift Lake, Peavine, and East Prairie. They are located in central and northern Alberta (see Appendix E). An additional four Metis settlements (Touchwood Siebert, Marlboro, Cold Lake and Wolf Lake) were rescinded between 1940 and 1960.

The Metis settlements in Alberta resulted from the Ewing Commission that began in 1934 and investigated the condition of the Metis of Alberta. The Commission recommended land, health, and education services for the Metis.[58] The Metis Betterment Act was passed on November 22, 1938 and the Metis settlements of Alberta were established.

The 2001 Census of Canada states that 188 365 individuals or five per cent of the Alberta population self-identify as Aboriginal.[59] Proportionally, the First Nations (Indian) group is the largest of the groups that fall under the Aboriginal umbrella, followed by the Metis. There has been a rapid increase in the number of Aboriginal people in Alberta due to changes in legislation such as Bill C-31[60] passed in 1985; a higher fertility rate in Aboriginal community than the non-Aboriginal community; and because many people are reclaiming their Aboriginal ancestry.[61]

Alberta's Aboriginal population is a young population with fifty per cent) under the age of twenty-five years.[62] Statistics Canada figures show that the average age of Alberta's Aboriginal population is 24.8 years old. This is approximately ten years younger than the average non-Aboriginal Albertan.[63]

Today, Aboriginals continue to participate in Alberta's wage-labour force. Statistics Alberta data shows that the Aboriginal people's labor participation rate in the Alberta labor force is 63 per cent; a mere 3 percentage points lower than the non-Aboriginal labor participation rate (66 per cent).[64] However, the Alberta unemployment rate is twice as high for the Aboriginal workforce than the non-Aboriginal workforce. These high unemployment rates are due to the lack of jobs on reserves but this situation is improving. In fact, the labor participation rate for Metis and Inuit is higher than that of non-Aboriginals.

Aboriginal people are bound to become a larger and more integral part of Alberta's economy and its future labor force. Two important factors that determine a nation's workforce are a working-age population (people) and a skilled workforce (skills). In the five years between 2001 and 2006, the Canadian workforce increased by 1.7 percent per year.[65] These workers entered the workplace in highly skilled occupations that require post-secondary qualifications. Immigrants accounted for almost seventy per cent of the growth in the labor market.[66] It is not necessary to look beyond our borders for workers. Aboriginal people are a virtually untapped pool of human resources – as employers, as employees and as consumers. Some of this untapped labor pool is local and if the development is in rural and remote areas of Alberta, the untapped labor pool is more likely to be Aboriginal.

Aboriginal people are recognizing society's need for an educated workforce and gaining credentials at a rate never before seen in our community. For many years, Aboriginal people faced many barriers and were discouraged from pursuing higher education. Most communities did not have a high school. This meant that students entering Grade 10 had to leave home. A Grade 12 education seems to be the minimum industry standard for employment and more Aboriginal people than ever are completing a high school diploma.

There has been an explosion of post-secondary educational attainment in the Aboriginal community. Aboriginal post-secondary student enrollment has increased steadily over the past four decades. Aboriginal students are now enrolling and graduating from many disciplines. The diversity of study is beneficial to the Aboriginal community and a departure from earlier enrollment, which showed a heavy concentration in the social work and education fields. The majority of Aboriginal enrollments are found in undergraduate studies, but there are increasing numbers enrolled in both graduate and professional programs such as law, medicine, pharmacy, and dentistry.

Some of these educated Aboriginal people choose to return to their communities thus becoming a local human resource. Some work for others while others work for themselves. Aboriginal entrepreneur rates are rapidly increasing – especially for Aboriginal women and youth.

The past two decades has seen tremendous growth in self-employment in Canadian society and this phenomenon has spilled over into the Aboriginal business community. Aboriginal Business Canada states that there are now more than twenty-seven thousand businesses owned and operated by Aboriginal people in Canada. Aboriginal entrepreneurship has increased more than 30 per cent since 1996.[67] Metis people have the highest rate of Aboriginal entrepreneurs.

Although Aboriginals business is dispersed in virtually every sector of the economy, more than two-thirds of Aboriginal businesses fall under four categories: professional (scientific, technical, education, health and social) at 23 per cent; retail/wholesale at 12 per cent; primary natural resources at 17 per cent; and construction at 17 per cent.[68] However, there is a trend toward more diversity in Aboriginal entrepreneurship. The "other" category increased from 11 to 18 per cent in five years.

The data show that Aboriginal entrepreneurship is increasing at a greater rate – nine times higher – than self-employment in the non-Aboriginal community. Self-employed Aboriginal people are found in all parts of Canada including urban, rural, and in remote locations. The vast majority of Aboriginal businesses (80 per cent) serve local markets.[69] Entrepreneurship in remote locations provides jobs and job-creation opportunities. There are more self-employed Aboriginals in British Columbia, Alberta and Ontario than other areas of Canada. Aboriginal entrepreneurship has created almost forty-nine thousand jobs between 1981 and 1996, according to an Aboriginal Business

Canada report.[70] Industry Canada reports that only a fraction of Aboriginal businesses (20 per cent) received government grants or contributions to start operations.[71] They further state that Aboriginal businesses are more likely to use equity than debt to begin their ventures.[72]

Alberta's Aboriginal populations contribute to the Alberta economy through employment, entrepreneurship, and making their lands and resources accessible. Aboriginal peoples will become an even larger part of the Alberta economy in the future.

Alberta's Aboriginal population is becoming increasingly more educated and credentialed. They are eager to be included in the economic activity occurring in their territory. This young and rapidly increasing population will be larger proportion of Canadian society, the workforce, the taxpayers who support Canada's social safety net, and the consuming public in the future. As an employee, if you do not know an Aboriginal employee now, you will get to know one very soon.

Aboriginal business ventures in rural and reserve areas allow Aboriginal people to remain in their home communities while creating jobs opportunities for themselves and others. They have an opportunity to earn a living for themselves and their families. Aboriginal business and entrepreneurship shows that they have and continue to contribute to Alberta's growth and development. Aboriginal people want to prosper from the exploitation of the rich natural resources of this province, just like non-Aboriginals.

Aboriginal people are a vital part of Alberta's social, cultural and economic fabric. McGregor's *History of Alberta* praised the efforts of the pioners and the immigrants for making Alberta a great province. The circle of praise must be widened to include the First Nations and Metis of the province who have also worked hard to make Alberta the great province it is today.

Notes

[1]Susan Berry and Jack Brink, *Aboriginal Cultures in Alberta: Five Hundred Generations* (Edmonton: Provincial Museum of Alberta, 2004), 1.
[2]Berry, *Aboriginal Cultures in Alberta*, 1.
[3]Gail Helgason, *The First Albertans* (Edmonton: Lone Pine Publishing, 1987), 17.
[4]Helgason, *The First Albertans*, 17.

[5]Helgason, *The First Albertans,* 20.

[6]Helgason, *The First Albertans,* 15.

[7]Sylvia Van Kirk, *Many Tender Ties: Women in Fur-Trade Society, 1670–1870* (Winnipeg: Watson & Dwyer Publishing Ltd., 1980).

[8]Van Kirk, *Many Tender Ties.*

[9]Olive P. Dickason, *Canada's First Nations: A History of Founding Peoples from Earliest Times* (Toronto: Oxford University Press, 1997), 174.

[10]R. Bruce Morrison and C. Roderick Wilson, *Native Peoples: The Canadian Experience,* 2nd ed. (Toronto: McClelland and Stewart, 1995).

[11]Clem Chartier, "'Indian': an Analysis of the Term as Used in Section 91(24) of the British North America Act, 1867," *Saskatchewan Law Review 37* (1979), 37–80.

[12]John Tobias, "Protection, Civilization, Assimilation: An Outline History of Canada's Indian Policy," in *As Long as the Sun Shines,* ed. Ian Getty and Antione Lussier (Vancouver: University of British Columbia Press, 1983), 39.

[13]John Leslie and Ron McGuire, *The Historical Development of the Indian Act* (Ottawa: Treaties and Historical Research Centre, 1978).

[14]Harold Cardinal, *Unjust Society: The Tragedy of Canada's Indians* (Edmonton: Hurtig Press, 1969).

[15]M. Elizabeth Atcheson, *Women and Legal Action: Precedents, Resources and Strategies for the Future* (Ottawa: Canadian Advisory Council on the Status of Women, 1984).

[16]Cora Voyageur, "Contemporary Indian Women," in *Visions of the Heart: Canadian Aboriginal Issues,* ed. David Allan Long and Olive Patricia Dickason (Toronto: Harcourt Canada, 1996), 93–115.

[17]Voyageur, "Contemporary Indian Women."

[18]Joe Sawchuk, "The Metis, Non-Status and the New Aboriginality: Government Influence on Native Political Alliances and Identity," *Canadian Ethnic Studies 21* (1985), 135–146.

[19]Government of Canada. Section 35 Constitution Act, Schedule B of the Canada Act, 1982, c.11 (UK).

[20]Douglas Sanders, "The Indian Lobby," in *And No One Cheered: Federalism, Democracy, and the Constitution Act,* ed. Keith Banting and Richard Simeon (Toronto: Methuen Publications, 1983), 301–332.

[21]Donna Hawley and Shin Amai, *The 1996 Annotated Indian Act* (Scarborough: Carswell Thomson Professional Publishing, 1995), 4.

[22]"An Act Providing for the Organization of the Department of Secretary of State of Canada for the Management of Indian and Ordinance Land," 1868.

[23]Voyageur, "Contemporary Indian Women."

[24]Brian Calliou, "The Imposition of State Laws and the Creation of Various Hunting Rights for Aboriginal Peoples of the Treaty 8 Territory," in *Lobstick: An Interdisciplinary Journal* (Grande Prairie: Grande Prairie College Press, 2000), 151– 193.

[25]Brian Titley, *A Narrow Vision: Duncan Campbell Scott and the Administration of Indian Affairs in Canada* (Vancouver: University of British Columbia Press, 1986).

[26]R. Douglas Francis, *The Imaginary Indian: the Image of the Indian in Canadian Culture* (Vancouver: Arsenal Pulp Press, 1993).

[27] John Foster, "The Metis: the People and the Term," *Prairie Forum 3* (1978), 79–90.

[28] Foster, "The Metis: the People and the Term."

[29] Nicole St. Onge, "Variations in Red River: the Traders and Freeman Metis of Saint Laurent, Manitoba," *Canadian Ethnic Studies 24* (1992), 1–24.

[30] Ken Hatt, "Ethnic Discourse in Alberta: Land and the Metis in the Ewing Commission," *Canadian Ethnic Studies 17* (1985), 64–79.

[31] Supreme Court of Canada, Re: Eskimo (1939), *Supreme Court Reporter 104.*

[32] Office of the Treaty Commissioner of Saskatchewan, "Five Treaties in Saskatchewan," in *Expressions in Canadian Native Studies,* ed. Ron Laliberte et. al. (Saskatoon: University Extension Press, 2000) 232.

[33] "Peace and Friendship Treaties," Historical Indian Treaties; <http://www.atlas.gc.ca/site/english/maps/ historical /indian treaties/historicalt> (accessed July 2005).

[34] John Leonard Taylor, *Treaty Research Report: Treaty Six (1876),* (Ottawa: Indian Affairs and Northern Development Canada, 1985).

[35] Taylor, *Treaty Research Report: Treaty Six (1876).*

[36] Taylor, *Treaty Research Report: Treaty Six (1876).*

[37] Doug Owram, Promise of Eden: *The Canadian Expansionist Movement and the Idea of the West 1856–1900* (Toronto: University of Toronto Press, 1980), 131.

[38] This 45-volume inventory has 18 000 pages and 10 000 maps. "Mineral Resource Potential of Indian Reserve Lands," Indian and Northern Affairs Canada (1990); <http://www.Inac.gc.ca.natres/caada.html> (accessed October 1998).

[39] Joyce Green and Cora Voyageur, "Globalization and Development at the Bottom," in *Feminists doing Development: A Practical Critique,* ed. Marilyn Porter and Ellen Judd (New York: Zed Books, 1999), 146.

[40] *First Nations of Alberta,* (Ottawa: Indian and Northern Affairs Canada, 2002).

[41] Taylor, *Treaty Research Report: Treaty Six (1876).*

[42] Richard T. Price, *Legacy: Indian Treaty Relationships (Edmonton:* Plains Publishing Inc., 1991).

[43] *First Nations of Alberta.*

[44] Hugh A. Dempsey, *Treaty Research Report: Treaty Seven (1877),* (Ottawa: Indian Affairs and Northern Development Canada, 1987).

[45] Walter Hildebrandt, Sarah Carter and Dorothy First Rider, *The True Spirit and Original Intent of Treaty 7* (Montreal: McGill-Queens Press, 1996).

[46] Price, Legacy: *Indian Treaty Relationships.*

[47] Price, Legacy: *Indian Treaty Relationships.*

[48] Frank Oberle, "Treaty 8 Renovation: Discussion Paper," Department of Indian and Northern Affairs, 1986.

[49] Dennis F. K. Madill, *Treaty Research Report: Treaty 8* (Ottawa: Treaties and Historical Research Centre, Indian and Northern Affairs Canada, 1986).

[50] David Leonard, "Decision at Lesser Slave Lake," *Legacy: Alberta's Heritage Magazine* (May-June 1999), 17–19.

[51] Wilfred Kesterton and Roger Bird, "The Press in Canada: A Historical Overview," in *Communications in Canadian Society, 4th ed.,* ed. Benjamin Singer (Toronto: ITP Nelson Canada, 1995), 30–50.

[52] *First Nations of Alberta.*

[53] Price, Legacy: *Indian Treaty Relationships.*

[54] Joe Sawchuk, Patricia Sawchuk and Teresa Fergason, *Metis Land Rights in Alberta: A Political History* (Edmonton: Metis Association of Alberta, 1981), 87.

[55] Price, Legacy: *Indian Treaty Relationships.*

[56] Frank Tough, "MatriX Project," in *Indigenizing Institutions* (Banff, Alberta: The Banff Centre Aboriginal Management and Leadership Program, Febuary 2004).

[57] Sawchuk, *Metis Land Rights in Alberta.*

[58] Sawchuk, *Metis Land Rights in Alberta.*

[59] Statistics Canada Alberta. Abo pop profile www12.statcan.ca/census-recense-ment/2006/dp-pd/prof/92-594/details/page.cfm? Lang=E&Geo1=PR&Code1=48&Geo2=PR&C

[60] Bill C-31 came into effect on April 17, 1985. This was an amendment to the Indian Act, which was deemed to discriminate on the basis of sex since only Indian women, and not Indian men, lost their Indian status upon marriage to a non-Indian. It was also meant to restore Indian status to those who had been enfranchised for joining military service, joining the priesthood, gaining a university degree or other reasons.

[61] Mary Jane Norris, "Aboriginal Peoples: Demographic and Linguistic Perspectives," in *Visions of the Heart: Canadian Aboriginal Issues,* ed. David Long and Olive Patricia Dickason (Toronto: Harcourt Brace, 2000), 176.

[62] The Daily, *Statistics Canada,* January 23, 2008.

[63] The Daily, *Statistics Canada,* January 23, 2008.

[64] *Aboriginal Population Profile from the 2006 Census*, Catalogue Number 92594XWE.

[65] Aboriginal Labour Force Characteristics from the 1996 Census

[66] Aboriginal Business Canada, Aboriginal Entrepreneurs in 2002 (Ottawa: Industry Canada, 2002); <http://strategis.ic.gc.ca/epic/internet/inabc-eac.nsf/en/ab003313e.html> (accessed January 2003).

[67] Aboriginal Labour Force Characteristics from the 1996 Census.

[68] Aboriginal Business Canada Aboriginal Entrepreneurs in 2002.

[69] Ibid

[70] Ibid

[71] Ibid

Aatsista-mahkan (Running Rabbit)

1833 - 1911
Siksika
Warrior,
Leader and
Head Chief

It must have been obvious to those who knew the young Aatsista-mahkan that he was destined for greatness. In 1833 Aatsista-mahkan (Running Rabbit), the younger brother of acclaimed Blackfoot chief, Akamukai (Many Swans), was born in central Alberta.[1]

As a teenager, Aatsista-mahkan (Running Rabbit) won the respect of his community. For his first raid, Akamukai (Many Swans) loaned him a protective amulet made of a round mirror and decorated with weasel skins, eagle and magpie feathers.[2] On that raid he captured two enemy horses for his brother, Akamukai. His brother eventually gave him the amulet after Aatsista-mahkan was successful on three subsequent raids.[3] As his success continued, Aatsista-mahkan's reputation grew among the community and he began being referred to as "the young chief."[4]

He had also gained a reputation as a person who could resolve conflict. For example, while camped at the Oldman River in southern Alberta, a young man accidentally shot and killed the daughter of the head chief Crowfoot. Aatsista-mahkan intervened on the young man's behalf and was able to persuade Crowfoot that the event was in fact an accident. He offered Crowfoot two horses for damages.[5]

He married the daughter of the Chief of the Fish Eaters Band, Seen From Afar, and would go on to have four wives and eleven children.[6] One of his more famous children, Duck Chief, would later also become a head chief.[7] At about the age of 38 years, Aatsista-Mahkan became chief of the Biters, a south Peigan band after the death of his older brother, Many Swans.[8]

He was a signatory of Treaty 7 in 1877.[9] At that point, Aatsista-Mahkan reportedly had about ninety members in his band.[10] He settled at the Blackfoot reserve in 1881 and began a farming lifestyle.The Indian Agent, Magnus Begg, noted that Aatsista-mahkan had quickly adapted to the settled life.[11] He became a prosperous farmer, by the standards of the day, and accumulated an array of farm implements including a wagon, mowing machine, and horse rake and a high-top buggy.[12]

The following year Aatsista-mahkan was named one of the two head chiefs along with Old Sun of the Blackfoot tribe. The two men replaced No-okska-stumik (Three Bulls) who had passed away.[13] While he shared leadership with Old Sun, he was considered the more progressive and often spoke for the entire tribe.[14] Aatsista-mahkan maintained his reputation as a wise leader, and was respected for keeping his family free of internal conflict and for controlling the tribal council with a firm grip.[15]

His character and judgment was respected by both the Blackfoot people and the government.[16] At his death he was honored as ranking with such leaders as Crowfoot and Old Sun.[17] Aatsista-mahkan died on or about January 24, 1911 at the Siksika reserve which is located east of Calgary.[18]

Profile by: Vivienne Biesel

Anderson, Anne

1906 – 1997
Metis
Language
Teacher and
Author

Anne Anderson had a mission to preserve the Cree language. She fulfilled a promise she made to her mother to not only speak and teach the language but to preserve it for future generations by writing it down. Anne became a prolific writer and wrote many books used for academic purposes. In total, she wrote ninety-two books dealing primarily with Cree language, herbal remedies, and history. She also wrote a Cree dictionary.[19] Her first book, *Let's Learn Cree,* was written with the help of her niece Elaine Rowe on Anne's kitchen table in her Jasper Avenue apartment. Elaine worked closely with Anderson for many years.[20] Anne's perseverance in keeping her language alive led her on many journeys which were both impressive and inspirational.

Anne Anderson was born on a river-lot farm four miles east of St. Albert in 1906. Her mother, Elizabeth Callihou, was Cree and her father, William Gairdner, was Scottish-French. She was the couple's eldest daughter and she had four brothers and five sisters. Her mother insisted that the children speak Cree at home. Anne and her siblings attended the Bellerose School. But at age ten, Anne went to Grey Nuns Convent a few miles from St. Albert for the lonely years before returning to the Bellerose School.[21] Her father passed away of an acute appendicitis when she was sixteen and this created a financial challenge for the large family. Anderson helped support her family by doing housework for neighbours.[22]

Anderson married William Callihoo in 1926 and went on to have two children: Patricia and Herbert. In 1947 she married Joseph

Anderson in Frog Lake where she worked as a supervisor for the Fishing Lake Metis Settlement.[23] She later married Alex Irvine in 1979.

Anne put an ad in the newspaper for a Cree tutor and received an overwhelming response, which led to the opening of the Native Heritage and Cultural Centre in 1984. Anne also was founder and president of Cree Productions Learning Centre in 1974. She taught Cree and Metis culture at the University of Alberta, Grant McEwan Community College, Fort Saskatchewan Jail, Charles Camsell Hospital, Fairview College, YWCA and Edmonton's Boyle Street Co-op.[24]

Anne Anderson was awarded an honorary doctorate in 1978 from the University of Alberta. She also won the Native Council of Canada Award, the Woman of the Year Award as well as the Order of Canada.[25] A park located at 105th Avenue and 162nd Street in Edmonton,Alberta has been named in her honor. Anne's wish to have a bronze statue of a buffalo, symbolizing survival, in the park was made possible by Lloyd Pinay from Peepeekisis Reserve near Fort Qu'Appelle, Saskatchewan.[26]

Anne Anderson's efforts gave many people a chance to preserve their language and understand who they are and where they came from. For this and her many other contributions to Alberta she will be remembered as a kind-hearted woman with a drive and passion who not only fulfilled her mothers dying wish but went beyond her dream.

Profile by: Marlaine Metchewais

Auger, Dr. Dale

1958 – 2008
Cree
Artist,
Playwright,
Storyteller

Dale Auger is best known as a visual artist, but he is also a singer, playwright, musician, photographer, storyteller,[27] and theatrical director. Dr. Auger was a Sakaw Cree from the Bigstone Cree Nation in northern Alberta and was born January 16, 1958 in High Prairie, Alberta, Canada. His education began as a young boy when his mother took him to be with the Elders. "I used to say to myself, 'Why is she leaving me with these old people?' but today I see the reason; I was being taught in the old way."[28]

Academics did not appeal to the young Dale and he dropped out of school in Grade 6. He returned to school as an adult, upgraded his education and entered Grant MacEwan College's Native Communications Program in early 1980s. He studied Fine Arts at Alberta College of Art and went on to pursue a Bachelor's degree in education. Auger continued his studies and ultimately received a Ph.D. in Education from the University of Calgary in 2000.

Auger explained how he strives to communicate with his art, "Because these worlds we live in, what we might know as the Indian world versus the white world, sometimes it has created such a complex place for itself that the basic human need to communicate cannot be there. Sometimes we don't communicate because we're so far apart."[29]

His work was regularly showcased and sold at the Calgary Exhibition and Stampede and his annual exhibit in Bragg Creek, "Dale Auger and Friends: A Premiere First Nations Art Event."

His paintings are held in private collections across Canada, and in the United Stated and England, as well as public collections such as the HRH Prince of Wales Collection at Buckingham Palace, Elizabeth Fry Society, Saskatchewan Indian Federated College, and many other public institutions.[30]

Besides being a renowned visual artist, Dr. Auger founded Mamawi (Cree for "all together"), a theatre group that re-enacted scenes of Aboriginal men and women hunting, recounting traditional stories, legends, and pre-contact history. He was often a featured guest speaker at such events as the Youth Empowerment and Recreation Symposium, where he spoke about the importance of culture, sense of community and self. He has appeared on several CBC and A Channel productions and appeared on "Medicine Walker" produced by the Aboriginal Peoples Television Network.[31]

Dale Auger passed away in September 2008. He left to mourn his passing his wife Grace, their three children and three grandchildren.

Profile by: Vivienne Biesel

Bad Boy, Margaret

1900 - 2001
Siksika
Teacher and
traditionalist

Margaret Bad Boy was a respected elder who played an important role in the Siksika Nation and in the Blackfoot Confederacy. At the time of her passing, she was reported to be one of Siksika's oldest and most respected elders.[32] She was a custodian of Siksika ways and felt that it was important to pass down traditions. She taught the young and old their heritage.[33]

Margaret Bad Boy was born the daughter of Three Suns and White Elk on the Siksika Reserve in 1900, and lived to be 101 years old.[34] She married Dick Bad Boy and the couple raised cattle and horses.[35] Although Margaret did not bear any children of her own she was known as the mother, grandmother and great-grandmother to many.[36]

Margaret was known for her great knowledge of the Blackfoot culture. Margaret was a medicine pipe holder and a member of several tribal religious societies. She was consulted about naming ceremonies, sundances, teepee transfers, and smoke ceremonies.[37] She was also instrumental in the repatriation of artifacts from museums since she one of the few people who could identify the items.[38]

Margaret was involved with many publications and language tapes that taught the Blackfoot language. Aakaitapitsinniksiists – Siksika Old Stories was part of an oral language skills series developed by the Siksika Nation and approved as part of the Alberta Learning elementary school curriculum. In this edition, Margaret Bad Boy and another Siksika elder, Beatrice Poor Eagle, tell stories about Napi – the Blackfoot trickster.[39]

Bad Boy had a real love for horses and of the Calgary Stampede. She began attending the Stampede as a child with her father and continued to go with her husband. The Bad Boys would travel into Calgary every summer to put up a teepee and enjoy the Stampede.[40]They also provided horses for what has been dubbed the world's largest outdoor event.[41]

In 2000, Margaret oversaw the transfer of a sacred shield for the Calgary Native Women's Shelter. She approached the shelter's founder about transferring the shield because she believed that the women in the shelter would need the strength and courage provided by the shield.[42]

She was described as, "one of the last of truest members of our community who lived culturally to the truest sense."[43] Margaret was known as the community helper whether it was to help the sick with her traditional remedies or for her kind ear to listen and give advice. People from all over the Blackfoot Confederacy from Alberta to Montana would come to her for advice.

Profile by: Carly Morton

Benson, Mel Edward

1949-
Cree
Resource
Developer

As a First Nation resource developer, oilman Mel Benson has travelled the world. He owns several businesses and fully supports and mentors his fellow Aboriginal people in employment and business.

Mel was born to Lena and James Benson on February 14, 1949. He was raised in a large family with three sisters and eight brothers in Lac La Biche in central Alberta. He is a member of the Beaver Lake First Nation.[44] Benson recognized the importance of education and he persevered to finish high school; he completed Grade 12 by correspondence courses and through night classes. Taking courses, attending seminars and constantly challenging himself and learning from successes and setbacks has helped him build his career.[45]

Mel Benson worked as an instructor at Alberta's first Native Studies Program at Grant MacEwen College in Edmonton before moving into the resource industry.[46] In the 1970s, as Esso Resources' socio-economic advisor during the planning for their Cold Lake heavy oil project, he developed industry-leading policies in the area of Aboriginal employment, education and training. He also worked as socio-economic and northern development manager on the Norman Wells expansion project – worth nearly $1 billion – and then it was on to the Beaufort Sea (1984) development as a project/operations manager in the operations department. He was the superintendent of drilling operations when he was transferred to the production department in 1985. For most of the 1990s he headed Imperial Oil's Drayton Valley oilfield. Again, both Aboriginals and the community benefited.[47] In December 1999, Mel retired from Houston-based Exxon International and returned to Calgary and began an oil and gas management consulting company which serves local and international companies and agencies.[48]

Benson was among fourteen individuals awarded an National Aboriginal Achievement Award (NAAA) for business at the National Arts Centre in Ottawa on March 28, 2003.[49] John Kim Bell, executive director of the NAAA, said Benson was "the most successful Aboriginal person ever to work in the oil and gas industry and that he ran all of Imperial Oil's oilfields at Drayton Valley. He oversaw 1 200 oil wells, eight natural gas plants, he had hundreds of employees under his managemen. Then he was hired to install a $4-billion pipeline in Africa. So as a business leader and entrepreneur, it is hard to get bigger than those numbers."[50] His other awards include a Development Award from the Government of Northwest Territory, an Alberta Justice Crime Prevention Recognition, a Red Cross Service Award, the Hobbema 4-Band Council Award, an Alberta Aboriginal Recognition Award, and the Dr. Ralph Steinhauer Award from the University of Calgary Native Centre.[51]

Benson believes that all of us as individuals, both adults and young people can and must give something back to society and support the less fortunate. He believes the Creator provided us with skills and gifts and an opportunity to share. Mel's advice to others, "work hard, be kind to yourself and those around you and remember to have fun."[52] Mel currently volunteers with Native Addiction Services in Calgary on a major fundraising effort, with construction underway for a thirty-six-bed facility. He now resides in Calgary. He and his former wife, Margaret, have three children, Cody, Claire, and Kristoffer, and many grandchildren.

Nominated by: Margaret Benson

Profile by: Cora Voyageur

Berube, Craig

1965-
Métis
Professional
Hockey Player

Spending a career running your body into others might not seem like a logical way to make a living. Craig Berube proves it could be done rather well and built a nice little seventeen-year career out of it. Berube was born in Calahoo, Alberta on December 17, 1965.[53]

Berube would spend time in the Pacific Coast Junior Hockey League (PCJHL) with Williams Lake before "getting a cup of coffee"[54] with the Kamloops Junior Oilers of the Western Hockey League during the 1982–83 season, playing in four games.[55] The next two years would show an improvement in Berube's game as he increased his point totals each year as a member of the New Westminster Royals.[56] Berube remained undrafted, however, and signed a free agent contract with the Philadelphia Flyers on March 19, 1986.[57] Berube finished his WHL career with the Medicine Hat Tigers, where he went to the 1986 WHL championship before losing to his former team in Kamloops, now known as the Blazers, in five games.[58]

Berube played his first NHL game during the 1986–87 season as a member of Philadelphia Flyers[59] and would also find his way into a half-dozen of the Flyers' playoff games as they made their way to the Stanley Cup finals before losing to the Edmonton Oilers in seven games. During his first five years he reached the one-hundred mark in penalty minutes, topping out during the 1990–91 season with 293 minutes.[60]

Berube found himself near his hometown as member of the Edmonton Oilers following a trade in May 1991. He would never play a game with the Oilers however, as he was the third member of a trade that sent Oiler all-stars Glenn Anderson and Grant Fuhr to the Toronto Maple Leafs. Berube would play out the rest of his career with the Calgary Flames, Washington Capitals, New York Islanders and a second stint with the Philadelphia Flyers.[61] In 1998, Berube went to the Stanley Cup finals with the Washington Capitals. He scored his first career playoff goal in Game Four against the Buffalo Sabres during the Eastern Conference final. The goal turned out to be the game-winning goal, giving the Capitals a pivotal series stranglehold. Berube, following the game, called that goal the biggest of his career.[62]

Berube wound up his career in the NHL with another tour of duty with the Calgary Flames following the 2002–03 campaign.[63] He retired from professional hockey following another thirty-three games with the Philadelphia Phantoms of the American Hockey League during the 2003–04 season.[64]

Berube finished his National Hockey League career with 64 goals and 99 assists for 163 points in 1 143 NHL regular season games.[65] He added three goals and an assist in 89 playoff games. An example of the rough and tumble image he garnered are the 3 149 minutes he spent inside a penalty box during his seventeen-year NHL career.[66]

Craig Berube is currently an assistant coach with the Philadelphia Phantoms of the American Hockey League.[67]

Profile by: Drew Calliou

Big Plume, Joseph Lloyd

1927 – 2004
Tsuu T'ina
Champion
Snooker Player

One of the greatest snooker players to ever grace Canada's pool halls was the late Joseph Lloyd Big Plume.[68] Born in 1927 and known as "Indian Joe" in pool circles, he knew many successes – was a good hunter, farmer, band councillor and family provider. In pool, he was the consummate artist of this exacting game – the total package. Joe credited his prowess at pool to his grandfather, a Labelle, as well as a Calgary Metis, Jim Whitford, and his dad, George, who took him into Calgary pool halls. "I started sneaking in (at age 14). I was big for my age," Joe said. From the 1950s to the 1980s, he was unsurpassed – a master player with hundreds of century runs and three perfect games (147 points) – something even some world champions could not boast about. He played many champions and spectators watched in awe and amazement as he worked his magic. World champions spoke about him with high regard, people like world champions Cliff Thorburn, John Spencer, Alex Higgins and, yes, the legendary Minnesota Fats, who he once defeated. Some of the greats he defeated included Thorburn, North American champion Georges Chenier and Canadian champions Bill Werbeniuk, Jim Wych, Tom Finstad, Jim Bear, Brady Golan, John Bear and others. In 1972 he lost a tough set 8–5 to Spencer, but came back to win 4–3 in a later match. Although he never won the Canadian crown, he managed to upset then-reigning champ Werbeniuk in the Canadian Championship quarter-finals.

Unlike many great champions, Joe did not seek fame and fortune. He was a family man who didn't want to be on the road. Many said he could have been the "king of pool," perhaps world a champion. However, he preferred to return home each day to be with family and community, the Tsuu T'ina First Nation, near Calgary. Spencer believed he would have ranked near if not at the top of the list as the world's best. He was an enviable "potter," and could play unbelievable shape. And, his smooth, flowing stroke was a work of art that made it all look easy. Indeed, he literally made those balls "dance." He was so adept, opponents feared to miss even one shot because he'd run the table on them. He competed in the World Amateur Championships and was third in the Canadian Championships, won the Alberta title several times and the city championship of Calgary many times. Joe was an icon, a free spirit who walked his own path at his own pace. Those who knew him were proud to say, "Yes, I knew Joe, saw him play; he was absolutely amazing, the best!" One thing's certain; anyone who ever played him always knew they were in for one "heckuva" game.

As for his home territory, he truly left his mark, was an inspiration, mentor and model for so many others – natives and non-natives alike – to follow. Many great players learned from Joe or were inspired by him. His gentlemanly manners also endeared him to many who remarked that he was the best ambassador. On a personal level, Joe sat on the Tsuu T'ina Band Council (1977–84). He and his wife, Dora, raised eleven children.

He had a wide circle of friends including farmers he partnered with to work his crops. He was gentle and easy-going and enjoyed a good laugh and friendships. If you were in the loop with Joe, you were a sure bet to be a long-time friend of his. Joe Big Plume passed away on March 2, 2004.

Profile by: Terry Lusty

Black Kettle, Maggie

1919 –
Siksika
Cultural
teacher and
traditionalist

Maggie Black Kettle was born in 1919 "somewhere out in the hills of Gleichen" the daughter of traditional Chief Sitting Eagle from the Siksika Reserve east of Calgary.[69] Maggie was raised with her family until the age of seven. At this time she was placed in the Cluny Residential School and she remained there until the age of sixteen. At fourteen her father passed away and her mother remarried.[70]

Like many children in the residential schools, her contact with her family was limited. Maggie received a weekly, two-hour visit from her mother and stepfather for the duration of her nine-year stay.

After graduation, Maggie married Dick Black Kettle and moved in with her new husband's family. Maggie and her husband worked side by side in the farmer's fields for the next ten years to earn a living for their seven children.

In 1966, Maggie moved to Calgary, where she found it hard to obtain employment. She settled for a job at the downtown Greyhound station coffee shop.[71] While there, Maggie learned that a local school needed a cultural instructor. Maggie applied for the position and thus began a twenty-year career teaching beadwork and the Blackfoot language to school children. Black Kettle also taught at Piitoayis Family School.[72]

Using the knowledge passed down to her from her grandmothers and her aunts she found that she was able to keep her Blackfoot heritage and help integrate it into Calgary's mainstream school system.[73] Involvement with the school children and the ability to pass on traditional skills was important to Black Kettle. It helped her regain some of the self-confidence she had lost while in residential school.[74]

After the death of her husband, Maggie became more involved with her heritage and beliefs by joining the Buffalo Woman's Society.[75] Along with the new membership into the society, Maggie also participated in sundances, powwows, and other traditional gatherings. This caused Maggie to travel to many places across Canada and the United States.[76]

Traditional fancy dancing is an activity that Maggie is proud to be a part of. She continues to compete and has won countless prizes for her dancing.[77] She has passed on her dancing skills to many of her children and grandchildren.

Maggie been involved with the film industry with a bit part in the movie, Wild America and two television shows, *Medicine River* and *North of 60.*[78] Maggie Black Kettle lives in Calgary.

Profile by: Carly Morton

Bourassa, John

1854 - 1941
Cree/Metis
Interpreter
Farmer

John Bourassa was the son of Louis Bourassa, a French-Canadian clerk for the Hudson's Bay Company, and Marguerite Otaikijik Lafleur, a member of the old Metis community on the Peace River.[79] Most of the Bourassa family members left the Peace River area in the 1870s, possibly due to the Hudson's Bay Company "down-sizing" their establishments. Some went to the Lac La Biche area while others went to the Fort Carlton and Round Hill areas of Saskatchewan.[80] However, John Bourassa migrated only as far as Fort Vermilion, where in 1876 he married Lucia St. Cyr, the daughter of Baptiste St. Cyr and Julia McCarthy/Mercredi, another fur-trade family.[81]

John Bourassa, like many Metis, was well-known for his linguistic skills. He was considered invaluable for his abilities to translate the difficult Dene languages of the Beaver and the Slavey. The 1892 Hudson's Bay Company Fort Vermilion Post Report describes John as "Interpreter, married, seven children resident, thirty-eight years of age, eighteen years service, Wages $243.33 with postmaster's allowance $35.28. Contract expires 1st June 1894. About the only Beaver speaker in the country capable of acting as Interpreter. Is reliable and trustworthy."[82] The historical record shows that not only was he employed as interpreter for the Hudson's Bay Company for some twenty years, but he also assisted missionaries, the 1899 Treaty Commission, and even the anthropologist, Pliny Earle Goddard, in his work with the Beaver people.[83]

John Bourassa was also one of the early farmers in the Fort Vermilion area, and according to family history, he specialized in raising cattle and growing wheat.[84] The 1906 map of the Fort Vermilion areas shows him as owning of Lot 9 and part of Lot 8 in the heart of present-day Fort Vermilion.[85] The 1906 census also noted that he owned sixteen horses, sixteen milk cows and twenty other cattle.[86] John and Lucia had a very large family and John was active on their behalf into his elder years. A house built by John in 1920 for one of his daughters, Maria St. Germaine, serves today as the Visitors' Centre for the Fort Vermilion Heritage Centre.[87]

Profile by: Theresa A. Ferguson

Bourque, Sharon

1963 –
Metis
Police Officer
& Community
Worker

Sharon Bourque is a hard-working and committed police officer with the Edmonton Police Service and an active community member. She is involved in many community activities and is always ready to step up to the plate when events need to be organized. Over many years, the Edmonton Aboriginal community has come to rely on her involvement.

Sharon Rosemarie Bourque was born on March 8, 1963 in Dawson Creek, British Columbia. She was one of two daughters born to Rose Asstevit and Joseph Bourque. She has one sister, Colette, and their single-parent father raised them both. She attended South Peace Secondary High School in Dawson Creek and graduated in 1981.[88]

She became interested in police work after attending a session hosted by the Royal Canadian Mounted Police (RCMP) at her high school career day. She began work as a civilian with the Edmonton Police Service for six years before joining as an officer in 1987. She was worked in varying capacities as a police officer.[89]

Bourque is a very active community member. For example, since 2000 she has been involved with the Esquao Awards coordinating an honour guard of Aboriginal women police officers (from the RCMP and Edmonton Police Service) to participate in the Grand Entry and assist with the award presentations.[90]

In fall 2000, she was a guest panelist and speaker at the 2000 Aboriginal Women's Human Rights Symposium hosted by the Institute for the Advancement of Aboriginal Women. She has been both a steering committee member and presenter at the Dreamcatcher Aboriginal Youth Conference held annually in Edmonton for Aboriginal youth between the ages of thirteen to seventeen years of age.[91] She has presented information on policing as a career, bullying, and Internet safety. She has been involved with the Edmonton Native Youth Justice Committee (ENYJC) as a committee member since 1996, where she has made numerous referrals to the committee when dealing with Aboriginal youth during the course of her policing duties.[92]

Sharon has been an instructor for the D.A.R.E. (Drug Abuse Resistance Education) program since 1997. Here she teaches the D.A.R.E. curriculum to Grade 6 students at Ben Calf Robe, Norwood, John A. McDougall, Mother Teresa, Parkdale, McCauley, Spruce Avenue, St. Alphonsus, and Eastwood schools.[93]

She facilitates and coordinates the Edmonton Police Service Native Insight Workshop for police officers and civilian members to learn about Aboriginal people and Aboriginal issues. Speakers are from the Aboriginal community and the workshop has been an overwhelming success.[94]

Sharon has earned many awards and recognitions for her work in the community and in her position as a police officer. In 1999, she received a Certificate of Recognition for Community Service from David Hancock, Q.C., Alberta Minister of Justice.[95] In 2000, she received an Appreciation Award in Recognition of Contribution to the Aboriginal People of Alberta from Native Counseling Services of Alberta as part of their thirtieth anniversary celebration. In 2001, she was a National Aboriginal Achievement Award Nominee. In 2004, she received a Certificate of Recognition from Heather Forsyth, Solicitor General, in recognition of her volunteer contributions to the Edmonton Native Youth Justice Committee.[96]

Sharon is married to Michael Shorter, a fellow police officer with the Edmonton Police Service. They have one daughter, Kendra, and they live in Sherwood Park.

Profile by: Cora Voyageur

Brady, James "Jim" Patrick

1908 – 1967
Metis
Political
Organizer and
Veteran

Jim Brady was best known for his role in establishing the political representation organization called the Metis Nation of Alberta, and for the creation of the Metis Settlements in Alberta. Although he only completed the ninth grade, he was a brilliant scholar committed to lifelong learning. He was a decorated World War II veteran, author and a self-taught geologist.

Jim Brady was born at Lake St. Vincent near St. Paul, Alberta on March 11, 1908. He was the second child in a family of three boys and five girls born to James Brady Sr. and Philomena (Archange). His grandfather, Lawrence Garneau, was a "comrade in arms of Louis Riel, during the struggle in 1870 and 1885."[97] Garneau became wealthy in the fur trade and Brady enjoyed a privileged childhood as a result.[98] Brady was raised at St. Paul de Metis, the largest Metis community in the province.

After leaving school, Brady became an itinerant worker and during this time he "became an avid student of the energetic philosopher-activists who abounded in the towns, on the farms and on the roads of Alberta and Saskatchewan,"[99] and where he developed an affiliation with socialist ideology. His socialist political leanings made him active with both the Communist Party (CP) and the Co-operative Commonwealth Federation (CCF).

In the early 1930s, efforts were made to bring the Metis peoples' desperate living conditions to the government's attention. In 1932, Jim Brady met with Malcolm Norris, Joe Dion, Felix Callihoo, and Peter Tomkins Jr., and together they formed the Alberta Metis

Association.[100] Brady was elected Secretary-Treasurer on December 28, 1932.[101] Over the next couple of years, the group lobbied the government and their efforts were successful with the creation of the Ewing Commission in 1934. The Commission's mandate was to investigate the Metis situation, "[k]eeping particularly in mind the health, education, relief and general welfare of such population.[102] Brady, Norris, and Tomkins testified on behalf of the Metis people of Alberta.[103] Commission findings served as a basis of the Metis Betterment Act and from which the Metis Settlements were created.[104]

Brady enlisted in Canada's armed forces on June 9, 1943. On November 22, 1943, after completing his training, he was sent overseas to Europe where he served as a gunner with the 50th Battery, 4th Medium Regiment (French Canadian), Royal Canadian Artillery.[105] While in Europe he "accepted a war medal on behalf of the 4th Medium Regiment from the Free University of Brussels."[106] He returned to Canada on January 9, 1946 and was honourably discharged on March 11, 1946 in Calgary.[107]

At the request of his friend, Malcolm Norris, he moved to Saskatchewan where he began work on behalf of the CCF government for the Saskatchewan Fish Board, and later established the Metis Cooperatives.[108] His outspoken support of Indian and Metis people led to his forced resignation and he became disillusioned with the CCF around 1950.[109] He moved to La Ronge, Saskatchewan and spent the remainder of his working life as a prospector.

In June 1967, Brady and another prospector disappeared while on a geological expedition to the Foster Lakes in northern Saskatchewan. Their bodies were never found and the mystery surrounding their disappearance remains unsolved.[110]

Submitted by: K. Patricia Colosimo

Calahasen, The Honorable Pearl

1951- Metis
Educator &
Member of the
Legislative
Assembly of
Alberta

Pearl Calahasen was born in Grouard, Alberta on December 5, 1951.[111] She was one of ten children born to Mary and Adolphus Calahasen.[112] She was raised in Grouard and attended the local school. She later attended the University of Alberta where she earned a Bachelor of Education degree and would go on to earn a Master of Education from the University of Oregon. She is an Adjunct Professor at the University of Alberta's Faculty of Education.[113]

Her professional, private-sector experience includes teaching within the private and public school systems, serving as a continuing education coordinator at Alberta Vocation College (Lesser Slave Lake), and working as a private consultant developing and evaluating education materials.[114]

Pearl Calahasen has been a champion of native education programs. She led the development of the first native language program introduced in Alberta schools and was responsible for developing the Cree language program for adult students.[115] As a consultant with Alberta Education, Calahasen was the principal advisor for the development of the native education policy, native curriculum materials, and native language program.[116]

Pearl decided to enter provincial politics running under the Progressive Conservative banner. She was first elected to the Alberta Legislature in 1989.[117] Pearl served as chair of the standing policy committee for natural resources and sustainable development, and Minister without portfolio responsible for Children's Services and

Associate Minister of Aboriginal Affairs.[118] Pearl was elected to her sixth term as the Member of the Legislative Assembly for Lesser Slave Lake in March 2008. She was appointed Alberta's Minister of Aboriginal Affairs and Northern Development.[119]

In addition to her role as MLA, Calahasen serves on the following committees: Private Bills, Public Safety and Services, and Public Accounts.[120]

Actively involved in community affairs, Calahasen has serves as a member of the Native economic development program as an Alberta Human Rights Commissioner, and as a volunteer tutor for illiterate adults. She canvasses for the Heart Fund and Cancer Society and has been actively involved in community sports as a player, coach, and administrator.[121]

Pearl is a long-standing member of the Metis Nation of Alberta, the World Congress on Education, the High Prairie Native Friendship Centre, the Alberta Teachers' Association, and the Metis Economic Development Board.[122] She is one of the founding members of the University of Alberta Native Student Club.[123]

She has earned many awards during her career, including the Governor General's Award (1992), Aboriginal Role Model Award (1998), honorary membership into the Kapawe'no First Nation (1999), Esquao Award from the Institute for the Advancement of Aboriginal Women (2002), and an Aboriginal Achievement Award (2004).[124]

Pearl is married and has one child.

Nominated by: Deanna Cardinal

Profile by: Cora Voyageur

Callihoo, Johnny

1882-1957
Iroquois-Cree
Activist and
Political
organizer

Johnny Callihoo devoted his life to improving the welfare of the Indian people of Canada. He was a proud Native Canadian whose dream was for Aboriginal people to be treated as equals.

Johnny Callihoo was born the son of Chief Michel Callihoo in 1882 on the Michel's reserve, near Villeneuve, Alberta. He was a treaty Indian of Iroquois-Cree descent.[125] Johnny attended the Dunbow Industrial School near Calgary and then attended school in St. Albert. He was fluent in English, Cree, and French. Despite the lack of formal education Johnny was an avid reader who taught himself about government policies and treaties, and became an expert on the Indian Act.[126]

Callihoo had many careers throughout his life. He was one of the first people to start farming on the Michel reserve.[127] He was a freighter who worked mainly the Edmonton to Fort McMurray route and around Athabasca and Lesser Slave Lake. He also delivered mail and payrolls using his team of horses.

In the 1930s, John urged Indian people to become politically active. In 1939 he helped found the Indian Association of Alberta (IAA) and acted as the president from 1939–1946.[128] The IAA fought for the rights of First Nations people including improved social benefits and more educational opportunities.[129]

John was greatly influenced by some of his contemporaries, including Metis leader Malcolm Norris, and First Nations leaders Albert Lightning and Peter Burnstick.[130] John formed an alliance with representatives of all Aboriginal peoples in Alberta – the Metis, the treaty Indians, and the non-treaty Indians. All agreed that social and economic conditions of reserves had to be improved.[131] He believed that the only way for better conditions was to improve education, social welfare benefits, and to grant full citizenship to Indian people.

He joined many off-reserve organizations including the United Farmers Association, the Alberta Wheat Pool, and other farm-based organizations whose members were usually non-Aboriginal.[132]

In 1953 Johnny was the recipient of the Queen Elizabeth II Coronation Medal. In Canada this medal was awarded to selected individuals who demonstrated greatness.[133] John fought for the rights and interests of Alberta Indians which included better medical care, access to education, and the protection of hunting, fishing and trapping rights.[134]

He was a clever leader and allied himself with social-justice activists. Mr. Callihoo's hard work resulted in mainstream society becoming more aware of the poor living conditions endured by Indian people.

In 1957, Johnny Callihoo died in his St. Albert home at the age of 75 years.[135]

Profile by: Michelle Voyageur

Callihoo, Victoria

1861 – 1966
Metis
Historian

Victoria Callihoo lived through many eras, which provided her with a wealth of information to pass on. Victoria Belcourt was born on November 19, 1861. She was christened Victoria after Queen Victoria, the reigning monarch, by Father Albert Lacombe. Her father, Alexis Belcourt, was a French hunter and her mother, Nancy Rowan, was a Cree woman who was recognized by many as a medicine woman. Victoria went on her first buffalo hunt when she was thirteen years old, at a time when buffalo were plentiful and described as "a dark solid moving mass."[136] Victoria did not get much schooling but could read and learned to write her name.

At seventeen Victoria Belcourt married Louis Callihoo, a French, Cree, and Iroquois farmer. The couple farmed at Villeneuve and later moved to nearby Lac Ste. Anne, Alberta. Louis and Victoria raised twelve children, six boys and six girls. The Callihoo family was busy since they not only farmed but also ran a sawmill. They later operated a hotel at Lac. Ste. Anne.[137]

Louis died in 1926 at a senior's home in St. Albert and Victoria found herself a widow at sixty-five years old.[138] She lived long enough to talk about her adventures to her great-grandchildren.[139] With a wealth of information to pass on she did just that and has left Alberta with great stories and histo ry that can be useful for all those who are interested in cultural history. Victoria provided information and stories with two of her stories published in the *Alberta Historical*

Review called "Life on a Farm" and the "Buffalo Hunt." Other stories are collected and preserved in the Provincial Archives.

For Victoria Callihoo, regular visits to the doctor did not occur until she was ninety-nine years old. She did not smoke, drink and was very healthy.[140] As a pioneer of old ways, Victoria Callihoo was able to live a simple life compared to modern day. The advancement of technology has led many of her family members in different paths; she still remained content with her life without all the technology. She did not speak on a telephone until she was over one-hundred years old.[141]

At the time of her death in 1966 at the age of 104, she was a beloved granny to 57 grandchildren, 165 great-grandchildren and 8 great-great-grandchildren.[142] Victoria has been involved in the Metis jigging tradition all her life even up until her 103rd birthday as she competed in the Red River jig at a native rally and won. At the age of seventy-four, Victoria competed in the Red River Jig and won first prize, which was a tanned buffalo hide.[143] Her love and zest for jigging reflects her grace and style in her many trophies.

Profile by: Marlaine Metchewais

Calliou, Brian

1958 -
Cree
Lawyer and
Administrator

Brian Calliou promotes legal and social justice of the Aboriginal people of Canada by seeking the reformation of policies and laws. Being an Aboriginal lawyer, Brian represents Indigenous people in their fight for social and legal justice.[144]

Calliou is Cree from the Sucker Creek First Nation in central Alberta. He was born on August 21, 1958, the oldest of five children born to a Cree mother, Yvonne (Calliou) and a British father, Austin Arlidge. He spent most of his formative years at the Sucker Creek reserve with his beloved grandparents, Elizabeth and Clement Calliou.

His educational journey began later than most. While the father of two (Carly and Drew), he decided to leave the security of his job as a plumber/pipefitter to attempt post secondary schooling. Although uncertain of his prospects, since he had not completed Grade 12, he persisted. The rest is history. Brian would go on to earn a University Transfer Diploma from Grande Prairie Regional College, a Bachelor of Arts in Political Science, a Bachelor of Law, and a Master of Law from the University of Alberta.[145]

It turns out that some of the problems with post-secondary schooling were not all academic. While attending the University of Alberta Law School, Brian and the other Aboriginal law students dealt with many obstacles including racism. It seems that some law students believed that the University had lowered its entrance requirements to admit Aboriginal students, and that somehow, the Aboriginal students were gaining advantages at their expense. The Aboriginal students, including Calliou, persisted and were able to complete their degrees.

Calliou's master's thesis explored the social and cultural environment surrounding the imposition of local and provincial game laws on First Nations people who had been promised unfettered access to the province's natural resources when they signed treaty only decades before.

He worked as a lawyer for many years including running his own law practice. He has taught as a sessional instructor at both the University of Alberta, where he taught Native Studies courses dealing with Aboriginal law, and at the University of Calgary, where he taught introductory Law and Society courses.[146] He has also served as a tutor for Aboriginal law students and as a mentor under the University of Calgary's Law Mentorship Program.

Brian is an active community member. For example, he has served as the chair of the Aboriginal Section of the southern Alberta Canadian Bar Association; executive member of the Indigenous Bar Association; member of the Legal Archives Society of Alberta. He was the chair of the Alberta Historical Resources Foundation Board (AHRF) for five years and served on its board of directors for an additional four years. As AHRF chair, Brian helped monitor issues related to the preservation of Alberta's heritage including controversial issues such as the renaming of Ha Ling's Peak and renovations to Edmonton's Rossdale Power Plant. He also served as trustee of the Canadian Native Friendship Centre (1995–1998), chair of the Boyle Street Community Cooperative (1994–1998) and member of the University of Alberta's School of Native Studies Advisory Council, (1989–1991).[147]

Through Brian's research on Aboriginal legal and social issues he exposes the non-Aboriginal community to important issues that affect Indigenous people. He has published many academic and non-academic articles dealing with Aboriginal issues in Canada. He has spoken at academic and industry conferences across Canada, the United States, Britain, and Europe.

He is the current director for The Banff Centre's Aboriginal Leadership and Management Program, which delivers training programs to Aboriginal agencies, organizations and to reserve administrators across Canada.[148]

Brian lives at Bragg Creek with his wife. He has two children and two grandchildren.

Profile by: Michelle Voyageur

Cardinal, Douglas Joseph Henry

1934 -
Métis
Architect and
Author

Against the horizon of the Prairies, his buildings fit into the landscape with an innovative artistry. The circle is the basis for these architectural designs that flow naturally into the landscape. The man behind these unique creations is Douglas Cardinal, a Métis architect who is recognized in fields ranging from educational philosophy and town planning to his pioneering work in the CADD (Computer Aided Drafting and Design) system of architecture. His buildings can be found across Canada in such communities as Hay River, Northwest Territories; La Ronge, Saskatchewan; Fort McMurray, Alberta; Grande Prairie, Alberta (Phase I of the Grande Prairie Regional College); and Red Deer, Alberta (St. Mary's, a Roman Catholic Church).[149] Perhaps his most noted commission was the Canadian Museum of Civilization located in Hull, Quebec – across the Ottawa River from the Canadian Parliament Buildings. Cardinal has also designed buildings in other countries around the world, including Australia, New Zealand, the United States and Bolivia.[150]

Douglas Joseph Henry Cardinal was born in Calgary in 1934 to Joseph and Frances Cardinal.[151] Although his parents were of Aboriginal descent (his father was mixed European and Blackfoot ancestry, while his mother was Métis), they did not openly acknowledge this aspect of their heritage.[152] As a result, Cardinal grew up in a "conspiracy of silence" regarding his Indian roots. Only the obvious native legacy of facial features belied his all-white upbringing."[153] When his mother became too ill to care for her family, he and his two younger brothers were sent to live at St. Joseph's, a Catholic residential school near Red Deer, Alberta. During his four years at residential school he received fine arts training from the Grey Nuns who ran the school. This training would figure significantly for him in later life.[154]

After completing high school in 1952, Cardinal was accepted into the University of British Columbia's (UBC) School of Architecture at the age of eighteen.[155] In his third year of study, he was dismissed from the UBC program after failing a studio design class.[156] After a Mexican holiday, Cardinal landed a job as a draftsman with a prestigious architectural firm, Jessen Jessen Milhouse and Greeven, in Austin, Texas.[157] He continued his university studies and graduated with an honours degree in architecture from the University of Texas in 1963.[158]

Early in his professional career, Cardinal took an active interest in native culture and religion. He started attending sweat lodge ceremonies in Hobbema and studied under a local medicine man. This spiritual awakening influenced his writing. His publications include: Of the Spirit: Writings by Douglas Cardinal (1977), and The Native Creative Process (1991).

Douglas Cardinal's architectural accomplishments have been recognized both nationally and internationally. Throughout his career he has received several honorary doctorates from Canadian universities, including the University of Windsor (1992), the University of Lethbridge (1994), Carleton University (1994), Trent University (1994), Concordia University (1998), and Emily Carr Institute of Art and Design (2000).[159] Cardinal has also received numerous architectural awards, most recently the Governor General's Award in Visual and Media Arts.[160] He was honoured with a National Aboriginal Achievement Award in 1995.[161]

Douglas Cardinal currently lives in Aylmer, Quebec, and runs an Ottawa architectural firm.[162]

Profile by: Vivienne Biesel

Cardinal, Gilbert "Gil"

1950 -
Metis
Filmmaker,
Director, and
Producer

Gilbert "Gil" Cardinal is a man known to many in the Aboriginal community and the film industry. He has written, produced, and directed movies, documentaries, and television shows since he began his career in the media industry in the 1970s. His focus on Aboriginal issues and the Aboriginal experience has helped increase Aboriginal awareness in Canadian society.

Gil Cardinal, a Metis, was raised in Edmonton, Alberta. At the age of two years old, Gil was ordered by the courts to be placed in a foster home. He was raised by a non-Aboriginal family, the Wilsons, and was not exposed to other Metis or Aboriginals.[163] This fact would be significant in later life.

Gil started his career in the film industry after taking the advice of a social worker who told him that he should enrol in the Radio and Television Arts Technology program at the Northern Alberta Institute of Technology (NAIT) in Edmonton, Alberta.[164] After graduating from the program he began work as a cameraman for the Access Network in Edmonton, Alberta. In the early 1970s, Gil Cardinal made his first documentary, A Portrait of the Pianist Mark Joblonski. After this first film, Cardinal was hired to direct the television series, Come Alive. By the 1980s Cardinal was freelancing for the National Film Board of Canada. It was here that he began to focus on native issues. Some of his earlier work included Children of Alcohol (1984), The Courage of One's Convictions (1985), Hotwalker (1986), and Foster Child (1987).[165]

With Foster Child, Cardinal produced poignant autobiographical documentary about his upbringing. This documentary followed his search for his birth mother. In it he learned that his birth mother, Lucy Cardinal, had passed away in 1974, and that she fought with poverty and alcohol for most of her life. Through this production he was able to find answers about his family background and was able to meet and reconnect with many of his relatives.[166]

Since Foster Child, Gil Cardinal has gone on to make many more documentary films including The Spirit Within (1990), Tikinagan (1991), and David with F.A.S. (1997).[167] Cardinal has also directed episodes for the television show North of Sixty. He co-wrote and directed the mini-series Big Bear (1998), and has done work for the British Broadcasting Corporation, Canadian Broadcasting Corporation, and Atlantis Films.[168]

Cardinal's work on Aboriginal themes and issues has been show-cased at numerous international film festivals and has won him a number of awards. He won a Gemini Award for best director for his film Foster Child, and in 1997 he received a National Aboriginal Achievement Award for Film and Television.[169] Cardinal received an honorary diploma from the Northern Alberta Institute of Technology in Edmonton in 2001.[170] He lives in Edmonton.

Profile by: Jeff Moulton

Cardinal, Harold

1945 - 2005
Cree
Author,
Activist, and
Politician

Harold Cardinal is admired for his persistence and dedication to challenging principles and creating opportunities for positive change for First Nations communities in Canada. His passion for seeking equality for First Nations peoples led him to wear many vocational hats, including author, politician, activist, scholar, professor, entrepreneur, and treaty rights consultant.

Harold Cardinal was born on January 27, 1945, to Frank and Agnes (Cunningham) Cardinal in High Prairie, Alberta. He was raised, along with his seventeen siblings, on the Sucker Creek Reserve in central Alberta.[171] After completing high school in Edmonton in 1965, he moved to Ottawa, Ontario, where he studied Sociology at St. Patrick's College. Cardinal first dabbled in politics as a student. He was the Associate Secretary for Indian Affairs for the Canadian Union of Students in 1967, and was elected president the following year.[172]

After returning to Alberta in 1968, he was elected the youngest president of the Indian Association of Alberta (IAA), where he served for nine controversial years.[173] During his time as president, he initiated many programs and policies to benefit Indians. In 1969, he authored *The Unjust Society: The Tragedy of Canada's Indians,* a stinging criticism of the reigning Liberal government's Indian policies.[174] In 1969, the federal Liberals drafted the Statement of the Government of Canada on Indian Policy (also known as The White Paper), which proposed sweeping changes to the relationship between the federal government and Canada's treaty Indians.[175] As IAA President, Cardinal commissioned the Indian's response, Citizens

Plus (also known as the Red Paper), the following year. For a short period in 1977, Harold held the office of Regional Director General of Indian Affairs – the first Indian to hold this position.[176]

After writing his second book, The Rebirth of Canada's Indians (1977), Cardinal left public life to become a director of an oil and gas company and a treaty rights and land claims consultant with Northern Alberta Indian bands.[177] During this hiatus from public life, Harold held posts as the Chief of the Sucker Creek Band and the Vice Chief for the Western Region with the Assembly of First Nations.[178]

Cardinal also returned to school. He obtained a Bachelor of Law degree at the University of Saskatchewan and a Master of Law degree from Harvard University. His thesis dealt with the underlying principles of Treaty 8. He received an honorary doctorate from the University of Alberta in 2000. He was also pursuing a Ph.D. at the University of British Columbia at the time of his death.[179]

Harold Cardinal continued to endeavour to achieve his lifetime goal of parity and justice for Native Canadians. In fall 2000, Cardinal ran unsuccessfully as a federal Liberal candidate in the Athabasca region.[180] In 2001, he received a Lifetime Achievement Award from the National Aboriginal Achievement Foundation (NAAF) for his association with the Red Paper and his book, Unjust Society: The Tragedy of Canada's Indians.[181] The NAAF declared that his "very presence helped Canadians at large opt for pluralism and tolerance during a very crucial time. He is a true Aboriginal – and a national treasure."[182] Harold Cardinal passed away in June 2005.

Profile by: Catherine Clennet

Cardinal, The Honorable Mike

1941 -
Cree
Member of the
Legislative
Assembly of
Alberta

Mike Cardinal is best known for his work with the Government of Alberta as a Member of the Legislative Assembly representing the Athabasca/Redwater riding. A large proportion of this riding, about 20 per cent, is made up of Aboriginal people.[183]

Mike Cardinal was born in Calling Lake, Alberta on July 17, 1941.[184] He was one of thirteen children born to Joe and Rose Cardinal.[185] He attended Alberta Vocational College in Calling Lake, from there he went on to work locally for a lumberyard from 1957 to 1968 before moving to the competitor to work as manager.[186]

In 1972 Cardinal took on his first government position as a mortgage officer with Alberta Housing Corporation. He then moved to the Alberta Human Resources Development Authority, were he developed the native housing relocation program. Cardinal took on the position of regional supervisor of Employment/Counselling Services with Alberta Advanced Education and Manpower for ten years.[187] Mike also served as a socio-economic consultant with North East Region, Alberta Family Social Services.[188]

Mike ran for the Conservative Party of Alberta in the Athabasca/Redwater constituency in 1988. He won election. Mike has won five consecutive terms as Member of the Legislative Assembly, serving as Minister of Family and Social Services, Minister of Sustainable Resources, Associate Minister of Forestry, Minister of Resources development and Minister of Human Resources.[189]

In addition to his role as MLA, he served on many committees including: Standing Committee on Energy and Sustainable Development; Government Reorganization Secretariat; Social Services Caucus Committee (Chair), Native Affairs Caucus Committee; Northern Alberta Development Council (Chair); Standing Policy Committee on Education and Training; and Standing Committee on Private Bills.[190] Mike did not seek re-election in 2008.

Mike is married to Mary Agnes and the father of two children. He lives in Calling Lake, Alberta.

Profile by: Carly Morton

Cardinal, Tantoo

1950 -
Metis
Actress and
Activist

Throughout history, artistic communities have served as vehicles for personal and political expression. Tantoo Cardinal[191] is an example of an actress who approaches her roles and uses her experience to help change how others view the Aboriginal community. Tantoo Cardinal's career spans radio, theatre, television, film, and politics. She is one of North America's most widely recognized Aboriginal actresses, with a list of awards under her belt.[192]

Cardinal was born in Anzac, Alberta, about 400 km northeast of Edmonton, Alberta. She was born in 1950, the youngest child of a Cree mother and a Caucasian father. Her parents separated shortly after her birth and she went to live with her maternal grandmother at six months old. She was nicknamed "Tantoo" by her Cree grandmother.[193]

Her political activism steadily grew when faced with the negative attitudes towards Aboriginal people in Edmonton, Alberta in the mid-1960s. While attending Bonnie Doon High School in Edmonton, Tantoo joined the United Native Youth that helped her forge links with other young Aboriginal people.[194] At this time, she was searching for her gift, her identity, and her community.[195] She had no status card, no reserve, and no Metis community.[196] She married Fred Martin in 1968.[197] In 1971, she won a small role in a CBC documentary on Father Lacombe.[198]

As a representative of the Canadian Aboriginal arts community, she has used her craft to communicate who she is as an individual and who her Aboriginal people are. Cardinal's approach to acting is

81

strongly influenced by her interest in the Aboriginal movement. Her life experiences have become a natural part in her performances and she states, "There is a well of emotional pain, although that feeds me as an actress, it can also be horrible."[199] Tantoo Cardinal's international recognition is a result of her films. Her impressive filmography, includes, in part, *Loyalties* (1987), *Dances With Wolves* (1990), *Where the Rivers Flow North* (1993), *Legends Of The Fall* (1994), *The Education of Little Tree* (1997), and *Smoke Signals* (1998).[200] Her stage roles include Jessica, an adaptation of Maria Campbell's autobiographical account, *Halfbreed;* and Floyd Favel's *All my Relations,* for which she won the 1990 Elizabeth Sterling Hayes Award for best actress.[201]

She has received many nominations and awards for her acting from both the Aboriginal and the mainstream artistic communities.[202] In 1998, she received the National Aboriginal Achievement Award for her contributions to the political and artistic communities.[203] She viewed this award not only as an acknowledgment of her work, but also as a celebration of her Aboriginal community.[204] She was awarded an honorary doctorate in Fine Arts from the University of Rochester in 1995 and from the University of Calgary in 2005.

Tantoo Cardinal feels that through acting, she can tell her people's stories, and tell them correctly. Her success is due to a mix of raw talent, smart choices, and the respect she has earned from her peers. She lives in Vancouver.

Profile by: Valerie Kynaston

Cardinal-Schubert, Joane Marguerite

1942 - 2009
Metis
Artist

Joane Cardinal-Schubert was an acclaimed artist, known as a multi-media artist, lecturer, poet and writer. Her work has been exhibited nationally and internationally.

Joane Cardinal-Schubert was born in Red Deer, Alberta in 1942. She is the fourth child among eight born to Joseph and Frances Cardinal.[205] Joanne was a sickly child and had to spend a lot of time in bed as a result. It was during this time that art became an escape from reality for her.

Joane began studying art in 1962. She attended the Alberta College of Art, at the University of Alberta, and graduated in 1977 from the University of Calgary with a bachelor's degree in Fine Arts.[206] After graduation Joane took a position as assistant curator at the Nickel Art Museum.[207] In 1986, Cardinal-Schubert was elected to the Royal Academy of Art.[208] In 1992, she was part of Indigena – an exhibition at the Canadian Museum of Civilization.[209]

To date Joane has had over twenty solo exhibits and forty group exhibits, many of these have been in major cities around the world.[210] She has received many Canada Council grants, scholarships, and awards for her work. She is a published author who has contributed to international art magazines, catalogs, and books.[211]

Joane created the theatre company Spider Tribe that has been recognized as aboriginal dedicated to the Aboriginal arts. She also is an editor of the Alberta addition for *FUSE Magazine*.[212]

Awards and recognitions that Joanne has received over the years include many scholarships, and Canadian Council grants. In 1985 Joane was inducted into the Royal Canadian Academy, then in 1993 she was awarded the Commemorative Medal of Canada for contributions to the arts. She received an Alumni Award of Excellence from the Alberta College of Art and Design in 2002. In 2003, Joane was conferred an honorary doctorate from the University of Calgary.[213] Joane Cardinal-Schubert passed away in September 2009. She left her husband, Mike, and sons Christoper and Justin to mourn her passing.

Profile by: Carly Morton

Carlson, Nellie Mildred

1927 –
Cree
Indian
Women's
Rights Activist

When Nellie Carlson was a young woman she promised her mother that she would speak for those who could not speak for themselves.[214] She has spent much of her adult life fulfilling that commitment. She has spoken for women and for children in her efforts for social justice.

Nellie Mildred Makokis was born on July 3, 1927 on the Saddle Lake reserve near St. Paul, Alberta.[215] She was one of only two surviving children of Frank and Marjorie (Jackson) Makokis.[216] She attended Blue Quills residential school and completed a Grade 8 education, which was standard for that time.

In 1947, Nellie married Elmer Carlson, the son of a Cree woman and a Swedish father.[217] As the product of a "mixed" marriage, Elmer was deemed "Metis" by the government and did not have Indian status. Although Nellie was born a Status Indian, her marriage to Elmer (a non-Indian) caused her to lose her Indian status as set out in Section 12(1) (b) of the Indian Act. This policy would prove significant in Nellie's future. Nellie and Elmer would have ten children, nine of whom survived to adulthood.[218] The Carlson family moved to Edmonton in the 1960s, where Elmer got work as a nursing orderly at the Charles Camsell Indian Hospital.[219]

Although she was the mother of a large family, Nellie found time to devote to social issues. In 1967, Carlson joined the Voice of Alberta Native Women Society and later served on its executive committee. In 1968 she got involved with a group that would evolve into Indian Rights for Indian Women.[220] Over the next sixteen years this group would lobby the federal government to make changes to the Indian Act, which discriminated against Indian women. This group of determined Indian women was not dissuaded when during a meeting the then Prime Minister, Pierre Trudeau, told them: "Go to [your] leaders. They will help you make the changes." To this remark, the women retorted: "This legislation came from this building. What good can our leaders do about something that the government created? You must help us change it."[221] The Indian Act was amended on April 17, 1985 so that Indian status could not be gained or lost through marriage.[222] The women's persistence paid off.

In addition to her interest in reinstatement of Indian women, Nellie was also involved in the furtherance of education for Indian children. In 1978, she and others established an advisory group called "The Sacred Circle" to enhance native education within the Edmonton Public School Board. Nellie also spent four years with the Social Justice Commission of the Roman Catholic Archdiocese of Edmonton. The group had the mandate to look at the social conditions of women in the inner city and the quality of life of the native people.[223]

Nellie has earned many awards. For example, in 1975, International Women's Year, she was honored by CFRN Television for her work to improve the social and political situation of Indian women in Canada. In 1988, Nellie was a recipient of the Person's award in recognition of her work for Aboriginal women's rights. In 1990, Nellie has a street in Edmonton named after her. In 1996, she won an Esquao Award from the Institute for the Advancement of Aboriginal Women for her work on Aboriginal women's issues.[224]

Nellie Carlson is now in her eighties and is as busy as ever. She serves as an Elder with many Edmonton service agencies. She lives with her husband, Elmer, in Edmonton.

Profile by: Cora Voyageur

Chalifoux, Thelma

1929-
Metis
Educator,
Activist, and
Senator

When Thelma Chalifoux was a young single mother struggling to put food on the table for her seven young children, she took to heart the words of her parents, who said, "If you keep the faith, you'll make it."[225] Chalifoux has worked hard to "make it" and become one of Canada's most ardent advocates of Metis culture and identity.

She was born the second of five children to a Metis father, Paul Michel Villeneuve and an American mother, Helene Margarite Ingerson, in Calgary, Alberta during the Great Depression. At eighteen years old, she married a man in the military. She found herself raising her young family on her own while her husband was dispatched to different assignments.

At the age of twenty-five, Chalifoux was abandoned by her abusive husband. She had a ninth grade education and seven young children for whom to care. Living by her belief that "the good Lord will look after us," she completed her education and raised her family. Chalifoux received her education at the Chicago School of Interior Design, the Southern Alberta Institute of Technology (Construction Estimating), and Lethbridge Community College (Sociology).[226]

Chalifoux's professional experience as a consultant, entrepreneur, and negotiator is extensive and impressive. Chalifoux has served as a land claims negotiator (1979–1982, 1996–1998), a consultant and senator for the Metis Nation of Alberta Association (1990–1995), and as a consultant for Chalifoux and Associates (1996–1998), a company that provides workshops on board development training to community and volunteer organizations. She also served as a panel member of the Alberta Provincial Appeals/Alberta Family and Social Services (1989–1998), and has been an active member of the Metis Nation of Alberta since 1961. Her career also includes a foray into journalism, where she had a stint as a newscaster, producer, host of a weekly show, and freelance writer.[227]

After becoming a distinguished recipient of the National Aboriginal Achievement Award in 1995, Chalifoux was appointed to the Senate by Prime Minister Jean Chretien on November 26, 1997. Senator Chalifoux was both the first Aboriginal woman and the first Metis appointed to the Senate of Canada.[228]

Hand in hand with her work as a senator, Chalifoux has worked to strengthen cross-cultural understandings by taking up positions in various sectors: community development, wellness, justice, education and economic initiatives. As a senator, Chalifoux has addressed issues of Metis housing, genetically modified foods, drug company relations with the federal government and environmental legislation.[229] More recently, Chalifoux gained notoriety for championing the proposed Louis Riel Act in 2001. The purpose of the Act is to honor Riel and the Metis people by commemorating the leader's unique and historic role in the advancement and development of Confederation.[230]

As chairperson of the Senate Standing Committee on Aboriginal People, Senator Chalifoux appointed a task force to discuss with Edmonton aboriginal groups, leaders, elders and youth the issue of urban aboriginal youth gangs.[231] The mandate of this task force is to seek solutions for the problems facing urban aboriginal youth. According to Senator Chalifoux, "We don't need another study . . . we need an action plan for change. The communities need to be empowered to take positive action in what is happening within their own communities."[232]

In discussing her role as a Senator, Chalifoux notes that, "my role here is partly education and partly bringing the issues forward, especially for the Metis because we are truly the forgotten people."[233] Thus, on the whole, she has endeavored to give Metis people a voice in government.

Senator Thelma Chalifoux is now in her eighties and has more than thirty grandchildren and numerous great-grandchildren.[234]

Profile by: Myles Wieselman

Chonkolay, Harry Gabriel

1909-1998
Dene Tha
Politician and
Community
Leader

It was the end of an era when Harry Chonkolay passed away in 1998 at the age of eighty-nine years. His passing marked the last of the hereditary Indian chiefs in Canada. He served as chief for the Slavey/Beaver Indians, that are now called Dene Tha for more than half a century.[235]

Harry Gabriel Chonkolay was born at Meander River on April 4, 1909 to Julie McKay (Tachatdje) and Romain Boniface Tchonkale. He was baptized twice – once in 1911 where he was named Gabriel and again in 1912 when he was named Harry. The 1912 name stuck.[236]

He married Elizabeth Mercredi in 1928. The couple would have eight children. In his early married life, Chonkolay worked as a trapper and hunter to support his family.[237] His wife Elizabeth was invaluable to him as a life partner but also helped him with correspondence since Harry Chonkolay did not have a formal education. However, the chief did speak five languages.[238]

Both the chief and his wife were enthusiastic supporters of education. In fact, later in life he served on the Board of Directors for Fairview College. He believed that education could help his people have a better life.

Chief Chonkolay was a respected leader of the Dene Tha in northwestern Alberta. The role of chief was handed down to Chonkolay from his uncle Talley. Harry was selected to lead the Dene Tha in 1938. He was only the fourth chief of the band. His Uncle Francois Tchatee (Dzadin) was a signatory of Treaty 8, signed on June 23, 1900.

When Chonkolay became chief in 1938, the Dene Tha did not have a reserve. He urged the federal government to grant reserve lands to his people. The reserve land was given in 1957.

As chief, Chonkolay worked closely with local politicians, the RCMP, MLAs, MPs and Indian Affairs to improve conditions for people living on the three reserves (Assumption, Bushe River and Meander River) that make up the Dene Tha band.[239]

He was a progressive chief and was able to bring many needed changes and services to the community. For example, he was able to successfully lobby the government for better roads, schools, health services, and housing.[240]

Harry Chonkolay's achievements did not go unrecognized or unappreciated. He was given the Alberta Achievement Award in 1987 and made a member of the Order of Canada in 1989.[241] The citation stated, "he has given valuable and inspirational leadership to his people in their transition from an entirely hunting and trapping society to one in-step with modern times."[242]

His health began to fail in the last few years of his life. Until then, he had lived an active and healthy life. In fact, he was buried in the same chief's suit he was given when he first took up the post in 1938.[243] Harry Chonkolay passed away at Fort Vermilion.

Hundreds of mourners from across Alberta, the Northwest Territories, and British Columbia attended his funeral.[244] At the time of his death, he had twenty grandchildren, thirty great-grandchildren and six great-great-grandchildren.[245]

Profile by: Cora Voyageur

Clark-Jones, Bertha

Metis
1922 -
Women's
Rights Activist
and Veteran

Bertha Clark-Jones has been a fixture in Aboriginal women's circles and in Aboriginal veterans' societies for a very long time. Her commitment to Aboriginal women's causes has kept her busy well past retirement age.

Bertha was the fifth of fourteen children born to Louis and Emilie (née St. Arnault) Houle. She was born to pioneering parents who moved to the Clear Hills area in northern Alberta to homestead.[246]

After completing high school, she moved to Grande Prairie and worked as a waitress. It was there that she began to hear news of unrest in Europe. She signed up to serve her country when she turned eighteen in 1940. She had tried to enlist a year earlier but was told that she was too young.[247] She was one of the very few Aboriginal women to serve in the Royal Canadian Air Force, women's division. She was a corporal and an acting sergeant with the RCAF.[248]

As a war veteran, Clark-Jones was entitled to a half-section of any unoccupied Crown land that she chose. She wanted to live at the Paddle Prairie Metis Settlement near High Level, Alberta, but her request was refused because she was a woman.[249]

Bertha became involved with Aboriginal women's issues in the 1960s. She was a founding member of the Voice of Alberta Native Women's Society – an Aboriginal women's advocacy group that tackled social and economic issues.[250] She served as its president. The organization's board and executive members travelled to communities all over the province to make Aboriginal women aware of their rights and the resources available to them.[251]

She is also an active community member. She is recognized as an Elder with the Metis Association of Alberta. She is a board member with the Child and Family Services Authority for Alberta.[252]

Some of the awards Bertha has received include the Golden Jubilee Medal in honor of all Metis war veterans. This medal was awarded to twenty Metis veterans by the Governor General in commemoration of the 50th anniversary of the Queen's reign in 2002.[253] The Fort McMurray Region gave Bertha a lifetime achievement award. Bertha has also been inducted into the Metis Hall of Honour. She received an Esquao Award in 1996, an award given annually to Aboriginal woman who have made a difference in their communities.

Bertha Clark-Jones lives in Athabasca, Alberta.

Profile by: Carly Morton

Collins, Joan

1948 –
Metis
Court worker
and advocate

Joan Collins set out to make a difference for her Aboriginal people. The proud Metis woman has not only beaten odds to get where she is but has helped countless numbers of people along the way.

Joan Collins was born to Mervin Airhart and Theresa L'Hirondelle on January 12, 1948, in Edmonton, Alberta.[254] She was the only girl among five children, which included Mervin Jr., Hugh, Ken and David.[255]

The Edmonton Native Youth Justice Committee helped push Joan's initiative for a sentencing circle where troubled youths could be encouraged to change their lifestyles by elders and role models. She eventually became the committee coordinator.[256]

The committee was founded in January 1994 to help troubled youths avoid jail time while attempting to put their own lives back on the straight and narrow. The program has had around eight hundred cases.[257] Collins has spent eighteen years with the Native Counselling Services of Alberta and calls herself a "Proud Metis."[258]

The program uses corrective measures such as healing and counselling to help youths avoid jail time and find out about possible reasons for their troubles with the law.[259] Children under the age of eighteen are given an opportunity to speak about social or personal problems they are facing which potentially result in their destructive behavior.[260]

"We set out to find out what else is going on in their lives, what is it that's bringing them to court," said Collins in a 2004 interview with the *Edmonton Journal*.[261]

One example was a seventeen-year-old Edmonton youth whose previous mishaps with the law could have potentially landed him in jail. Instead he was ordered to attend the sentencing circle where it was discovered he suffered from headaches caused by hunger. The agency helped provide for the family and the boy was able to keep himself out of trouble.[262]

The Aboriginal woman has also commented on how sentencing circles were used far before English common law made its way across the Atlantic.

Collins served on the Board of Directors of the Canadian Native Friendship Centre in Edmonton from 1978 through 1983 as well as a member of the advocacy group, Indian Rights for Indian Women, for two years beginning in 1976. She is the mother of two sons, Darren and Brian.

Joan Collins was awarded the YWCA's Woman of Distinction award in 2001 for Social Services and Advocacy.[263] She continues to work as a court worker for the Province of Alberta. She recently became a grandmother – an event that she is proud of.[264]

Nominated by: Pamela Anderson

Profile by: Cora Voyageur

Cree, Raphael

1893-2002
Cree
Elder,
Advocate

Over the 108 years of his long life Raphael Cree, a respected elder and community advocate, witnessed the transformation, misfortune, and triumphs of Alberta's First Nations people. His life spanned three centuries.

Raphael Cree was born in 1893 at Muskeg Lake, Saskatchewan. He was a First Nations member of the Paul Cree Band. His parents moved their family from Manitoba to the Fort McMurray area. His father Paul Cree was the chief of the Paul Cree band.[265]

In 1899, the six-year-old Rapheal Cree along with his family and his people witnessed the signing of Treaty 8. His uncle Chief Seapotakinum represented the Paul Band people.[266] Raphael married his wife Louise in 1925. The couple had three children. Raphael and Louise would be married for seventy-one years until she passed away in 1996.[267]

Mr. Cree was an active hunter and trapper for most of his life; he was a successful trapper until the 1980s. He trapped muskrat, fox, beaver, lynx, and mink. As a result of his extensive life knowledge Mr. Cree gave advice to many. He spoke four languages: English, French, Cree and Chipewyan.

Rapheal began fighting for a land claim in the early 1990s. At that time he delivered a statement of claims to Indian Affairs. With the help of others like his son Elmer Cree and John Malcolm, Cree demanded that the claims of the Paul Cree band be addressed.

He has been a role model for Aboriginal people as he brought to light the misfortunes that the Indian people were handed at the time of the signing of Treaty 8. To many this era of Canadian History has been forgotten, through Mr. Cree's courage and determination and his will not to forget the past has allowed other Indian bands to come forward with their injustices that were implemented by Indian Affairs.[268]

Raphael Cree has been a respected elder in the Fort McMurray area for years; in 1998, he received a Regional Aboriginal Achievement Award for the Elder of the Year Category.

Raphael Cree passed away in 2002, one week before his 109th birthday. He leaves behind numerous family and friends.[269] It is claimed that Mr. Cree was the last living witness to the signing of Treaty 8.[270]

Nominated by: Robert Cree

Profile by: Cora Voyageur

Crop Eared Wolf (Makoyi-Opistoki)

1845 - 1913
Blood/Kainai
Chief

Crop Eared Wolf was one of the prominent chiefs of the Blood people in the early part of the twentieth century. He fought hard to keep Blood lands intact, and resisted any and all attempts by early white settlers to annex or purchase their ancestral lands.

Crop Eared Wolf was born into the Many Children band around 1845, the son of Sun Old Man (Natos-api). When he was still a boy, both his parents died and he was adopted by his sister and her husband, Red Crow (Mékaisto), who was Chief. He became a member of the Fish Eaters band. Soon, Crop Eared Wolf earned the respect of his adoptive father, as they were alike in both looks and temperament.[271]

As a young man, Crop Eared Wolf was a feared warrior. In one fight against the Cree near Fort Macleod, he killed a man and captured three horses, a blanket and two saddles. His raiding career was all but ended in 1865, when a Cree warrior shot him in the leg. He walked with a limp for the rest of his life.[272]

After this mishap, Crop Eared Wolf began ranching and farming with great success. He started breeding horses, and then turned to farming with his adoptive father, Red Crow, cultivating potatoes and grain. In 1894, they both began cattle ranching, and owned two thousand head of cattle by the turn of the century.[273]

Red Crow wanted Crop Eared Wolf to succeed him as Chief, even though his other son, Willie Red Crow wanted the position. He foresaw the Blood people would need the quiet yet forceful leadership of Crop Eared Wolf over the coming years. Soon, the surrounding white settlers were trying to take over the Blood reserve lands. By 1907, the Blood were forced into a referendum to decide whether or not to sell off 2 400 acres on their southern boundary. Crop Eared Wolf canvassed the reserve, lobbying all residents to vote against this sale. The Indian agent, Robert Wilson, was angry, but Crop Eared Wolf was politically astute and went over his head to the Indian commissioner, David Laird. The government policy soon changed, no doubt due in part to Crop Eared Wolf's actions, and surrender votes were abandoned in favor of urging the Blood to cultivate the land themselves. This was highly successful, and with Crop Eared Wolf's full support, 2 500 acres were under cultivation by 1909.[274]

Crop Eared Wolf lived out his days as a successful rancher, watching his people prosper independently. He always worried about future land seizures or sales, and made his people promise never to sell any of their land. His son, Shot Both Sides, succeeded him.

On September 22, 1995, the RCMP returned to the Blood Tribe a painted buffalo robe depicting Crop Eared Wolf's early deeds. It came into the possession of the RCMP in 1945 when donated by a private citizen. In return, the Blood Tribe provided the RCMP with a replica.[275]

Profile by: Lee Tunstall

Crowchild, David

1899 – 1984
Tsuu T'ina
Politician and
Rodeo
Competitor

David Crowchild was born on the April 12, 1899 on the Tsuu T'ina Reserve in southern Alberta to Mark Crowchild and Sarah Big Plume. David's father was Cree from northern Alberta and his mother was Tsuu T'ina and the daughter of Chief Big Plume. Marrying into the band caused Mark to be adopted into the Tsuu T'ina band.[276]

David started school at the age of eight at the St. Barnabas Anglican Residential School located on the Tsuu T'ina Reserve on the outskirts of Calgary. He would remain there until 1917 when he grad-uated at the age of eighteen.[277] After David finished school, he took up farming and raising horses on about thirty acres. It was at this time that David became interested in the rodeo scene.[278]

David married Daisie, a Sioux from Portage la Prairie, Manitoba in 1929.[279] Daisie had been married before and had three children. David and Daisie went on to have five more children.[280]

Horse riding became one of David's greatest passions; he took part in bronco riding, wild horse racing, calf roping, chuckwagon, democrat racing and cattle calling competitions. Later he worked behind the chutes.[281] He participated in every Calgary Stampede from 1923 to 1972.

David became interested in the economic problems of his people in 1945. He and his wife attended and became active in the Indian Association of Alberta meetings from the late 1940s through the 1950s, and he became the secretary for the IAA.[282] During this time David meet John Laurie, later adopting him as his "brother."[283]

In 1946 David became Chief and was elected to a seven-year term. He was a progressive leader and brought many changes to the community. For example, he brought management systems to the band including regular reporting, minute taking, and making minutes available to the public. He modernized the school system and built relationships with surrounding Calgary schools so reserve children could continue their education off the reserve.[284] David improved the reserve road systems. He also pioneered the corporate farming system and also the expansion of the cattle operation on the reserve.[285]

David's religious upbringing led him to take part in the Moral Re-Armament in the late 1950s. This involvement opened up a whole new world to him. He travelled the world extensively, including trips to Brazil, New Zealand, Japan, South Africa, Italy, and Switzerland.[286]

David received many awards and recognitions for his work, such as being named Honorary Chief for Life in 1953. In 1971 a roadway in Calgary was named Crowchild Trail. In 1982 he was awarded the Centennial Medal of Canada.[287] He also received a citizenship award from the Calgary Council of Christians and Jews for improving relations between Aboriginal and non-Aboriginal cultures.[288] David Crowchild passed away in 1984 at the age of eighty-three.[289]

Profile by: Carly Morton

Crowfoot, Bert

1953 -
Siksika
Newspaper
Publisher

The media empire known as the Aboriginal Multi-Media Society of Alberta (AMMSA) has been in existence for over twenty years and was founded by Siksika First Nation member, Bert Crowfoot.

Born and raised on the Siksika reserve near Calgary, Alberta, Bert is one of ten children born to Cecil and Francis Crowfoot. His parents ran a successful farming operation and instilled a solid work ethic in each of their children.[290] Bert points to his family's achievements as proof of his parents' wisdom: there are twenty-two degrees among ten children.[291]

Bert graduated from Brigham Young University in the 1970s in physical education, then moved back to Alberta where he coached softball.[292] He began his media career in 1983 with the publishing of a bi-monthly magazine focused on northern Alberta. He incorporated it under the Alberta Societies Act as a non-profit enterprise, which it remains today: the AMMSA.[293] During the mid-1980s the government started spending less money on the subsidies that many Aboriginal publications relied on. Bert developed a five-year plan for economic self-sufficiency.[294] *Windspeaker* was born during this time of reorganization and remains the AMMSA's flagship publication.

To make AMMSA self-sufficient and strong, Bert Crowfoot had to find an economically viable way to fund the papers that AMMSA publishes. One of the significant revenue generators for AMMSA is a province-wide radio bingo operation. Bingo revenues are used to finance AMMSA's rapidly expanding Alberta-wide radio operation.[295] Bert's operations employs both Aboriginal and non-Aboriginal journalists. Award-winning Ojibwa playwright Drew Hayden Taylor, and political scientist Taiaike Alfred, director of the Indigenous Governance Program at the University of Victoria, are just two examples of the caliber of writers that Bert attracts to his publications.

Bert describes his management style as "hands-off" and believes that good, solid journalism sells papers.[296] Bert has a reputation for never killing a story and has let Windspeaker run unflattering stories about his friends and even his brother.[297] Aside from the national paper, Windspeaker, Bert has also added a few provincial papers to AMMSA's list of publications: Alberta Sweetgrass, Raven's Eye (BC), and Saskatchewan Sage.

Another one of Bert accomplishments with AMMSA is a new website that is now up and running, which allows people to conduct research. It includes articles from all past and present publications. There is a fee to use the site but there are still some areas that will be free.

In his spare time away from his little empire Bert is also a coach for a girls' softball team. Bert Crowfoot is a hard-working entrepreneur who is a role model for Aboriginal people. He was able to continue in the media business when many Aboriginal media outlets shut down after government funding was cut. One of Bert Crowfoot's philosophies is to "surround yourself with good people, empower them, and get out of their way."[298] Bert Crowfoot lives in Edmonton.

Profile by: Casie McGonegal

Crowshoe, Joseph and Josephine

Joseph 1909 –
1999 and
Josephine 1920 –
2002
Peigan (Blackfoot)
Ceremonial Elders,
spiritual leaders,
and farmers

Joseph and Josephine Crowshoe dedicated their lives to preserving First Nations traditions, culture, and history. Working together, they were recognized as spiritual leaders. They were the last ceremonial elders of the Peigan Nation.[299] Through years of oppression, they ensured the survival of the sacred Peigan ceremonies.[300] Through cross-cultural exchanges they promoted understanding between Aboriginals and non-Aboriginals.

Joseph Crowshoe was born in a teepee near the Old Man River on January 3, 1909.[301] He was raised in traditional Peigan culture. Josephine Crowshoe was born in 1920.[302] They were members of the Peigan (Blackfoot) First Nation Community in southern Alberta.[303] The Crowshoes were married on June 28, 1934.[304] They had eleven children and raised another six.[305] They operated their family farm for many years.

Joseph was a member of the Anglican clergy and keeper of the Blackfoot Short Thunder Medicine Pipe bundle.[306] Josephine was the keeper of the Sun Dance Medicine bundle.[307] Both are important in performance of the Sun Dance ceremony. During the dark days when First Nation people were forbidden to use their language or practice their religion or traditions, the Crowshoes found ways to preserve their heritage. By day, they worked on their farm. At night, Joseph organized members of the Blackfoot community and taught them ancient Blackfoot knowledge.[308] In later years, they jointly received the National Aboriginal Achievement Award for saving the knowledge and practices of the Blackfoot people.

In 1951, Joseph was elected to the Peigan Band Council. He served on the band council until he retired in 1979.[309] He was a founding member of Peigan Indian Days and the Farmer's Association of the Peigan Nation. He was advisor to the Universities of Calgary and Lethbridge in their Native American studies programs. He assisted Dr. Frances in editing the Blackfoot language diction-ary.[310]

When Head-Smashed-In-Buffalo Jump was built he ensured it would become an interpretive centre. As well, he was advisor to archaeological expeditions, museums and cultural events. He was spiritual guide to the Bowden and Drumheller Correctional Institutions.[311] His memberships included Elders Advisory of Sun Dance in Little Eagle, South Dakota. Mr. Crowshoe also received an Alberta Achievement Award, a Citation of Citizenship, and honorary Doctorate of Humanities from the University of Montana and an honorary Doctorate of Laws from the University of Calgary.[312] In addition, he was a Lifetime Councillor for the Peigan Nation and part of a palaeontology mission to China as well as a member of cultural exchanges with Aboriginals of Australia and New Zealand.[313] Josephine Crowshoe began a lunch program for school children on the Peigan Reserve in 1950. She was an advisor to the production, *Children of the Eagle,* dealing with child sexual abuse.[314] On a cultural exchange to Australia and New Zealand, she was Elder Ceremonialist representing First Nations.[315]

The Crowshoes worked to educate Aboriginal and non-Aboriginal people about Native tradition culture and history. "They played a crucial role in preserving the tradition, history, and spirituality of the Blackfoot people for more than sixty years" is how they were described when they received the Order of Canada in 1992.[316]

In the Blackfoot nation they were given the highest tribute from the four tribal groups, that is, the Old Man and the Old Woman.[317] They led their people with dignity and wisdom. Joseph passed away on October 28, 1999.[318] Josephine passed away in 2002.

Profile by: Margaret Burgess

Crowshoe, Dr. Lindsay

1969 –

Blackfoot

Physician

Dr. Lindsay Crowshoe, a member of Peigan First Nation, is a well-regarded medical doctor and academic and a recipient of the prestigious National Aboriginal Achievement Award in 2001 at the age of thirty-two.

Dr Crowshoe provides clinical, emergency and hospital services in rural Alberta. He currently practices primary-care medicine on the reserve at Siksika two days a week. He has made fly-in visits to towns and villages not accessible by road. He is also occupies a full-time faculty position teaching Aboriginal health research. In his position as Assistant Professor within the Faculty of Medicine at the University of Calgary he helped create an admissions policy for students entering medical school and helped create a model for health-service delivery to Aboriginal communities.[319] Dr. D. Grant Gall, Dean of the Faculty of Medicine, called him an "outstanding individual" because he can teach medical students and residents about Aboriginal culture and brings tremendous awareness to Aboriginal people about important opportunities and issues around healthcare.[320]

One of Dr. Crowshoe's goals is to integrate Aboriginal health curricula within a large medical framework in a systematic and balanced manner so that medical learners are better able to integrate their medical knowledge with real understanding when seeing Aboriginal patients.[321] One of the means of education he has used is interactive theatre.[322] He established the Indigenous Health Pathways Forum Theatre,[323] where medical students have the opportunity to address issues of race and culture. He has taken his students to culture camps with Elders and advisors to learn through ceremony.

In addition to practicing medicine and teaching, Dr. Crowshoe works with the Calgary Health Region one day a week, helping to create the medical component of an urban Aboriginal health centre.[324]

His clinical interests and priorities focus on issues of addiction, mental health, and children's health, emphasizing prevention and education. His goal is to improve Aboriginal health, working to develop appropriate primary health models for Aboriginal communities and increasing physician knowledge and capacity regarding Aboriginal people's health. He believes that the health of Aboriginal people and non-Aboriginal people alike would be better improved if doctors integrated their efforts with those of other professional-service providers such as social workers, policymakers, lawyers, and child welfare workers.

He is an expert advisor on Fetal Alcohol Syndrome[325] and has co-authored and published his research on the epidemiology of severe trauma among status Aboriginal Canadians.[326]

Dr. Crowshoe is one of those rare multi-talented individuals. Besides being a devoted doctor and scholar, he is also an accomplished guitarist, with one of his songs placing number six on the Canadian country charts. He is known in some communities as the doctor with the guitar, or "the singing doctor."[327] He is also a talented athlete who has won scholarships for his ability; he helped the University of Calgary Dinosaurs win the Vanier Cup in 1988.

Profile by: Vivienne Beisel

Crowshoe, Reg

1951-
Peigan
(Piikani)
Cultural
Educator, Chief

A leader, author, and cultural educator, Reg Crowshoe is an important figure in the First Nations community. He strongly believes in preserving Aboriginal heritage and promotes cultural awareness.

Reg Crowshoe was born in 1951, on the Peigan Reserve. He was one of eleven children born to Josephine and Joseph Crowshoe. As a child he attended a residential school on the Peigan reserve and then went to a residential school in Drumheller to complete high school.

As the son of acclaimed spiritual leader, Joe Crowshoe, Reg comes from a prominent lineage of transferred bundle keepers of the Piikani Nation. Joe Crowshoe, Reg's father, made efforts to teach the aboriginal ways to non-Aboriginals, including inviting them to participate in ceremonies. Reg has continued his father's legacy of teaching others about First Nations culture.

Reg was among the first Aboriginal police constables in Alberta. He has worked as a social service administrator and served one term on band council and was elected Chief in 2006. He was an advisor during the development of the Head Smashed-In Buffalo Jump Interpretive Centre, located near Fort Macleod. Crowshoe also helped develop the Native Cultural Festival for the Calgary 1988 Winter Olympics.

In 1990 Reg began his work with the Peigan renewal project, Keep Our Circle Strong. As a result of his work with this program Reg

Crowshoe has developed a sentencing centre for Peigan young offenders.

Among Reg's other contributions, he is the President of the Board of the Niitisitapi Tourism Society of Alberta, Executive Director of the Oldman River Cultural Centre (which he established in 1974), board member of the Calgary Exhibition and Stampede Indian Village Committee, and a member of the Alberta Strategic Tourism Marketing Council. In addition, Crowshoe co-authored *Akak'stiman: a Blackfoot Framework for Decision-Making and Mediation Processes* with Sybille Manneschmitt in 2002.

Working with a Metis police officer with the Calgary Police Service, Mark Dumont, Reg assisted in developing an Aboriginal Awareness Camp at Brocket, near Calgary. The goal of this camp is to provide police officers with an opportunity to learn about the Aboriginal culture. Organizations throughout Western Canada have benefited from Reg's cross-cultural programs and camps. He is collaborating with Canadian museums to have cultural artifacts returned to Aboriginal communities.

In 2000 Reg received an Award of Excellence from the Calgary Police Services, recognizing his efforts to improve the relations between the police and the Aboriginal community. Reg was awarded an honorary Doctorate of Laws from the University of Calgary in 2001.

Today Reg and his wife Rose live on the Peigan reserve. They continue to bring the native and non-native people together through their police, health, and justice camps.

Profile by: Michelle Voyageur

Cunningham, Chester Raymond

1933—
Métis
Legal Agency
Founder

Chester Cunningham reformed how the criminal justice system was applied to Aboriginal defendants. He accomplished this through the creation of the Native Counselling Services of Alberta (NCSA) in Edmonton in the early 1970s. NCSA was designed to explain individual rights and the judicial system to Aboriginal defendants. His program was so successful that it has been emulated in most Canadian provinces and territories and has gained interest overseas. Cunningham has also been active community member by sitting on numerous boards and agencies. He has also received many honors and awards for his dedication and hard work.

Chester Cunningham was born in Slave Lake, Alberta to Walter and Maria Cunningham, the third of ten children.[328] As a young man, Chester's father, Walter was a well-known interpreter in the Slave Lake region.[329] Chester attended high school in Wayne and St. Paul, Alberta where he excelled in sports, particularly baseball. In 1952 he left school to play semi-professional baseball. After his baseball career ended, he worked in the construction industry throughout Alberta.[330] He married Elzaida McGhee and together they have seven children.[331]

The 1960s was the turning point in Chester's career when the Canadian Native Friendship Centre in Edmonton hired him to work as their program director and assistant director.332 While visiting the courthouse to observe proceedings he became aware of the lack of understanding that Aboriginal defendants had about the court system. "They were putting four of them in the docket, asking their names, reading the charges, accepting a plea – never any verbal communication. It was always a nod of the head, and they were being sentenced."333

Cunningham approached several judges to see what could be done to rectify the situation and to create a more equitable situation for the Aboriginal defendants. The judges were very receptive and offered assistance.[334] As a result, the Native Court Worker Program was initiated. This program explained the judicial system to Aboriginal defendants and provided them with information about their individual rights.[335] This responsibility was added to Cunningham's list of duties.

In 1969, Chester resigned from the Friendship Centre when the Native Court Worker Program needed to grow beyond the boundaries of the Friendship Centre. Chester saw that social problems such as alcoholism, which plays a large role in Aboriginal justice, needed to be addressed. This resulted in the establishment of the Native Counselling Program in 1970.[336] It was so successful that the level of Aboriginal inmates in Alberta penal institutions dropped from fifty-six per cent to twenty-eight per cent in the first five years of operation.[337] Subsequently, the Metis Association and the Indian Association of Alberta asked him to set up a province-wide program. Cunningham has assisted other Canadian provinces and territories to set up their own Native Counselling Services programs.[338]

In addition to his work with the Native Counselling Service. Some of his contributions include serving as a trustee for the Alberta Family Life & Substance Abuse Foundation, a board member for the Law Enforcement Review Board, a board member of the Aboriginal Multi-Media Society of Alberta, and a committee member for the Canadian Bar Association.[339]

He has also received a number of awards, some of which include an honorary Doctor of Laws degree from the University of Alberta in 1989. He received the Order of Canada in 1991, a National Aboriginal Achievement Award in 1993, and the Governor General's 125th Anniversary Medal in 1997.[340] He lives outside Edmonton with his wife, Elzaida.

Profile by: K. Patricia Colosimo

Cunningham, Henry

1868 – 1955
Metis
Fur trader,
Farmer, and
Politician

Henry Cunningham has earned a place in Metis history because of his contribution to improving the lives of Metis in the early part of the twentieth century. At that time Metis were in a difficult, almost desperate, position. They were neither recognized by Aboriginals nor accepted by whites. Having a non-land base of their own, they were described as "road allowance people."[341]Henry Cunningham worked to bring their condition to the attention of authorities.

Born at St. Albert, Alberta, Henry was the son of John Patrick Cunningham and Rosalie L'Hirondelle.[342] In 1895 he married Mary Rachel Rowland in St. Albert.[343] Another brother, Reverend Edward Cunningham, performed the marriage ceremony.[344] Henry worked as a farmer in the St Albert area. He and Mary raised seven children.[345] For a time Henry took his family to Wabasca where he worked as a fur trader.

When Henry Cunningham and his family moved back to the St. Albert area, he became interested in politics. On the local level, he became involved in municipal politics. In 1904 he ran and was elected to the first town council of St. Albert. He served a two-year term.[346]

Throughout this time he was interested in the plight of the Metis in Alberta.[347] As a result of Henry Cunningham and others efforts at lobbying on behalf of the Metis, the Metis Nation of Alberta was organized in 1932.[348] This organization was formed to represent the Metis' interest and concerns. Metis concerns included obtaining land, improving education standards, having better health services, and advancing social and economic conditions. The Ewing Commission of 1934 investigated the condition of Metis life in Alberta.[349] Cunningham was elected to the first executive of the newly formed Association as third vice-president. He remained in that post between 1932-1934 when he was replaced by Peter Tomkins.[350]

After his retirement, Henry and his wife Mary stayed on the farm. In 1947, his wife of more than fifty years, Mary, passed away. She was buried at St. Albert. Henry was hospitalized at the age of eighty-six and passed away in 1955. He too is buried at St. Albert.[351]

Profile by: Margaret Burgess

Daniels, Christine

1931 – 2005
Cree
Homemaker
and Counsellor

Christine Daniels was a prominent leader in the Aboriginal community for many years. She inspired others to organize and take action. She was proud of her culture and shared her knowledge with others. Throughout her life she worked hard to keep her culture alive. Her deep reverence for her Creator guided her always in her many activities. The young, the addicted and the incarcerated benefited from her strength and wisdom.

Christine Whiskeyjack was born on the Saddle Lake Reserve near St. Paul de Métis on June 22, 1931.[352] At the age of eighteen, she married Stanley Joseph Daniels on December 31, 1949. They had four daughters: Joanne, Teresa, Dorothy (deceased), and Lenore.

In 1970, after being a homemaker for several years, Christine decided to write a book about her early experiences on the Saddle Lake Reserve. The book, *White Man's Law*, (later the title was changed to *Many Laws*) was an instant success. She travelled throughout Canada giving interviews. The warm reception her book received encouraged her to a life of promoting her culture and helping others.[353]

In the late 1970s Christine received training in addiction counselling and worked for many years for AADAC Foundation Lodge. She spent five years as an elder and consultant with the Native Counselling Services of Alberta. She also worked as a Native Liaison Worker with the Edmonton Maximum Security Institution. In addition, she has been affiliated with the ACADRE Network, an Aboriginal health program at the University of Alberta.[354]

Christine Daniels was a founding member of the Voice of Alberta Native Women's Society (VANWS) in the mid-1960s. She coordinated the VANWS community leadership courses for Aboriginal women.

In 1975, Christine received the Mayor Cavanaugh Health and Welfare Award for her community work. One year later, she founded the White Braid Society Dancers and Drummers Group that went on to international acclaim.[355] Christine received the Premier's Excellence Award for her cultural work and community involvement in 1987.[356] When the Institute for the Advancement of Aboriginal Women (IAAW) formed an Elders Council, Christine was named a member.[357] Christine's many achievements in helping Aboriginal girls and women earned her the Esquao Award from the Institute for the Advancement of Aboriginal Women.[358]

After a lifetime of tireless efforts to improve the lives of her people, Christine retired and lived in Edmonton until her death in 2005. It is interesting to note that the White Buffalo Dancers insisted that Christine accompany them to meet Queen Elizabeth II on her visit to Edmonton in May, 2005.[359]

Profile by: Margaret Burgess

Decoteau, Alexander "Alex' Wuttanee

1887- 1917
Cree
Olympian,
Police officer
and Soldier

Alexander Decoteau was one of Alberta's first Olympians and the first Indian person to become a member of a municipal police force in Canada. He was a celebrated long-distance runner, representing Canada in the 1912 Olympic Games. He was killed in 1917 during the World War I battle of Passchendaele.[360]

Alex was born on the Red Pheasant Reserve on November 19, 1887 near Battleford, in what was then the Northwest Territories. His father, Peter Decoteau (probably more rightly "Dakota") was one of Poundmaker's warriors at the Battle of Cutknife Hill in 1885. When his father died in 1891, Alex and his brother Peter attended the Battleford Industrial School in Saskatchewan. It was here that Alex was encouraged to become an athlete by visiting Irish police officers in 1903. Later, Alex moved to Edmonton to live with his sister, Emily Latta, and her husband David, who was an Irish-born veteran of the North West Mounted Police.[361]

Alex's athletic career began in earnest in 1909. That year he won six races, including the Cross Cup in Calgary. He eventually won the Cross Cup five times in six years, and the Cup was awarded to him permanently after his fifth victory. During the 1910 provincial championships held in Lethbridge on July 1, Alex won all four events he entered. He also won the coveted *Calgary Herald* Christmas Road Race in 1910, 1914 and 1915, and again was presented with the trophy permanently. In 1912, Alex easily qualified for the Olympics and became the only Albertan on the Canadian team that travelled to

Stockholm, Sweden. He qualified for the 5 000 metre final but he developed leg cramps and could not finish.[362]

Decoteau also had a distinguished career in the Edmonton Police Force, being the first Aboriginal officer on a municipal force in Canada when he joined in 1911. He became one of the first motorcycle police officers in Canada, and was assigned to lock the High Level Bridge every night.[363] In 1914, Alex was promoted to Sergeant, again the first Aboriginal Canadian to hold this rank.

Alex resigned from the police in 1916 to enlist in the war effort. He entered as a private in the 202nd (Sportsmen's) Battalion. Still finding time to run, Decoteau participated in two races while stationed in England. He won the first and was presented with King George V's own pocket watch, as the trophy did not arrive in time. When he entered a race the following day, he arrived to find it was a bicycle race which in true form, he won regardless. Decoteau was sent to the front in 1917, and was killed by a German sniper's bullet on October 30, 1917, at age twenty-nine. He was buried in Flanders Field at Ypres, Belgium, but in 1985 his reserve held a special ceremony to bring home his spirit.[364]

Alex Decoteau was inducted into the Edmonton Sports Hall of Fame in 1967,[365] the Saskatchewan Sports Hall of Fame in 2000 and in 2001, he was posthumously awarded the Pioneer's Award by the Alberta Sports Hall of Fame.[366]

Profile by: Lee Tunstall

Dickason, Dr. Olive Patricia

1920 -
Metis
Journalist,
Historian, and
Professor
Emeritus

The Metis have always stood with one foot in both worlds, straddling the cultural divide. Knowing this, it seems most fitting that a Manitoba-born Metis woman would build bridges of understanding between the native and non-native people of Canada and between the young and old. As an indefatigable and youthful spirit of ninety years, the acclaimed historian and academic, Olive Dickason, has managed to rewrite Canadian history while battling against institutional ageism.[367] In fact, her efforts in bridging both cultures and generations within Canada have been and continue to be remarkable in reshaping the attitudes of Canadians.

Dickason was born in Winnipeg, Manitoba in 1920 to a Metis mother, Phoebe Cote, and an English father, Frank Williamson.[368] Dickason's background is as varied as her career path. As a child, Dickason began her studies in an Oblate convent.[369] During the Great Depresssion, Olive's mother fed the family using her "bush survival skills" after her father lost his banking job. It was also Olive's mother who persuaded her to continue her studies through correspondence.[370] This encouragement would eventually lead to a university degree for Dickason.[371]

For the next twenty-four years, Dickason worked as a journalist at various prominent newspapers including the *Globe and Mail*.[372] An increasing awareness of her mixed heritage spurred Dickason to return to university and study history. Christopher Moore writes that Dickason's penchant for rewriting Canadian history was sparked by her indignation at textbooks which cast natives in a secondary role to the so-called "discovery of Canada" and more insultingly as "savages."[373] Her decision to pursue a graduate degree in native history was questioned since "the University (of Ottawa) in those days doubted that aboriginal history was real history."[374] Determined to give voice to her native heritage, Dickason would eventually graduate with a doctorate, and thus the right to teach the seldom-heard Aboriginal side of Canadian history. Her battles had just begun.

In 1985, the University of Alberta informed the then sixty-five-year-old Dickason that she was obliged to retire under the terms of her contract. Dickason replied, "I was just getting started."[375] She took the northern institution to court under the new Charter of Rights and Freedom and by the time a ruling was reached seven years later, in 1992, she was ready to retire of her own accord.[376]

Dickason has taken the historical establishment to task using her powerful arsenal of words. Some of her more notable writings include *The Myth of the Savage* (1977) and the highly acclaimed *Canada's First Nations: A History of Founding Peoples from Earliest Times* (recently released in its third edition). Interestingly, although Dickason's mainstream accolades would include the esteemed Order of Canada (1996), her proudest moment came when she was awarded the National Aboriginal Lifetime Achievement Award in 1997.[377] Dickason's commitment to the truth has initiated a genuine dialog between the Aboriginal and the non-Aboriginal people of Canada – taking that first step together toward real understanding.

Profile by: Yvonne Pratt

Dion, Joseph Francis 'Joe'

1888 - 1960
Metis
Teacher,
Politician,
Author, and
Historian

Joe Dion was an Indian man who voluntarily gave up his status under the Indian Act. Throughout his life he was concerned with the situation of Aboriginal people, Metis and First Nations, alike. He was one of the founders of the Metis Association of Alberta and served as its president. He also served as a vice-president for the Indian Association of Alberta. Dion was hired by the Government of Alberta to determine the boundaries of the Metis settlements and he also assisted in drafting the regulations to govern these colonies. Although he was politically active, he is also remembered as being a schoolteacher. In addition, he was an author, and he documented the history of the Cree people. His writings can be found in the book entitled, *My Tribe, The Cree*, published posthumously.

Dion was born on July 2, 1888 on the Onion Lake Reserve in Saskatchewan. He was the nephew of Big Bear, one of the most powerful chiefs to support Louis Riel in 1885.[378] Dion's parents, August Dion and Marie Mountain, lost many of their children in an epidemic that hit Onion Lake in 1903.[379] This loss resulted in his parents moving their remaining children to the Kehewin area of northern Alberta.[380] In 1912, he married Elizabeth Cunningham from St. Albert.[381] After his marriage, Dion chose to franchise and "gave up [his] treaty status in order to gain the rights of an ordinary Canadian citizen."[382] In 1915, he built the first school on the Kehewin reserve and became its teacher.[383] He taught there for twenty-four years.[384]

On May 24, 1930, Dion attended a meeting of about thirty Metis people held on the Frog Lake Indian Reserve.[385] During this meeting he discovered that no action had been taken by the government in response to issues raised at these Metis meetings. From 1930 to 1932 he acted as a spokesman for the Metis and brought their concerns forward to government. In 1931, two hundred Metis met to ask the Alberta government for land and better living conditions. Dion and the MLA delivered a five-hundred-signature petition to the Alberta government. In 1932, the Metis passed a resolution demanding land from the government.

On December 28, 1932, Dion attended a provincial Metis convention where the Metis Association of Alberta was formed. Dion was elected to the first executive council as its president.[386] The Metis Association of Alberta lobbied the provincial government over the next few years and in 1934, the Ewing Commission was formed to investigate the Metis situation. As a result of the lobbying, the Metis Betterment Act was passed and Metis colonies were established.[387] The government hired Joe Dion and another member of the Metis Association of Alberta executive to select the locations of the colonies and to develop the regulations that would govern the colonies.[388]

Joe Dion was sympathetic to the cause of all Aboriginal people. In addition to his work with the Metis Association of Alberta, Joe Dion was active with the Indian Association of Alberta (IAA) and its precursor, the League of Indians of Western Canada.[389] He attended the first official meeting of the IAA in 1939 and was elected to the position of vice-president.[390] In 1944 the IAA was reorganized and once again, Joe Dion was elected to the position of vice-president.[391]

In addition to his political activities, Joe Dion formed a Metis dance troupe in 1930 that toured Alberta and eastern Canada.[392] He wrote a weekly column in the *Bonnyville Tribune* that described the history and traditions of the Cree people[393] These columns were eventually organized into a book entitled *My People, The Cree,* published by the Glenbow-Alberta Institute in 1979.[394] Joe Dion was a deeply religious man, and in 1957 he was awarded the Gold Medal "Benemerenti" by Pope Pius XII for "his work among his people."[395]

Joe Dion passed away on December 20, 1960, on the Kehewin Indian Reserve where he had spent all his adult life.

Profile by: Tina Dion

Donald, Bella "Georgina"

1932 – 2006
Cree/Metis
Community
Worker and
Cultural
Ambassador

Bella "Georgina" Grandbois was the youngest of seven children born to David and Denise on November 10, 1932 at Calling Lake, Alberta. She grew up in nearby Athabasca as part of a close-knit family. Her mother passed away when Georgina was young and her sister, Lena, took on the role of surrogate parent. The Grandbois clan moved to Edmonton in 1949.[396]

Shortly after moving to Edmonton she met her future husband, Ross Donald. The couple were married on February 3, 1951.[397] They raised six children: Beatrice, Wayne, Dennis, Lyle, Joanne, and Brian. They celebrated their 49th wedding anniversary before Ross passed away in March, 2000. At the time of Ross's death, they had twenty-six grandchildren and thirty-three great-grandchildren.[398]

Georgina worked at odd jobs in the early years of her marriage, including housekeeping, to help make ends meet. In 1964, Georgina began volunteering at the Canadian Native Friendship Centre (CNFC) in Edmonton. The volunteer stint worked its way into a full-time job for Georgina two years later. Georgina would work at the CNFC in varying capacities for the next thirty years.[399]

In 1966, Georgina was hired as a referral worker. She enjoyed this position because it allowed her to meet many new people, make friends, share ideas, and refer those requiring assistance to the appropriate agencies. In the 1960s, the Canadian Native Friendship Centre was the first point of contact for many Aboriginal people moving to the city. It provided many services to the newcomers including a food bank, clothing distribution, housing referrals, and provided job referrals. Georgina worked in this position for eight years.[400]

In 1974 Georgina was promoted to Assistant Director of the Canadian Native Friendship Centre and to Executive Director two years later. During this time, the CNFC services expanded to include social and recreational programming.[401] Sports programs included boxing, basketball, volleyball, hockey, and baseball. They also provided meeting rooms and hosted banquets and other social activities such as dances. Board member Stan Daniels got the Centre involved in the Annual Heritage Festival.[402] This participation continues to this day.

Throughout her involvement with the CNFC, Georgina's first love was dancing. When she became the CNFC's cultural director in 1986 she, with the help of Moise White, initiated Canadian Native Friendship Centre Junior Dancers. Georgina's goals were simple – teach the youth to dance and promote the Metis dance culture.[403] After only two weeks of practicing, these young dancers competed in the 24th Annual All-Native Festival.[404] The dance troupe is still a popular activity at the Centre and has performed across Canada.

After retiring from the CNFC in 1996 she took a more active role at the Native Seniors Centre, serving as president. She was very proud of the progress that the Centre has made, especially in the last few years with all the programs that are in place for the Native Seniors.

Georgina has earned many awards over the years. For example, in 1986 she was made a lifetime member of the Canadian Native Friendship Centre in recognition of her work. In 1989, she was given a Certificate of Recognition from the Metis Association of Alberta for the "Promotion and Preservation of our Distinct Metis." In 1993, she was inducted into the Metis Nation of Alberta's Hall of Honour. In 2002, she was awarded the Queen's Jubilee Medal.[405] Georgina passed away in 2006.

Profile by: Cora Voyageur

Eagle Speaker, Casey[412]

1951-
Blood
Youth Worker

Casey remained true to his roots in Alberta. His family tree spans two First Nations communities in southern Alberta: his father was a Blood Indian, Clifford Eagle Speaker, and his mother was Cecilia Water Chief from Siksika, a reserve located about sixty miles east of Calgary.[406] The names of his ancestors reflect equal parts of history and leadership. Members of his family held prominent roles in various societies, such as the Horn Society.[407] With that, Casey brings the strengths of Blackfoot cultural history into the present.

The family name Eagle Speaker has always had an impact on Casey. The eldest of nine siblings, Casey was born in Yakima, Washington and over his life resided in Seattle, Washington, Portland and Salem, Oregon, and Billings, Montana.[408] The name Eagle Speaker allowed him to fit into the Aboriginal communities in the United States. He met his wife, Pixie, in 1970 and the couple married in 1972.[409] They would have three children: Tonya, Mary and Jesse. Casey expanded their family to include forty-three foster children and his own eleven grandchildren.[410] Fostering children prove to be a source of inspiration to change careers.

To provide for his family, Casey has worked as landscaper, construction worker, welder, and earned a supervisor position in the sheet metal business. He moved into social services to become a youth and family counsellor with Native Alcohol Services and then with TCS Family Services.[411] Ever-expanding responsibilities led him to take on roles as one of the founding board members of Four Direction Foster Parents Association and chair of Aboriginal Community Council with Alberta Association of Services for Children and Family, which he chaired for seven years.[412] He skirts over the accolades he has received for his contribution to this organization. He also served on the board of a local native women's shelter. His career in community services has steered him to his current position with Hull Child and Family Services, where he is currently responsible for cross-cultural programs, working with youth and families, and liaison with local Aboriginal agencies.[413]

Casey has been awarded the Dr. Joseph Crowshoe award in education from the University of Calgary's Aboriginal Student Council and the Chief David Crowchild award for cross-cultural awareness from the City of Calgary.[414]

His spiritual strength abides in him. In his role as father and grandfather and provider for his family dwells the strength of his spiritual development. In the late 1980s he linked up with Morris Crow, his spiritual guide and mentor, and embarked on a spiritual path. His participation in Sundances over the fifteen years have led him to take on the responsibilities as a lodge holder, pipe carrier and Sundance leader.[415]

Casey garners respect from members of Calgary's Aboriginal community for his commitment to supporting and helping people. "Its been a long journey, but a good one," says Casey when he reflects on his life and achievements.[416]

Profile by: Wayne Courchene

Erasmus, Peter

1833 – 1931
Metis
Interpreter
and Civil
Servant

Peter Erasmus played a prominent role in the settlement of whites in western Canada, including the settlement of Alberta. He was a part of the Palliser expedition, an interpreter for Methodist missionaries, an eyewitness to the events of the Riel Rebellion, and an interpreter during the Treaty 6 negotiations.[417] He provided a link between the Aboriginal peoples and the new settler population.

Peter Erasmus was born in Kildonan, a Red River settlement near Fort Garry, on June 7, 1833, to an Ojibway mixed-blood mother and a Danish father.[418] He had a good education for his time and by his mid-teens, he was teaching school in a northern district.[419] He trained with the Anglicans at St. John's College in Winnipeg for service as a missionary and eventually served the Wesleyans.[420] Erasmus worked as a guide and interpreter for many Anglican missionaries including Robert Rundle, Thomas Woolsey, John McDougall, and Henry Bird Steinhauer. He was fluent in six Aboriginal languages as well as English, French, Greek, and Latin.[421]

From 1857 through 1859, Erasmus joined Captain John Palliser and his expedition that conducted exploratory surveys for the British government in the Canadian west, working closely with Dr. James Hector.[422] Erasmus recruited other Metis to help in the tour. Erasmus was involved in many other livelihoods including gold mining, hunting, fur trading, freighting, and farming. He was also a Hudson's Bay Company trader at Whitefish Lake in central Alberta.[423] He was a great sleigh dog handler and used them extensively in the winter.[424] Erasmus married his wife Charlotte and after the Palliser expedition he moved in 1861 to Whitefish (Goodfish) Lake to settle down. He and Charlotte had six children: four boys and two girls. Charlotte died in 1880 and two years later he married Miss Stanley of Whitefish Lake; they had three more daughters.[425] In 1908, he moved his family to Gleichen, Alberta, near the Siksika (Blackfoot) Indian Reserve, where he worked as a clerk and interpreter and as an official for the Department of Indian Affairs until 1911.[426] Erasmus worked fifty years in government service.

In his later years, he moved back to live a quiet life at Whitefish (Goodfish) Lake Reserve. At the age of eighty-seven, he told his recollections to a Metis journalist, Henry Thompson, who helped to write it into a manuscript, which eventually found its way to the Glenbow Archives, which published it as a book, *Buffalo Days and Nights*.[427] The book provides Erasmus' personal comments regarding Captain Palliser and Dr. Hector, as well as his recollections of the Treaty 6 negotiations. The book of memoirs illustrates Erasmus's bias in favor of the treaty, reports the First Nations' transition to farming, and demonstrates his dislike of the Hudson's Bay Company.[428]

Mount Erasmus is named in his honor.[429] His house was moved to Fort Edmonton Historic Park and is open to the public. Erasmus was a link between two ways of life and he played a role in facilitating the change from the buffalo economy to settlements, reserves and an agricultural economy in Alberta.

He died at the age of ninety-seven at Goodfish Lake, near Spedden, Alberta on May 27, 1931.[430] His unmarked grave lies beside the church at Whitefish (Goodfish) Lake.

Profile by: Brian Calliou

Fedyk, Cora

1930 –
Metis
Community
worker

Cora Fedyk has shown outstanding commitment to promoting awareness of Aboriginal culture and the Aboriginal perspective. She has spent countless hours as a volunteer in a variety of areas. All her work is characterized by unfailing good humor, graciousness, and dignity.

Cora Fedyk was born in 1930 at Estevan, Saskatchewan.[431] She lived in Saskatchewan until 1974 when she married William Fedyk. They moved to Red Deer, Alberta, where Cora still resides.[432] Cora's husband, William, passed away in 2003.

During her more than thirty years in the Red Deer area, Cora has had a long record of community involvement. She has been a Metis Nation Senator, a Metis Nation Zone III Elder and a Youth Justice Committee member. She is a member of the Red Deer Elder Council and a strong supporter of the Metis Nation Local #84.[433] In addition, she has assisted at the Red Deer Friendship Centre. At the Red Deer Remand Centre she has assisted with the Niwichihaw Addiction Program by attendance at their Aboriginal Healing Circles.

In 2002, she won an Esquao Award for her community involvement from the Institute for the Advancement of Aboriginal Women (IAAW). This award is given to Aboriginal women who brought positive changes to their community and are an inspiration to others.[434] Two years later she received a certificate for her work from the Institute for the Advancement of Aboriginal Women. The Institute has also appointed her Elder on their Council.[435]

When a committee was formed for the Burial of Ancestors at Rocky Mountain House, Cora was one of its members. The work on this project took over a year to complete, and was finally finished in 2005.

Those who know Cora call her "Our Kokum."[436] They describe her as a cheerful, caring woman who gets things done. They say she is always available to those who need encouragement and help.

Now in her late seventies, Cora continues to volunteer and be active in the affairs of the Metis and Aboriginal community in Red Deer.

Profile by: Margaret Burgess

Fletcher, John Thomas

1937 – 1995
Peigan
Athlete,
Builder, War
Veteran

John Thomas Fletcher is known as an athlete, builder, and war veteran,[437] but perhaps best known for being instrumental in establishing the North American Indigenous Games.

He was born December 19, 1937 at Brocket, Alberta to Beatrice Alphonse and Thomas Bullpen. From 1942 to 1949, he attended Shingwauk Indian Residential School in Sault Ste. Marie, Ontario.[438] For junior and senior high school he went to The Sioux, Michigan, from 1950 to 1957. The 6′ 3″ Peigan Indian was a sports superstar in school. He was an All-State football, basketball, and track and field athlete from 1950 to 1957. He went on to become team football captain at the University of Wyoming from 1958 to 1960.[439] He attended baseball pro camp with the St. Louis Cardinals and played with the Jacksonville Bears of Florida in the International Football League. He was such a sought-after athlete that he turned down an invitation from the Edmonton Eskimos of the Canadian Football League. He then attended the Michigan College of Mining Technology, and from 1969 to 1970 studied at UCLA.[440]

Fletcher admired the accomplishments of Indian athlete Jim Thorpe and became friends with Thorpe's family. He assisted the family to regain the medals that were stripped from him at the 1912 Olympic Games.[441]

Partway through his studies, Fletcher joined the war effort in Vietnam. "Big John" was a paratrooper with the world-renowned

101st Airborne Division "Screaming Eagles" from 1963 to 1965, serving for thirteen months in Danang.[442]

He returned to America and sports, this time devoting his service as executive board member of the National Indian Athletic Association (NIAA) from 1971 to 1973, later inducted into the NIAA Sports Hall of Fame.[443] In the 1970s, Fletcher joined Willie Littlechild from Hobbema and together they established the Indian Sports Olympics in the 1970s, Friends of Sports in the 1980s, and the North American Indigenous Games in the 1990s.[444]

Fletcher also devoted himself to community service and activism. He served on Edmonton's mayoral Aboriginal committee and devoted time to the Children's Health Centre at the University of Alberta.

If there was an issue that was unfair or detrimental to his people, he was never afraid to stand up and be counted. He participated in activities related to the American Indian Movement and Wounded Knee, the illegal transfer of Leonard Peltier from Canada to the United States, the conflict at Oka, the Oldman River Dam, the police and military siege at Gustafson Lake in British Columbia, and much more.[445] He died of a heart attack on September 1, 1995, while addressing the Shuswap Indian protest at Gustafsen Lake, B.C.[446] He was married to Mona for twenty-five years and they had four childrenr.[447]

Profile by: Cora Voyageur

Fortin, Terry

1944 -
Metis
Teacher and
School
Superintendent

Terry Fortin, a Metis, has played a significant role in the area of education in Alberta, with thirty-five years experience in teaching and administrative positions. As Superintendent of Schools, he inspired and challenged youth to become life-long learners.[448] He is still active in Alberta and national education, especially in the area of Aboriginal education.

Terry Fortin was born in 1944 in Edmonton. Terry was adopted by his aunt and uncle – his mother's older sister and brother-in-law – and raised with the assistance of his Cree-speaking grandparents.[449] Later, his adoptive parents moved to Dawson Creek, British Columbia, where he went to school for the next eight years. His adoptive mother died while he was in ninth grade and his father moved the family to Grand Centre, Alberta, where Terry attended Cold Lake High School.[450]

After completing high school, Fortin completed a Bachelor of Education degree from the University of Alberta with a specialization in secondary mathematics. He would earn a Master of Education from the University of Calgary, focused on human resources. Terry also supplemented his learning by taking leadership courses from Gonzaga University in the US.

Terry Fortin taught at a number of schools including ones in Lacombe, Calgary, Edmonton, and in the Netherlands. While teaching he moved into administrative leadership roles. He was promoted to head of the mathematics department at Bishop Carroll High School in the Calgary Roman Catholic School District. He became assistant principal at the Three Hills School and eventually Principal at the Catholic Central High School in Lethbridge. Terry then accepted a position as director of education for the Prince Albert Catholic Schools and moved up to chief superintendent of Edmonton Catholic Schools in 1994. He also served as an adjunct professor at the University of Alberta.

In 1999, Terry Fortin was seconded to Alberta Learning to lead a two-year Native Education Policy Review. This review built upon the 1987 Native Education Policy and resulted in the current First Nations, Metis and Inuit Education Policy Framework. Terry also served on the Indian and Northern Affairs Canada Minister's National Working Group on Education that produced Our Children – Keepers of the Sacred Knowledge.[451]

He has also worked with the Kainai Board of Education, evaluating their Board and staff in-services, and with the Stoney Board of Education on their in-services.[452] His other work in the Aboriginal education area is diverse, and includes: membership on an Indian and Northern Affairs Canada expert panel on education; ecumenical representative on the Indian Residential Schools Resolution Chief Adjudicators Reference Group; chair and final report author for the Holy Spirit Division Native Education Task Force; along with a variety of studies, reviews and reports on Native education or Aboriginal schools.[453] Terry also has presented his perspective, knowledge and experiences to many native education conferences, panels and other public forums.

Terry Fortin retired as superintendent of Edmonton Catholic Schools in 1999.[454] However, he is still very active as a consultant and volunteer in the area of Alberta's education, and especially native education, professing his strong belief that teachers can inspire confidence and lifelong learning in our children and that each child has a gift.[455]

Profile by: Brian Calliou

Fosseneuve, Louison "Shot"

1841-1914
Entrepreneur
and River
Transporter

Louison was born the son of Baptiste Fosseneuve and Julie Morand/Morin in Red River and came to the Athabasca District in 1865 in the service of the Hudson's Bay Company.[456] According to local history, Louison was called "Shot"due to his skills as a buffalo hunter.[457] Initially he was stationed at Dunvegan.[458]

In 1867 he married Catharine Decoine, the daughter of Francois Decoine and Josephte Desjarlais in Lac La Biche[459] and they were transferred to Fort Vermilion. Catharine unfortunately died in early 1869 after two months of illness.[460] Louison stayed at Fort Vermilion as a Hudson's Bay Company employee until 1871[471] and then moved permanently to the south side of the lake at Lac La Biche in 1872. There he married Therese Ladouceur, daughter of Joseph Ladouceur and Julie Auger.[462]

In Lac La Biche, Louison Fosseneuve worked as a trader and then in 1889 turned to the river transport business.[463] Louison became one of the first to shoot the rapids along the Athabasca River, thus contributing to the opening up of the Athabasca Landing-Fort MacMurray route for transport to the north. Missionaries and others have recorded many stories about his feats of strength and his ability in the arduous tasks of river transport.[464] The Roman Catholic missions seem to have had particular reason to be thankful for his skills. Fosseneuve built boats for the mission so that they could avoid the heavy fares charged by the Hudson's Bay Company for the use of their scows[465] and provided guiding and river pilot services for them including the guiding of the first group of Sisters of Providence from Lac La Biche to Fort Providence. In the late 1890s, the route became heavily travelled with the Klondike gold rush, and the expansion of the Canadian government into northern Alberta in the form of the North West Mounted Police and the Department of Indian Affairs. The *Lac La Biche Chronicle* states that, "'Sure Shot' the buffalo hunter became 'Shot' the scowman and eventually 'Captain Shot' the highly respected businessman."[466]

Louison's fame as an entrepreneur in river transport in the "romantic" North was also a topic for writers. He apparently was the inspiration for Robert Service's poem, "Athabasca Dick" and he appeared in the writings of Emily Murphy.[469]

Profile by: Teresa Ferguson

Friedel, Marge

1936 -
Metis
Cultural
Worker

Marge Friedel is a very busy retiree. In fact, she is probably busier since she turned sixty-five than she was before retirement. But this energetic community worker would not have it any other way.

Marge Friedel was born on July 24, 1936 at Lac St. Anne, Alberta, to her mother Lilly LaRocque and father Montrose Cunningham. She had two sisters, Marina (Joyce) and Delores, and one brother, Roderick.[470] She attended Evansburg High School, graduating from Grade 12 in 1954. She held various jobs such as working in a cookhouse in a foothills coal mining town. On April 22, 1957 she married Clifford Friedel and they had five children: four girls, Tracy, Melanie, Leslie and Luanne, and one boy, Dale.[471]

Marge Friedel, who was already busy in community service, had a dream to see Aboriginal culture respected and reflected within Alberta's health care system. She was prompted by the way her ninety-year-old aunt was treated disrespectfully by caregivers while hospitalized during an illness. This incident caused Freidel and her daughter Leslie Moncrieff to create the Tender Ties Agency in March 1997. This agency teaches health care workers about Aboriginal culture and teachings.[472] The Tender Ties Agency partnered with Northern Alberta Institute of Technology to set up the Metis Women Nursing Assistant/Emergency Responder training program, which runs twice a year for eighteen weeks. It is a unique program that combines learning about Aboriginal culture, spirituality, traditional ceremonies, and insight into Aboriginal wisdom, along with the regular health care training.[473]

Friedel is busy with her job as elder at the Amisk Wachiy Academy, an Aboriginal high school in Edmonton, where she works with children on a one-to-one basis to gain their trust and support them in the learning process. In addition to the Amisk Wachiy position, she also carries out her role as a cultural coordinator at the Northern Alberta Institute of Technology, through the Tender Ties Agency.

Marge is also very involved in community service, volunteering her cultural knowledge, experience and perspective to a variety of Aboriginal and community organizations. She served on various boards such as the Alberta Child Welfare Certification and Accreditation Board in Edmonton, and as a representative on the Provincial Elders Council for the Metis Nation of Alberta. She had also worked with the Native Counselling Services in the community service area. Other community involvement included a member of the Elders Circle for ACADRE (Aboriginal Capacity and Development Research Envelope), the Fetal Alcohol Syndrome initiative of the Metis Nation of Alberta, and she also co-chaired a session at the United Nations Indigenous Women Conference in China, in 1995.[474]

Marge Friedel was honored as an Elder by the Metis Nation of Alberta, when they awarded her the Metis Person of the Year in 1993 for her contributions to the Metis peoples.[475] Marge currently lives in Edmonton, and continues to contribute to Alberta's Aboriginal community by providing spiritual and cultural guidance.

Profile by: Brian Calliou

Garrioch, Alfred Campbell

1848 - 1934
Metis
Clergyman,
Missionary,
Linguist,
Author

In 1874, Alfred Campbell Garrioch came to Alberta from Manitoba as a schoolteacher for the Anglican mission under Bishop Bompas, and stayed to work for almost twenty years as ordained minister and linguist. Raised in Portage la Prairie, Garrioch credited the stories of his mother with drawing him to northern Alberta.[476] Eliza Campbell Garrioch was born in Fort Dunvegan on the Peace River, the daughter of Chief Trader Colin Campbell and his Metis wife, Elizabeth McGillivray. After Campbell and his family retired to the Winnipeg area, Eliza met and married John Garrioch, also a Metis child of a Scottish Hudson's Bay Company employee.[477]

Alfred Garrioch's first year in the north was spent at Fort Simpson, Bompas' home mission. From 1876 to 1885 he was at Fort Vermilion, establishing the mission, Unjaga, with church, mission house, a farm and the Irene Training School. He also started working on his Beaver language translations. The school was not a success by the standards of the mission and Garrioch lamented that only the children of the Hudson's Bay Company employees and a few Beaver orphan children were enrolled, but sympathized with the Beaver Indians who objected to an education that created a distance between themselves and their children.[478]

In 1885–86 Garrioch travelled to London, England to discuss the dissemination of his Beaver-English dictionary and took advantage of his time there to court and marry an English bride, Miss Crabbe. From 1886 to 1891, the Garriochs lived at Fort Dunvegan, establishing the mission, St. Saviour's and attempting to serve the Beaver Indians during one of the worst decades of their history. Plagued by epidemic illnesses throughout the 1800s, particularly by a severe form of tuberculosis called scrofula, their population was stricken again with a series of epidemics in the 1880s plus the accompanying famines. Eastern Canadian doctors advised that nothing could be done about the scrofula.[479] The Garriochs attempted to support the local people by running a soup kitchen. Garrioch wrote that the rice flour and canned meat were funded by a lady in England and vegetables were added from the mission garden.[480]

The Garriochs returned to the Winnipeg area in 1891 and Alfred continued to serve as an Anglican clergyman. After his retirement, he wrote about his time in northern Alberta. Of his four publications, two deal with Manitoba history[481] and two deal with northern Alberta: the autobiographical *A Hatchet Mark in Duplicate,* (Toronto,1929) and *The Far and Furry North,* (Winnipeg, 1925). These publications and his unpublished correspondence and other papers[482] are a mine of information on this period in northern Alberta history.

Profile by: Teresa Fergason

Genaille, Sheila

1947 -
Metis
Activist

As national president of the Metis National Council of Women, Sheila Genaille has spent most of her adult life advancing the rights and interests of Metis women. For this work she has received: a certificate of recognition from the Metis Nation of Alberta; the Governor General's 125th Commemorative Medal; the Governor General's Award in Commemoration of the Person's Case, 1997;[483] an honorary doctorate (civil) from St. Paul University, Ottawa, 2003; the Queen's Jubilee Medal, 2003; St. Alberta Citizen of the Year award, 2003; and a place on the YES Canada Committee.[484]

Sheila Genaille is a seventh-generation Metis born January 20, 1947 in Russell, Manitoba to Vina Morriseau and William Alexandre Genaille.[485] She was the middle child of eleven children. Her father was WWII Canadian army veteran who served in Europe.[486] Her family struggled financially and she dropped out of school because her family could not afford to buy clothes that met the requirements of the dress code. Ten years later she completed her high school diploma in Alberta. She attributes her strength of character, strong sense of self worth, and commitment to the guidance of her parents.[487]

She has faced many obstacles, including discrimination from all levels of government, including Aboriginal leaders. She identifies these barriers as gender- and race-related: the fact that she is a woman coupled with the fact that Metis people are seen as "second-class Aboriginal people."[488] Her work has focused primarily on the issue of gender discrimination, as well as unemployment, poverty, education and literacy, violence against women and their children and the preservation of the environment.

As national president of the Metis National Council of Women, Ms. Genaille advanced the interests of Metis women at the Dobbie Beaudoin Commission, Ottawa; the First Peoples and the Constitution Conference, Ottawa; the First Ministers Conferences, Ottawa, Charlottetown, and Baddeck; the Royal Commission on Aboriginal Peoples; Education Round Table, Ottawa; Economic Development Round Table, Ottawa; Health Round Table, Vancouver; Justice Round Table, Ottawa; Provincial/Territorial Meeting of Ministers Responsible for Aboriginal Affairs in Regina.[489] She represented the Metis Nation at the United Nations, Year of Indigenous Peoples, New York and represented Metis trappers in Europe, London, Brussels, and Geneva.[490]

She is also an historian and while working as the research director for the Metis Nation of Alberta, she was responsible for the Metis Cultural Centre, archives, and library. In conjunction with the University of Alberta and Canada Employment and Immigration, she developed and implemented a training program in the museology, archival, and library fields for Aboriginal people. She volunteered at the Alberta provincial Archives for six years and served as president of the Alberta Genealogical Society, Edmonton Branch, the Louis Riel Historical Society, the Edmonton Metis Local 1885, and the Alberta Metis Women's Association.[591]

If that is not enough, Sheila is the co-chair of the Indigenous Women of the Americas: Canadian Committee, a coalition of indigenous groups from Canada that formed links with indigenous women's groups in Central and South America. She has lectured at universities, conferences, and historical societies over the past twenty years, including Carleton University, the University of Ottawa, St. Paul University in Ottawa, and Grant MacEwan Community College in Edmonton.[492]

Profile by: Vivienne Biesel

Gladstone, James Basil

1887 – 1971
Kainai
Senator and
Rancher

Senator Gladstone was instrumental in leasing reserve lands to non-Aboriginal people who wanted to grow crops. This brought much needed wealth to the Kainai Reserve in the Depression years and gave the people an economic foundation on which to build.

James Basil Gladstone was born at Mountain Mill in 1887. His mother was a member of the Kainai Nation while his father, William Shanks Gladstone, was a Scot who came to Canada as a Hudson's Bay Company boat builder.[493] His Kainai name was Akay-Na-Muka, which translates to Many Guns – a common Kainai family name.[5494]Gladstone attended school at the St. Paul Anglican Mission on the Blood Reserve in southern Alberta and then transferred to Calgary Industrial School when he was sixteen years old. At the school he trained as a typesetter and worked briefly at the *Calgary Herald*.[495] He also worked as a wrangler and a Royal Canadian Mounted Police scout and interpreter in 1911.[496]

Gladstone married Jane Healy, the daughter of Joe Healy, a prominent Kainai chief. The couple had six children: Lucy, Fred, Nora, Horace, Doreen and Pauline. Gladstone and his sons ran a 720 acre ranch north of Cardston with four hundred head of cattle.[497] Always the innovator, he brought the first tractor on to Kainai land and introduced modern ranching techniques to the reserve.

James Gladstone was a founding member of the Indian Association of Alberta, a political representative organization that advocated Indian rights and Indian issues. He served as its president and held the position for nine years, from 1948 to 1957.[498]

He was surprised and very pleased when he received a call from the then Prime Minister, John Diefenbaker, inviting him to join the Senate of Canada. In March 1958 he was sworn in, and would remain in this position until he retired in 1971. Gladstone wore traditional regalia to his swearing-in ceremony in Ottawa. He stated, "I have always tried to do the best I could for the Indians in the past and now I will have greater opportunities and greater responsibilities. My work in the Senate will be aimed at improving the position of Canada's Indians."[499] In 1961, he was appointed co-chair of a joint Senate/House of Commons committee on Indian Affairs.[500]

Gladstone was known for his sense of humor, his accurate memory and his ability to see the broad picture in society. He was a gentle person and highly respected. He was the subject of a book, *The Gentle Persuader,* written by his son-in-law, Hugh Dempsey. James Gladstone passed away in 1971 at eight-four years of age in Fernie, British Columbia.

Profile by: Cora Voyageur

Gladue, Joey Wayne

1981 – 1999
Cree
Metis Dancer

Joey Gladue, or "Jigga" as he was known to many of his friends, was a bright light in the Metis cultural community until his life was cut short by a car accident in 1999. His love for Metis traditional dance was matched only by his prowess, and he is remembered by all who knew him as a skilled dancer and a kind and wonderful young person.

Joey came from a loving family who are members of the Alexander First Nation located forty kilometres northwest of Edmonton. His parents, Margaret and John Gladue, had seven children including Joey, who was the fifth child. At a young age he showed a love for dancing and when he was just four years old he went to the annual Heritage Festival in Edmonton with his mother and watched the Metis dancers for hours on end.

Joey won the Batoche, Saskatchewan jigging championship for four consecutive years, for which he earned the title, "Mr. Batoche."[501] He mastered many Metis dances, including the traditional broom dance, the belt dance, the Orange Blossom Special and the Red River Jig.[502] Elder Moise White first began to give Joey lessons, and then referred him to Georgina Donald of the Edmonton Metis Cultural Dance Society when he quickly saw the boy's potential. Joey's dance career blossomed with the troupe, and he was able to travel all over North America.

Gladue also became a mentor to other, younger dancers, starting with his younger brothers, Marco and Raymond. At a community level, he took great pride in his work with the Kipohtakaw Wheelers from his own community, the Alexander First Nation. The Wheelers once placed third in Batoche with Joey leading them.[503]

On Friday, September 3, 1999, Joey was travelling to a dance competition in Prince Albert, Saskatchewan with his mother, stepfather, one younger brother and a family friend. Near Hafford, Saskatchewan, a tanker truck ran a stop sign and crashed into their vehicle. Joey was killed at the young age of eighteen.[504]

After his untimely death, the community established the Community Scholarship Program in honour of Joey Gladue and Elder Delia Gray. The scholarships are designed to encourage Aboriginal students in Alberta to continue on to higher education, as well as continue their involvement in and build a stronger Aboriginal community.[505]

Even though he was a young man when he died, Joey Gladue touched many lives. He was known to be an excellent role model for other Aboriginal youth, due to his cheerful disposition and his undying love for dance. His ambition was from a young age to be the best dancer in the world. No small goals for Joey Gladue. According to his mother Margaret, he still lives on in his brothers' dancing, his words of wisdom, his love for his family, and his love for dancing.[506]

Nominated by: Margaret Gladue

Profile by: Lee Tunstall

Gray, Delia

1917 – 1999
Metis (Cree)
Community
Worker and
Activist

During her eighty-two years, Delia Gray made significant contributions to the betterment of the lives of her people. Throughout her life, she took pride in her ability to speak Cree. She promoted its use as well as working tirelessly to promote native culture and arts.[507]

Delia Gray was born in a log cabin in Wabasca to Metis parents. She was educated in St. Albert. From her tenth to sixteenth year she was ill with tuberculosis. During her formative years, her grandmother taught her traditional ways and traditional remedies as well as Cree language and Cree hymns.[508]

In 1935 she moved to Edmonton and worked at Edmonton General Hospital. In 1945 she married Robert Gray and they had seven children. When the family moved to the Paddle Prairie Metis settlement in 1957, she became a social worker.[509]

When Delia and her husband Robert returned to Edmonton in 1962, she continued being active in community life. With her husband, she helped to develop the Canadian Native Friendship Centre. After sitting as a board member for several years, she was made a lifetime member.[510]

Another of Delia Gray's accomplishments was establishing the All-Native Festival in 1964. The festival promotes Aboriginal talent in the arts of singing, Metis fiddling, dancing and jigging. This festival ran until 1996.[511]

In 1970 Delia and Robert Gray were instrumental in starting native Catholic masses at St. Joseph's Cathedral in Edmonton. These masses were later continued at Sacred Heart Church services.[512]

Delia Gray was recognized as a Metis leader in many ways during her active life. In 1991 she was appointed to the Metis Nation of Alberta Zone IV Regional Council Elder's Senate. In 1996 she was named Provincial Elder. She was also appointed to the Elder's Senate of the Metis Association of Alberta. As well, she was a recognized elder for the University of Alberta Native Studies Program. Her work included assisting Cree language instructors and acting as a consultant for Cree language textbooks.[513]

Delia also held numerous memberships. From its beginning she was a member of the Aboriginal Veteran's Society of Alberta. She has held memberships at the Catholic Women's League, the Legion of Mary and the Native Senior's Centre. In addition, she has belonged to the Montgomery and Kingsway Legion's Women's Auxiliary for five years.[514]

Delia Gray died in November 1999. In 2000, the Delia Gray Memorial Scholarship was established in her honor and in recognition of her contributions to the native community. Two scholarships are awarded to post-secondary students in the field of music. All Aboriginal students are eligible but preference will be given to Metis students. The first scholarships were presented to the recipients at the Delia Gray Memorial Gala on November 16, 2001.[515]

Profile by: Margaret Burgess

Halfe, Louise Bernice (Skydancer)

1953 –
Cree
Writer and
Poet

As a Canadian writer, Louise Halfe has many awards to her credit. She has participated in distinguished writer programs in both Canada and Australia.[516]

Louise Halfe was born on the Saddle Lake First Nations Reserve and attended Blue Quills Residential School in St. Paul, Alberta. She completed her secondary education at St. Paul's Regional High School. She received a Bachelor of Social Work from the University of Regina. She also earned a certificate in addiction training from Nechi Institute at St. Albert.[517]

Halfe's work re-examines Canadian history from a First Nation's perspective. Her aim is to provide information for Aboriginal people to learn their history and then to use that knowledge to heal past wounds. In particular she deals with the role of women in the fur trade, residential school abuse, and the loss of culture.[518]

Her use of storytelling, native spiritualism, and childhood memories helps her audience understand her message. They learn the impact that European contact has had on their lives. Her work emphasizes understanding and healing. One reader stated, "She chases out the shadow images that haunt our lives."[520]

Halfe received her first recognition as a poet in Jeanne Perreault and Sylvia Vance's *Writing the Circle: Native Women of Western Canada,* an anthology of writings by native women. In 1993, she won third prize in the League of Canadian Poets national poetry contest.

Bear Bones and Feathers, her first book of poetry, won the Milton Acorn Award in 1996. It was short-listed for the Spirit of Saskatchewan Award, the Pat Lowther First Book Award, and the Gerald Lampert Award. Her second book, *Blue Marrow*, was short-listed for the 1998 Governor General's Award. Her poetry has appeared in several anthologies and magazines, including the New West Review.[520]

Louise is able to connect with other indigenous people throughout the world through her work since many confront the same problems as Canadian Aboriginals. In 2003, she was one of the five Canadian Aboriginal writers who toured Australia as part of Honouring Words: Second International Indigenous Author's Celebration Tour. They gave readings, lectures, workshops and media interviews throughout Australia's east coast.[521]

Louise believes she has a responsibility to show future generations how the power of words can bring change and improvement. Her approach has benefited herself as well. She finds in her own people a source of strength and dignity, which she can use in her own life.

At the present time, Louise lives in Saskatoon, Saskatchewan with her husband and children.

Profile by: Margaret Burgess

Hope, Adrian

1903 - 1986
Metis
Poet, Film
Stuntman,
Politician

Adrian Hope was an advocate of Metis rights, a poet, cowboy, and movie stuntman. He raised the Metis profile, not only in Alberta, but also in Canada, by virtue of his own fame.[522]

Adrian Montrose Douglas Hope, also known as the "Canadian Kid," was born in Morinville, Alberta, in 1903. He is the second oldest of nine; his mother was a Cree woman and his father, Harry Hope, was a Scot. Harry was an employee of the Indian Affairs Branch and worked as an Indian Agent until he passed away in 1916.[523] Adrian spoke both Cree and English fluently. Adrian married at the age of twenty-two and had three daughters.

Prior to his political aspirations, Adrian was a rodeo cowboy who won championships until he had an accident that took one of his legs. It was during his recovery from the accident that Adrian decided to seek a new direction, not only for himself, but also for his Metis people. Adrian began his political career in 1928 by getting involved in Metis issues.

He was one of the founding members of the Metis Association of Alberta and the Northwest Territories, officially incorporated on December 28, 1932. Adrian also provided the majority of testimony on behalf of the Metis for the Ewing Commission.[524] The Ewing Commission was a Royal Commission created to look into the Metis situation and eventually led to the Alberta Metis Betterment Act.[525] Shortly thereafter, the provincial government set apart land for Metis settlements on which families would have tenure and opportunities to pursue agriculture.[526] It was the first of its kind in Canada and eight of the initial Metis colonies remain today. One Metis settlement is called Kikino, which means "home" in Cree.[527]

In 1961, Adrian was elected president of the Metis Nation of Alberta and served on the executive committee of the Federation of Metis Settlements. Adrian was a very proud Metis and once stated, "We are the progeny of the best of two races. The explorers and traders were the strongest and the bravest of the European males, and they selected the strongest and most beautiful of the Indian women as their mates. We are the children of these unions."[528]

Many in Canada will remember Adrian Hope for his love of his people. For many, he is best known as a poet and storyteller who chronicled the life, times, and feelings of his beloved Metis people.[529] The School of Native Studies at the University of Alberta awards the Adrian Hope Award annually to a student for outstanding academic achievement in native issues and insights.

Adrian lived at the Kikino Metis Settlement until he passed away in 1986.

Profile by: Casie McGonegal

Janvier, Alexandre Simeon "Alex"

1935 -
Dene
Artist and
Educator

Alex Janvier is considered one of Canada's greatest artists. He is one of the first native artists to paint in a style that blends "traditional native styles with abstract modernism."[530] Painting since the early 1960s, Janvier broke into the mainstream art world and paved the way for future Aboriginal artists.

Alexandre Simeon "Alex" Janvier was born to hereditary chief Harry Janvier and his wife Mary on February 28, 1935 at the Cold Lake Reserve in northeastern Alberta, where the approximately one thousand reserve residents lived by a traditional lifestyle and subsisted by hunting, trapping and fishing. Janvier describes Cold Lake as "where the Plains ended and the North began."[531]

At the age of eight, Alex Janvier attended Blue Quills Indian Boarding School in St. Paul, Alberta, where he felt the cultural shock of his new environment. Speaking only the Chipewyan language, Janvier quickly learned English and by age twelve, people at school were calling him an artist.[532] Janvier recalls himself as a child on the reserve using a stick to draw on the ground and comments that others had as much talent as an artist as he did.[533] It was at Blue Quills that he was provided the opportunity to work on his artistic ability and it was there that he learned how to paint. An art teacher from the University of Alberta, Karl Altenberg, was a regular visitor to St. Paul, and he gave young Janvier the encouragement to expand his "artistic horizons."[534] Janvier says that at age fourteen, "they conspired to rush art on me."[535]

Janvier attended the Alberta College of Art in Calgary, Alberta and completed a Bachelor of Fine Arts degree in 1960. He held a number of jobs after graduating from art school and he was an activist in the Indian rights movement. Janvier taught for the Faculty of Extension at the University of Alberta from 1960 to 1962.[536] In 1964, Alex Janvier's work was showcased at the Jacox Gallery in Edmonton.[537] By 1966, Janvier was working as an arts and crafts consultant, travelling Alberta searching for new talent, encouraging young Aboriginal artists with artistic ability and setting up exhibitions of their works for the Department of Indian Affairs. During Expo 67 in Montreal, Janvier helped organize the Indian Pavilion for which he also provided a large circular mural.[538]

In 1968, Janvier met his wife, Jacqueline Wolowski, while teaching adult classes at Saddle Lake Indian School near St. Paul. With Wolowski, also a teacher, Janvier taught an adult life skills class until 1970 at Alberta Newstart Inc. at Fort Chipewyan.[539] During Janvier's many years of teaching he still found time to paint, but in 1971, he decided to turn painting into his full-time job.

Alex Janvier achieved notoriety when he began using his band treaty number, 287, along with his name to sign his paintings. However, for a period in the 1960s, he used his treaty number alone as his signature. With the use of the treaty number, Janvier mocked the system in which the people were numbers controlled by a distant bureaucracy. This was a reflection of his own attitude of the government as paternalistic and depersonalized.[540]

Among Janvier's many works, Morning Star, painted in the early 1990s, is viewed as a masterpiece and is located in the dome of the Grand Hall of the Canadian Museum of Civilization in Hull, Quebec. Janvier has had many exhibitions: Land Spirit Power at the National Art Gallery (1992); Alex Janvier: First Thirty Years Retrospective at the Thunder Bay Art Gallery (1993); and most recently the Edmonton Art Gallery held Alex Janvier: New Works (2002).

Artist, educator, political activist, these are the many talents of Alex Janvier and he has been recognized for his numerous contributions. In 1993, Janvier was inducted into the Royal Canadian Academy of Artists and the following year inducted into the Northeastern Indian Hall of Fame.[541] On March 10, 2002 at the Ninth Annual National Aboriginal Achievement Awards in Winnipeg, Alex Janvier received the Lifetime Achievement Award. He lives in Cold Lake. He was awarded Honorary Doctorates from the University of Alberta and the University of Calgary in 2008. He was inducted as a member of the Order of Canada in 2007. He lives in Cold Lake.

Profile by: Phyllis Chau

Jobin, Louis

1860 – 1934
Metis
Political
activist,
Pioneer, and
Businessman

Louis Napoleon Jobin was born on December 14, 1860 at St. Charles, Manitoba to Ambrose Jobin (born 1817 in Montreal) and Marguerite Mandeville (born 1831 on the Great Plains also known as the Northwest Territories). Louis had four sisters, Cécile, Marie, Madeleine, Caroline, and four brothers, Joseph, Ambrose, Pierre, and Patrice.[542]

During the Riel Rebellion of 1885, Louis, Joseph and Ambrose joined Louis Riel in his cause for a better understanding with the Canadian government for acknowledgement of the Metis people. At the height of the rebellion, Riel sent Joseph Jobin to Chief Poundmaker for reinforcements; Poundmaker agreed to help the Metis, although the Metis men were warned to stay away from the Indian women.

On March 2, 1885, Riel formed a provisional government with fifteen members, with Ambrose being one of the executives. During the Battle of Batoche, several Metis were wounded in the conflict.

After Riel's arrest by the Canadian army, several of his comrades fled to Montana in the United States. Louis Jobin went to northern Alberta to Slave Lake (later to be named Grouard in memory of the Oblate missionary Bishop Grouard). On April 11, 1905, he homesteaded in Big Prairie just east of High Prairie, Alberta. After securing land he returned to St. Albert for his wife, Olive Dumas. Louis purchased a building from a nearby town and it took six teams of horses to pull it up the hill to Big Prairie. Louis and Olive raised eleven children in this house.

Louis Jobin's family was active in the community, competing in sporting activities held once a year in High Prairie. Louis was involved in the formation of the Agricultural Society in 1910. He became vice-president of the association and also became the director of the Cream Producers Association. He was well known in the community and because of this, the family was referred to as "well to do."

At the age of seventy-three years, fate dealt Louis a final blow when John Ferguson gunned him down on March 15, 1934. He died of two gunshot wounds. By the time his wife Olive found his body, it was already covered with freshly fallen snow. Family members and friends assisted the R.C.M.P. in tracking down Ferguson, who had persuaded Louis's sixteen-year-old daughter Marcella to leave with him. They were discovered in the cellar of Ferguson's home.

On October 6, 1934, Ferguson was hanged and laid to rest in the Fort Saskatchewan jail cemetery.

Olive Jobin left the farm in the early 1940s and moved to High Prairie with her daughter Lena.

Profile by: Yvonne Jobin

Johnson, Connie Beverly

1960-
Cree
Community
Worker

Connie Johnson is an example of optimism and fortitude. This is someone who just does not know the meaning of the word quit.

Connie Beverly Johnson was born to Joe and Rose Cardinal on May 26, 1960, at Athabasca, Alberta. The Cardinals were from Calling Lake, a small community north of Athabasca. She was the twelfth child in a family of thirteen children.[543]

In 1979, she married a local fellow who was also raised in the community, Gerald Johnson. They would go on to have six children: Justin, Chantel, Pisim, Wasi, Cody, and Wapan.[544]

Connie worked as a clerk at the general store in Calling Lake before beginning school in 1985 at the Sunrise program at Slave Lake, Alberta. At the age of twenty-five and then the mother of four children, Connie decided to begin a post-secondary education. Connie was not alone in her educational pursuit, and was joined by her sisters, Gladys and Claris, who were both enrolled in the Bachelor of Education program. Since graduation in 1990, Claris has taught at the elementary school in Calling Lake and Gladys is now the principal of the Wabasca Community School in Wabasca/Desmarais.

After completing the first two years of a university transfer program at the Sunrise Program she and her family moved to Edmonton to continue her education at the University of Alberta. During this time, she had two more children. She eventually earned a Bachelor of General Studies degree from Athabasca University.

Johnson had trouble with her eyesight since childhood. After a visit to the ophthalmologist, she received a diagnosis worse that anyone could have imagined. Connie was diagnosed with an eye disease called histoplasmosis, a disorder that would eventually leave her with low vision.[545] In 1998 Johnson registered with the CNIB and was given instructions on how to cope with her ever-decreasing eyesight. Not to be deterred, Connie continued to work as school and community liaison worker at the Calling Lake Elementary School.[546]

Through most of their time at school, Connie's sister Gladys was stricken with kidney disease. She underwent dialysis treatment and would eventually require a kidney transplant. The doctors tested all of the Cardinal siblings to see who would be the best kidney match for Gladys. As it turns out, the best match was Connie and in June 1997, Connie donated a kidney to her sister. Gladys has since made a full recovery.[547]

When the University of Calgary began its Rural and Aboriginal Social Work Program at Slave Lake in 2000, Connie decided that she needed a new challenge. She registered in the program as a disabled student and with the help of sight aids such as talking books, a computer program called zoomtext, and readers, she was able to complete a Bachelor of Social Work. Her degree was conferred at the spring convocation in June 2006.[548]

Connie Johnson lives in Calling Lake, Alberta with her six children and a grandchild named Kimwan.

Profile by: Cora Voyageur

Kane, Margo

1950 –
Cree/Salteaux/
Blackfoot
Multidisciplinary
Performing
Artist

For more than twenty years Margo Kane has been known in both rural and urban native communities for her compelling performances as a multi-disciplinary artist. She dances, sings, writes, directs, and produces meaningful works. Her varied career has included video, film, radio, and television with theatre performances and gallery shows.[549]

Margo Kane was born in Edmonton. She was a Metis child who was adopted as a baby by her aunt and uncle. Her aunt was killed in a car accident and her stepfather then raised her. She was not told she was Indian until she was in grade seven. She was the only native child in a white family and was brought up as white.[550]

Although Kane was an honor student and excelled in dancing and singing, she became confused over her cultural identity. Her love of dancing proved to be the catalyst for change.

As a first step in recovery, Kane enrolled at Edmonton's Grant McEwan College for the Performing Arts, where she excelled at acting, dancing, and singing. Scholarships to the Banff School of Fine Arts and to the Circle on the Square Theatre School in New York City gave her the opportunity to grow as an artist.[551] By taking charge of her life, Kane embarked on a brilliant career. As well, she found a spiritual path, which led her to self-fulfillment and spiritual strength.[552] Kane first attracted attention in the late 1970s when she acted in the Ecstasy of Rita Joe. As a role model for the National Native Alcohol and Drug Abuse Program, she travelled to prisons and recovery centres. In addition, she became the first native artistic director of Spirit Song Native Theatre School.[553]

The next stage in Kane's career was to create theatre pieces from her own experiences and identity, using her own unique methods. In 1987, she produced, Reflections in a Medicine Wheel. In it she played dual roles, an old native woman and her young granddaughter. The old woman passes on her wisdom to the younger one.[554]

Moonlodge (1990) grew out of Kane's experience with women's circles in native communities. She created it as a play to remind people of the importance of women in their lives and to empower women.[555] In 1992 Kane started her own performance company, Full Circle: First Nations Performance. As its artistic director she has gathered together a pool of artists from various disciplines to share their knowledge and inspiration with others. Workshops and studio performances provide training and research projects for those involved. Full Circle's mandate is to promote collaboration between Canadian and international artists.[556]

Full Circle's innovative projects include Community Talking Circles, Artist Development Workshops, and two major performances by Kane in *The River Home* (1994) and *Confessions of an Indian Cowboy* (2002).[5557]

Margo Kane has succeeded in her goal of being an honor and inspiration to her people. Her single-minded dedication towards raising awareness in the native community has given her a deepened sense of belonging to the larger native community. She now resides in Vancouver.

Profile by: Margaret Burgess

158

Lafleur, Joseph "Dollar"

1860 - 1953
Cree/French
Canadian
Fur Trader,
Farmer

Born the son of Jean Baptiste Lafleur and Marie Bisson dit Mayatis,[558] Joseph Lafleur was a member of a very old fur-trade family in the Peace River. The French-Canadian Jean Baptiste Lafleur had traveled with Peter Pond to the Athabasca River in 1786. In 1787 he was sent with Charles Boyer to build the first post on the Peace River, probably in the area of what is now Fort Vermilion.[559] The Metis generation of Lafleurs began with the marriage of this Jean Baptiste to a woman known to us only as Angelique.[560]

Joseph left Dunvegan in 1878. According to family history, he was accompanying his father on a trip to Montreal. They were caught by the ice at Fort Chipewyan and Baptiste, then an old man, died at the New Year's Day levee in Chief Factor Macfarlane's house. Macfarlane then offered Joe a home and he worked there until 1888, tripping and transporting mail.[561]

Joseph Lafleur married Pauline Mercredi in Ft. Chipewyan in 1885.[562] He worked in Fort Smith from 1888 to 1894 as a cattle-keeper and laborer.[563] In 1894, Joe and his family moved to Fort Vermilion, possibly because the Hudson's Bay Company was reducing staff in the Athabasca area[564] and undoubtedly because of the greater opportunities at Fort Vermilion in both farming and fur trading. Joe and Pauline had a large family to support. In his 1899 scrip application, Joe Lafleur described himself as a farmer on a squatter's claim.[565] According to the 1906 census, Joe and Pauline owned stock to the extent of four horses, five milk cows and ten cattle.[566]

159

Joseph Lafleur was called "Dollar" because he always kept his money with him. According to family history, a bank had defrauded him of his savings at one point.[567] Although labourers for the Hudson's Bay Company were not usually described as "very well-off,"[568] Joseph undoubtedly inherited his father's estate. The "bon-homme" Jean Baptiste Lafleur II was thought to have considerable savings.[569]

Joseph Lafleur became a local hero during the diphtheria epidemic in 1928 at Little Red River, a community just east of Fort Vermilion. He and his son-in-law, William Lambert, rode out by horse and sleigh from Fort Vermilion to Peace River to request medical assistance. Reports on the duration of that trip vary from eight to twelve days, but it was clearly an ordeal. There was no trail at that time, so they followed the river. Apparently the horse team and sleigh fell through the ice several times, each time necessitating stopping to build a fire and dry everything out. The community honored Joe with an engraved .303 Savage rifle and William Lambert with an engraved gold fob watch.[570]

Profile by: Theresa Ferguson

Lewis, Willard

1975 -
Cree
Boxer

Willard Lewis is a boxing champion and the pride of northern Alberta. Driven by the desire to be the first native boxer to win a world title, he has won numerous titles as an amateur and professional boxer. Lewis is known as "Red Thunder Rock, a name the grandfathers gave him in a dream during a sweat lodge ceremony in Fort McMurray in 1996.[571]

Lewis got his start in boxing at an early age. He was raised on the Beaver Lake Reserve in northern Alberta.[572] He was interested in boxing since he was eight years old and joined the Hobbema First Nations Boxing Club.[573] A non-drinker, very self-disciplined, and idolized by children, he has been a great role model for Aboriginal youth.[574]

Lewis's dedication and drive certainly deserve admiration. As an amateur, he had won five Canadian titles.[575] By the age of nineteen, he had won the national amateur heavyweight championship in Winnipeg, Manitoba. In 1998 at the age of twenty-three, after turning pro, he was undefeated with a 12-0 record, eight of those wins by knockout.[576] He also won the bronze medal at world junior Olympics in Romania in 1991 and would have done better had it not been for a broken and profusely bleeding nose. That year he won the Canadian cruiserweight title.[577] 1999 was a successful year for Lewis. He won the WBO cruiserweight title, then went on to win the WBO NABO cruiserweight title.

With this strong record of wins behind him, his next goal was to fight Dale (the Cowboy) Brown, who held the North American Boxing

Federation title and who was also pursuing a world title. Lewis (16-2-1, 8 TKOs) ultimately fought Dale Brown (21-2-1, 15 TKOs) on July 2, 2000 to defend his cruiserweight title, but he returned home from Montreal defeated by the Cowboy in a seven-round technical knock-out. He was disappointed with what he called "the most devastating defeat of my entire career." He didn't make excuses but thought that Dale Brown had an edge because he had funding and could devote his entire energy to training, while Lewis had to pursue his goals while working full-time as a welder in northern Alberta to provide for his wife Helena and their two children.[578]

Earlier on in his career he had been supported by Sawridge First Nation Chief, Walter Twinn, and Department of Indian Affairs, who gave Lewis a public relations position with Indigenous Sports Council in Edmonton. Twinn agreed to pay for his training in Edmonton and Las Vegas.[579] With Twinn's support, he trained under Jerome Coffee and Eddie Mustafa, Steve Delgado and Danny Carbajal. He also had to opportunity to spar in Las Vegas and Phoenix against tough Mexican fighters, returning to Canada with improved techniques. His trainer, Jerome Coffee, has every confidence that he has what it takes to be the champion of the world.[580]

The loss to Dale Brown did not discourage him for long. Willard Lewis rose from the ashes and persevered until he won the Canadian super middleweight title in 2002.[581] Willard "Red Thunder Rock" Lewis has made his family (particularly his father Percy Lewis) and his community proud.[5982]

Profile by: Vivienne Biesel

L'Hirondelle, Louis "Maurice"

1910 - 1994
Metis
Politician and
Administrator

Louis "Maurice" L'Hirondelle was born on May 4, 1910 to Peter L'Hirondelle and Sophie Berland of Lac La Nonne, Alberta.[583] Maurice is the oldest of eight children, with the L'Hirondelles having three more boys (Edward, Roy, and Lawrence) and four girls. (Mary, Doris, Emily, and Emma).[584]

On May 31, 1935, L'Hirondelle was married to Marguerite Majeau at Mearns, Alberta.[585] The L'Hirondelles were married for fifty-nine years before Maurice's death, and raised fifteen children.[586]

L'Hirondelle's political career began as an eighteen-year-old, when in 1928 he formed the Lac La Nonne Metis Local and served as secretary to this organization.[587] Along with his father Peter, Maurice was one of three founding delegates behind the first Metis Association in the region.

In the 1960s, L'Hirondelle was involved in a mandate calling for economic self-sufficiency on Alberta Metis settlements. L'Hirondelle was so involved with this cause he spent many personal and family resources promoting the Alberta Federation of Metis Settlements and the causes for which it stood.[588] His promotion and efforts on behalf of the Federation led to his presidency. One of L'Hirondelle's first acts was to see to the Federation's registration under the Society Act of Alberta.[589]

The Federation's mandate was to deal with three major issues: natural resource revenues, local government development, and the re-establishment of four Metis settlements (Cold Lake, Touchwood, Marlborough, and Wolf Lake).[590]

One of the major accomplishments of L'Hirondelle's presidency was an economic development strategy for the Metis settlements. L'Hirondelle actually led the Federation into litigation against the Alberta provincial government regarding the management of trust funds accruing from the sale of sub-surface natural resources. During his presidency, L'Hirondelle served a pivotal role as a witness at pre-trial hearings called Examination for Discovery.[591]

L'Hirondelle continued with his determination to gain economic self-sufficiency. In 1990 the Metis settlements agreed to settle out of court for local government development along with a financial package.[592] The Metis settlements of Alberta would be far different than today without L'Hirondelle's insightful passion for his people. His efforts have brought the Metis settlements closer to the dream of self sufficiency and self-reliance.

L'Hirondelle received many awards for his dedication to Metis settlement efforts. Some of these awards include recognition from the Fishing Lake Settlement Council, The Metis Nation and Securing Metis Settlement Areas in Alberta, the East Prairie Settlement Council. L'Hirondelle also received the Alberta Achievement Award for Outstanding Service in Metis Associations.[593]

L'Hirondelle finished his political career by providing information and consultation services concerning Metis issues and culture to various institutions, including the University of Alberta, prisons, and schools.[594]

Maurice L'Hirondelle's legacy and profound effect on the Metis peoples of Alberta can still be seen in the foundations he helped build years ago. He passed away on September 23, 1994.[595]

Profile by: David Christiansen

Lightning, Albert (Buffalo Child)

1900 - 1991
Cree
Statesman and
Spiritual
Leader

Albert Lightning was a man others looked to for quiet leadership and traditional knowledge. He was an active participant in the Indian Association of Alberta and as an elder, helped many younger people discover their Aboriginal heritage.

Lightning was born on July 7, 1900 at Pigeon Lake, west of Hobbema. His Cree name was Paskwaw Mostos Awasis, or Buffalo Child. History has shrouded his parents, but we know he was married young but lost his first wife, Mary Baptist, to the flu epidemic of 1917.[596] He eventually moved to the Ermineskin Reserve and ranched there. His second wife was said to be chosen by Albert's horse, which he sent into the crowd to choose a woman who would be a good wife.[597] His family included two daughters and four sons, with numerous grandchildren.

Lightning was an avid sportsman in his youth, and an avid spectator as he aged. He particularly enjoyed hockey and was often seen at the hockey arena. He also loved animals and was especially gifted with horses. He was one of the first professional rodeo cowboys from the Hobbema area.[598]

A founder of the Indian Association of Alberta, Lightning was elected its president in 1956. His family had also been involved in the landmark Samson Case in the 1950s, and they had been threatened with expulsion from the reserve. There were allegations that his ancestors had accepted scrip, but his family was eventually cleared and allowed to remain.[599]

After leaving active politics behind, Lightning concentrated his time and efforts on developing and sharing his cultural teachings. He made more than eight hundred flights during his life to do just that. His leadership and diplomatic skills continued to travel far beyond his own people, and he was fluent in Cree, Blackfoot, Stoney and English. The traditional enemies of the Cree, the Blackfoot, even honored him with a Blackfoot name. He was known as Iron Shirt, due to the fact that when a Blackfoot tribe member threatened to kill him, he told them to go ahead.[600] He also often travelled to the Stoney Reserve at Morley to spend time with his friend Chief John Snow. Non-Aboriginal peoples also valued his wisdom and travelled far to spend time with him.[601]

In 1969, Lightning was instrumental in organizing the first North American Ecumenical Conference at Crow Agency in southwestern Montana. By the 1970s and into the 1980s, the conference had evolved into an annual summer event where people from varied racial and religious backgrounds came together to share and discuss their spiritualities. Albert was always quick to share his spiritual wisdom and healing gifts with any and all who desired them. He believed strongly in natural law and that truth will never lead anyone astray. [602]

Albert Lightning lived a long and full life. He was a wise spiritual leader and healer, an astute statesman and a true warrior for Indian rights.

Profile by: Lee Tunstall

Little Bear, Leroy

1944 –
Blood
Educator and
Administrator

Leroy Little Bear has established himself as a scholar and an educator in the field of Native Studies in Canada. He was born in Lethbridge in 1944 and raised on the Kainai reserve. He attended Saint Mary's residential school on the Blood reserve. He later earned a Bachelor of Arts degree from the University of Lethbridge in 1971. He continued his education at the University of Utah where he earned a Juris Doctor degree (the equivalent of a Canadian Bachelor of Laws, an LLB) in 1975.

Little Bear joined the faculty at the University of Lethbridge in 1975. He was a founding member of the Native American Studies program and served as its chair. He served in this position until he retired from the University of Lethbridge in 1997. He watched the number of Aboriginal students grow from a handful in the mid-1960s to about two hundred in the late 1980s.[603]

In the 1980s he co-authored three books with fellow University of Lethbridge professors Menno Boldt and Anthony Long: *Pathways to Self-Determination: Native Indian Leaders Perspectives on Self Government in Canada* (1984); *Quest for Justice: Aboriginal Rights in Canada* (1985); and *Indian Nations in Conflict: Provinces and Indian Nations in Canada* (1988).

Leroy helped establish a similar Native American Studies program at Harvard University in Massachusetts in 1998. He remained at Harvard from January 1998 to June 1999.[604] While at the University of Lethbridge he helped set up an Aboriginal management program that addressed First Nation band management and administration issues. Leroy commented, "Educating native students was my way of making a difference. If I can graduate ten or fifty students then that makes a difference."[605] He further stated, "Native survival is all about adaptability and education give you the basis to develop adaptability."[606]

Leroy contributed to the Royal Commission on Aboriginal People reports. He has been affiliated with The Banff Centre's Aboriginal Management and Leadership Program. At the Banff Centre he serves as a faculty leader and teaches classes on indigenising institutions.

He has served as a legal and constitutional advisor to the Assembly of First Nations and has served on many influential committees, commissions, and boards dealing with First Nations issues.[607] He received the National Aboriginal Achievement Award for education in 2003. He also received an honorary doctorate from the University of Lethbridge in 2004.[608]

Leroy Little Bear lives in Lethbridge.

Profile by: Joan Ryan

Littlechild, George

1958 -
Cree
Artist

George Littlechild is recognized as one of foremost First Nations artists in Canada. He is known for bright, bold colours, playful images, serious undertones, collages of mixed media, and strong connection to ancestors.[609] His mixed-media paintings record his personal and family history as well as his reclamation and re-connection with his ancestral culture. His trademark is the use of high-chroma color, environmental installations and photo collages. He has a unique style of incorporating haunting vintage photographs in collages, juxtaposing archival photographs with images of today's world.[610]

George Littlechild was born on August 16, 1958 in Edmonton,[611] a descendant of Chief Bobtail, Chief Ermineskin, Chief Samson, and Chief Louis Bull.[612] His mother was Rachel Littlechild Cree from Ermineskin First Nation, and his father was James Price, a Scottish/Micmac from New Brunswick. At a young age, George was taken from his mother and placed in foster homes. At the home of Mrs. Winnie Olthius, his artistic talent was recognized and encouraged. His foster parents arranged for private art lessons with a non-native artist who had experience painting Aboriginal subjects.[613]

He found a voice through his artwork and earned numerous scholarships to prestigious art schools including the Banff School of Fine Arts. George earned an art and design diploma from Red Deer College in 1984 and a Bachelor of Fine Arts degree from Nova Scotia School of Art and Design in 1988.[614] He also studied art at The Banff Centre in 1988. At the age of thirty he was named Alberta artist of the year. He won a number of scholarships including the First Place Scholarship Award, Alberta Indian Arts and Crafts Society: Asumena (Cree for "once again").[615]

In recent years, Littlechild's interest in his heritage has led him to re-learn his past and explore socio-political issues related to residential school and reserve system.[616] Through his art he seeks to educate and alleviate prejudice. His art is currently on display in art galleries and museums around the world, as far away as Japan, Germany, and Australia. There are numerous public, private and corporate collections of his work in museums, galleries, and educational institutions across the country.

He is the author and illustrator of several children's books, including the award winning publications *This Land is My Land* and *What's the Most Beautiful Thing You Know About Horses?* In 1996 he was honored with the British Columbia Cultural Services Award.[617]

George Littlechild is an educator, lecturing at universities and conducting adult art workshops. He also runs art programs in elementary and secondary schools in Vancouver, where he lives. He uses art and education to promote pride in his students' heritage and to celebrate the uniqueness of each person.[618]

Profile by: Vivienne Beisel

Littlechild, Jacob Wilton "Willie"

1944 -
Cree
Lawyer and
Politician

Jacob Wilton "Willie" Littlechild is truly a trailblazer. He has a string of firsts attached to his name. For example, he was the first Aboriginal lawyer called to the Alberta Bar and one of the first indigenous Members of Parliament, and he was the first indigenous person appointed as Queen's Counsel by the Alberta Law Society.[619]

Jacob Wilton Littlechild was born on the Ermineskin First Nation at Hobbema on April 1, 1944. He was one of ten children born to Smith and Justine (nee Minde) Littlechild.[620] After completing school on the reserve he attended St Anthony's College in Edmonton where he finished Grade 12 in 1964.[621] He later attended the University of Alberta where he earned several degrees including a Bachelor and a Master's degree in Physical Education and a Bachelor of Law degree.[622] He was called to the Alberta Bar in 1977.[623]

He married Helen Peacock, from the Enoch Cree Nation in 1970. They have three children, Teddi, Neil, and Megan, and four grandchildren, Shayna, Keeshon, Cleveland, and Summer.

"Willy" was instrumental in founding the North America Indigenous Games Association along with Peigan athlete John Fletcher. The games help aspiring Aboriginal youth; its first event was held in Edmonton and consisted of track and field events as well as archery, baseball, boxing, canoeing, soccer, swimming and a rodeo.[624]

He was inducted into the University of Alberta Wall of Fame as well as the Indigenous Sports Hall of Fame and the Canadian Hockey Wall of Fame between 1967 and 1999. As a sports advocate, "Willy" was involved in international and national sports gatherings and events. "Willy" was also a member of the International Red Cross and helped set up water safety programs in Jamaica.[625]

"Willy" Littlechild was elected as a Member of Parliament for the Wetaskiwin constituency from 1988 to 1993.[626] While an MP, he served as a member of the Standing Committee on Aboriginal Affairs.[627] He also served on committees involved in education, health and justice issues. He was appointed to the United Nations Forum on Indigenous Issues and was also chairman of the Justice Reform Commission on First Nations Peoples and Metis in Saskatchewan.[628]

He held several awards during his academic career: scholarship awarded by INAC; National Fitness and Amateur Sports bursaries; scholarship in Indian Law; Tom Longboat Trophy and Indian Athlete of the year in 1965, 1967, 1974 and 1975.[629s]

In 1999, "Willy" was awarded the Order of Canada for his contributions to his own and other indigenous communities.[630] Willy decided not to seek re-election as an MP because he wanted to be home with his family. He continued his law practice until he was elected as the Alberta Assembly offirst Nations In 2009 he was named a comissionaire for the Residential School's Truth and Reconciliat Commission. He lives in Hobbema.

Profile by: Joan Ryan

Lusty, Terry

1942 –
Metis
Historian,
Teacher and
Photographer

One can always depend on Terry Lusty to attend and document events in Alberta's Aboriginal community. He has been reporting and photographing powwows, and awards dinners for the past couple of decades. To date he has amassed a photographic archive of Alberta Aboriginal history.[631]

Terry Lusty was born in St. Norbert, Manitoba in February, 1942. His mother died when he was three years old and he was raised in a residential school and in a series of foster homes.[632] At age sixteen, Lusty struck out on his own. He worked a series of odd jobs and would eventually move to Calgary. While working at the Calgary Native Friendship Centre he began work as a writer and a photographer. His first writing assignment was a newsletter.[633]

Terry began singing in the residential school choir as a child. His love of singing continued while attending Daniel McIntyre Collegiate High School in Winnipeg, where Terry was part of the award-winning school choir.[634] Terry began playing guitar and became an accomplished musician. He has given command performances for the likes of Buffy St. Marie.[635]

He would later receive a Bachelor of Education degree from the University of Calgary. Terry was instrumental in Aboriginal curriculum development for Alberta Learning.[636] He taught school in Wabasca and in Fort Chipewyan. He served on ministerial committees for MLAs Horst Schmitt and Mary Lemessereur.[637]

Lusty has a passion for Metis history. He authored two books on the topic and co-authored *An Annotated Bibliography of the*

*Meti38*with John Friesen[638] and, *Louis Riel, Humanitarian,* published in 1973.[639] He He has lectured at schools and universities and facilitated workshops on Metis culture and history.[640]

Since the mid-1980s, Lusty has worked as a freelance writer and photographer. He was a regular contributor to the *Windspeaker* newspaper with his Metis history column. He has also written for *Sweetgrass, Aboriginal Voices, Grassroots,* and *Indian Country.*[641] Terry has photographed some of country music's biggest stars including Vince Gill, Johnny Cash, Dolly Parton, and George Jones. He has also taken pictures of famous people such as Wayne Gretzky, Chief Dan George, Pope John Paul II, and Jordin Tootoo.[642]

He is an active community member and has served on a number of boards and committees over the years. He has participated on the Edmonton Urban Aboriginal Affairs Committee, the Indigenous Sport Council of Alberta, Dreamspeaker Festival, the Canadian Native Friendship Centre, and the Aboriginal Youth and Family Wellness and Education Society.[643]

He was awarded the Premier's Award for Excellence in 1998, the Aboriginal Role Model Award in 1997, and was a nominee for the National Aboriginal Achievement Award in 1997.[644] Terry has three children and he lives in Edmonton.

Profile by: Cora Voyageur

Mandamin, Judge Leonard Stephen (Tony)

1944 -
Ojibway
Lawyer, Judge

His Honor, Judge Mandamin, has been a lawyer for more than twenty years. He has had a distinguished career and has held several important offices in Alberta. His most important achievement to date has been in the area of restorative justice in the Aboriginal community. He helped establish the Peacemaker Court, a precedent-setting project on the Tsuu T'ina Reserve near Calgary. This court, the first of its kind in Canada, combines Aboriginal peacemaking values and Canadian law.[645] Judge Mandamin presides over this First Nations Court on the Tsuu Tina Reserve. He is also a judge at the Calgary Criminal Division of the Provincial Court.[646]

Judge Mandamin was born on the Wikwemikong First Nation Reserve on Manitoulin Island in Ontario. The members of the reserve are Odawa, Ojibway, and Pottawanimi. He earned a Bachelor's degree in electrical engineering from University of Waterloo in 1971, and a Bachelor of Laws from University of Alberta, conferred in 1982.[647]

Before he enrolled at the University of Alberta to study law, Mandamin was employed by the Indian Association of Alberta in the early 1970s. It was at the Indian Association of Alberta that he met his future wife, Joyce Blackman. After their marriage, they moved to Ottawa where Tony worked for the Aboriginal Citizens Group housed at the Secretary of State. After returning to Edmonton in 1974, he worked at the Department of Regional Expansion until 1979.[648]

He began law school in 1979 and graduated in 1982. After graduation he articled with the Edmonton law firm of Ackroyd, Bradley, Piasta, Roth and Day. In 1984, he set up his own law firm, Mandamin and Associates, on the Enoch Cree Nation on the western outskirts of Edmonton. His practice included work for Alberta First Nations on treaty rights and land claims.[649] His Badger case was heard at the Supreme Court of Canada.

As a lawyer, Mandamin specialized in Aboriginal restorative justice and has done much to promote the idea. In the early 1990s he organized two major Aboriginal Justice conferences in Edmonton, both of which attracted hundreds of delegates.[650]

He shared his Aboriginal law expertise through teaching. At the Banff School of Management he served as faculty coordinator for several Aboriginal justice seminars. While he was also an adjunct professor at the University of Alberta's School of Native Studies, where he taught courses in Aboriginal law.[651]

Mandamin's community work was extensive, as he served on the Edmonton Police Commission from 1991 to 1995, first as a commissioner and later as its chairman. The Commission established sentencing circles for teenaged offenders during that time. The Aboriginal Youth Justice Committee was formed during his term as chairman; the committee continues to this day and has expanded to include adults.[652] He was also a trustee of the Canadian Native Friendship Centre in Edmonton.

Judge Mandamin has long been an advocate for a separate Aboriginal justice system. He stresses that Aboriginal justice is not more lenient on Aboriginal offenders but emphasizes accountability and responsibility. In a special ceremony held on the Tsuu Tina Reserve on October 15, 1999, L.S. "Tony" Mandamin was sworn in as the first Aboriginal judge to serve in an Aboriginal court in Canada.[653] He is the third Aboriginal judge in Alberta after Thomas Goodson (1991) and Dick Fowler (1994).[654] He was appointed to the Federal Court of Canada in 2007.

He has an office on the reserve as well as in the Provincial Court in downtown Calgary. He lives in Ottawa, is married and has one daughter.

Profile by: Margaret Burgess

Margetts, Jenny

1936 - 1991
Cree
Educator
and Activist

When Jenny Shirt was young, a teacher told her that even one committed person can make change.[655] This statement was never more true than with Jenny Margetts. Her sense of social justice and her commitment to equal treatment for Aboriginal people in Canada caused her to spring to action. Her efforts continue to benefit the Aboriginal community to this day.

Jenny Shirt was born on the Saddle Lake First Nation, near St. Paul in central Alberta, on June 14. 1936. She was one of eight children born to Felix Shirt and his wife, Louisa (Doghead).[656] She, along with her brother and sisters, attended the Blue Quill Indian Residential School until she was sixteen years old.[657] While in residential school Jenny decided that she wanted to become a nun. She entered the Dominican convent in Quebec as a novice at the age of seventeen and remained for three years. During this time she studied early childhood education.[658] While working as a kindergarten teacher at Goodfish Lake, near St Paul, Alberta, she decided not to continue with the Order.[659]

In 1959 she met her future husband, Gordon, in Grand Centre. The couple were married the following year and would go on to have two children, Tim and Karen. The family moved to Edmonton in 1967.[660]

Jenny held a number of jobs after graduating from secretarial college but she was drawn to working with children. As a child welfare worker she grew disenchanted with the system. The more she got to know about the child welfare policies the more she disliked them. Her husband Gordon recalled that she got so angry when children were apprehended. Crying children were being ripped from the arms of tearful grandmothers.[661] She believed that something needed to be done and that an advocate was needed to represent those who could not fight for their rights.

In early 1968 she began working with a University of Alberta law student, Jim Robb. She asked him to look into aspects of the Indian Act that discriminated against Indian women – most notably Section 12(1)(b). This section stated that if an Indian woman married a non-Indian man she would lose her Indian status. However, if an Indian man married a non-Indian woman, she would become an Indian under the Indian Act.[662] Later that year, Margetts and other Indian women, including Nellie Carlson, Kay Anderson, and Philomine Ross, organized a lobby group that would evolve into Indian Rights for Indian Women.[663] At one meeting with the then Prime Minister Pierre Trudeau, Nellie and Jenny teased Trudeau when he arrived for their scheduled meeting flanked by bodyguards. They asked him whether he was afraid of "two little Indian women from Alberta."[664] Trudeau asked the bodyguards to leave the meeting. The tenacity of this dedicated group of Indian women caused the passage of Bill C-31, proclaimed on April 17, 1985.

Her concern and love of children caused her to create the Awasisd[665] Program at Prince Charles School in Edmonton in 1980. This cultural program was the first of its kind in Canada. It provided traditional and cultural teachings to kindergarten students in Edmonton's public school system. The program continues to acquaint children with their Aboriginal background and helps instil in them pride in their heritage.

Jenny received many awards for her efforts. She was honored by Status of Women Canada during International Women's Year in 1975. She also won the Aboriginal Order of Canada from the Native Council of Canada in 1992. Most recently, she was named one of Edmonton's one-hundred most influential citizens.[666] Her husband attended a gathering at city hall hosted by the mayor, Bill Smith, and the Lieutenant Governor, Lois Hole. Gordon was presented a commemorative gold medal and a leather-bound book entitled *Edmontonians of the Century*, featuring Jenny's profile.[667] The medal and the book are proudly displayed in the Margetts home.

Sadly, Jenny passed away at the age of fifty-five years. However, her legacy lives on.

Profile by: Cora Voyageur

McDonald, Dorothy

1946 - 2005
Cree
Politician,
Environmentalist
and Activist

Dorothy McDonald was born in 1946 in Fort McKay, a community located sixty-five kilometres north of Fort McMurray. She was the fifth child of Phillip and Victoria McDonald. Her father was the hereditary chief of the Fort McKay First Nation and he ruled the community for more than twenty-five years.

Her move into leadership after her father's death seemed a natural thing for her to do. Like most women chiefs in Canada, McDonald was raised in a political family. She became her community's first female chief when she was elected in 1980; she would go on to win three elections. During this time the community and the region was undergoing tremendous change due to resource development in the area.

She implemented a three-pronged approach to help her community regain control of its future. Her goals included protection of traditional lifestyles for hunters and trappers, the establishment of an economic base to move the community away from dependence on the Department of Indian Affairs and acquiring better employment and training opportunities for community members. This approach benefited the community and helped improve the community's social and economic well being.

Dorothy was always concerned about the environment and her time as the elected leader of her community was not easy. During her tenure as chief she ruffled feathers in industry and government with her tenacity. The community members had longstanding grievances

179

over environmental issues and compensation for trappers who lost land to resource development. She ensured that resource development in the area was not unfettered or unregulated.

In 1982, the Fort McKay band under McDonald's leadership brought five charges against Suncor Inc., while the Attorney General added an additional fifteen charges under the Fisheries Act and the Clean Water Act. The following year a provincial court judge found the company guilty of violating the Fisheries Act while charges under the Clean Water Act were dismissed.

Dorothy McDonald was honored by her community when its adult education centre was named after her in 1999. The learning centre is a satellite campus of nearby Fort McMurray's Keyano College, and offers upgrading and other educational programming to the community members.

In 2003, Dorothy was the recipient of an Esquao Award from the Institution for the Advancement of Aboriginal Women. This Lifetime Achievement award recognized her decades of advocacy on behalf of the environment and her community. Dorothy McDonald lived in Fort McMurray with her husband, Rod Hyde and her children and her grandchildren lived neaby.She passed away in 2005.

Submitted by: Cora Voyageur

Moostoos, "The Buffalo" aka Louison Willier

1850 – 1918
Cree
Trapper,
Fisherman and
Headman

Moostoos was the spokesman for the Cree at the Treaty 8 talks with the federal government in June 1899. He was an eloquent speaker. His negotiating style was conciliatory but he was firm in his resolve to get the best possible deal for his people.[668]

Moostoos was born at the western end of Slave Lake, Alberta. He was the eldest of ten children born to Masinigoneb and Marie Kowikkiu. His younger brother Kinasew (Kinoosayo) worked with Moostoos in protecting the interests of First Nation people during that crucial part of the twentieth century – a time of great change on the western prairie.[669]

The change came when the federal government wanted to open up the Canadian west to white settlement. Eastern interests saw the great economical advantages of the rich western farmlands. The same land was the ancestral home of the Cree, Dene, Metis, and others. An agreement needed to be reached. Treaty 8 was the result of the negotiations, which took place in June 1899 at Willow Point on Lesser Slave Lake.[670]

The spokesmen for the Cree were Moostoos and Kinasew. The government representative was the Treaty Commissioner, David Laird. The federal government wanted safe passage for white settlers as the area was opened up for mining and farming. For their part, the Cree spokesmen strove to keep their traditional way of life intact and to protect future generations.[671]

Laird confirmed the freedom of the First Nations people to hunt, fish and trap. Kinasew wanted additional benefits for the Cree. Moostoos supported him but stressed the need for peaceful relations between First Nations and the whites. In addition, Moostoos pointed out the need for education for his people. He received a positive response from Commissionaire Laird. After two days of talks, Treaty 8 was signed.[672] In the ensuing years, Moostoos and Kinasew worked diligently to ensure that the government kept the promises made under the treaty.[673]

In 1900 Moostoos, Kinasew and other headmen asked the government for reserve land east of the Driftpile River on Lesser Slave Lake. Because each of the brothers and other headmen had different followers the government established two reserves in 1910. Kinasew had the Driftpile Reserve. Moostoos was given a reserve at Sucker Creek. For the rest of his life he served as a leader of the Sucker Creek band as well as being their medicine man and healer[674]

The band members at Sucker Creek regarded Moostoos as their Chief rather than leader. They revered him for his knowledge, wisdom and strength. He had the unique ability to foresee and accept changes without compromising the traditions and rights of his people. He died in 1918 during the Spanish Flu epidemic that hit the First Nation community.[675]

Submitted by: Margaret Burgess

Norris, Malcolm

1900 – 1967
Metis
Politician,
Veteran

Malcolm Norris was best known for the political roles he played in the establishment of formal organizations on behalf of Aboriginal people in both Alberta and Saskatchewan. He helped establish the Metis Association of Alberta and was also active with the Indian Association of Alberta (IAA). He also started the Metis Association in Saskatchewan. In addition to his work with the Aboriginal community, he was a tireless worker for the CCF party in Saskatchewan. He was a World War II veteran and a geologist.

Malcolm Norris was born on May 25, 1900 in St. Albert to John Norris and Euphrosine Plante, who was Metis. John Norris had made his fortune in the fur trade and Norris enjoyed a privileged childhood.[676] As a child, Norris was introduced to the concept of ethnic tolerance and developed an appreciation of the political and social viewpoints at an early age. He also developed an appreciation of Indian people and of his own Metis heritage, as stories of the Riel rebellion and First Nations were told.[677]

Malcolm Norris was a scholar, and by the time he was an adult he was fluent in English, French, and Cree.[6788] He expected to attend university but his father's death ended these plans when it became apparent that appropriate provisions had not been made for Malcolm's education.[679] Norris joined the Royal North West Mounted Police (RNWMP) and was sent to Regina for training. His career ended after he completed his training because the RNWMP instituted the minimum age requirement of eighteen.[680]

In 1919, he began working for the Hudson's Bay Company (HBC) in Fort Vermillion before transferring to Little Red River in 1921 to work as the assistant postmaster. During his early days in northern Alberta he met Mary Celina Tardiff, whom he married 1921.[681] Together they had four children.

Norris was elected to the first executive council of the Metis Association on December 28, 1932 as the first vice-president.[682] Over the next couple of years, the executive committee lobbied the government until December 12, 1934, when the Ewing Commission was formed to investigate the Metis situation.[683] Norris was one of the executive committee members to testify on behalf of the Metis people of Alberta.[684] As a result of their efforts, the Metis Betterment Act was passed and Metis colonies were established.[685]

In 1939, Norris worked with Johnny Calihoo to form the Indian Association of Alberta (IAA). The purpose of the organization was to "improve the social and economic conditions on reserves."[686] In 1940, during World War II, he joined the Royal Canadian Armed Forces and was first stationed in Ontario before he was transferred to Calgary in 1942.[687]

He was a vocal supporter of Aboriginal rights and constantly encouraged the people to fight for their rights. He then became the director of the Prince Albert Indian/Metis Friendship Centre and formed the Metis Association of Northern Saskatchewan and became its first president.[788]

Norris suffered a stroke in 1966 that left him unable to walk. But he did not lose his ability to speak, and when he gave his last political speech at the Centennial Workshop for Native People in Prince Albert, there was not a dry eye in the house.[689] He withdrew from politics in 1967 and moved to Calgary. On December 5, 1967 he suffered a heart attack and passed away.[690]

Profile by: K. Patricia Colosimo

Norwest, Henry

1884 – 1918
Cree
World War I
Sniper

For a man who started his working life as a saddler and cow-puncher, Henry Norwest turned into one of Canada's greatest military heroes in the First World War. His success as a sniper in World War I made Norwest the most effective of the Canadian troops of the front, if not the best in the British forces.

Henry Norwest was born in Fort Saskatchewan on May 1, 1884.[691] He was one of four children born to Cree parents Louis Norwest and Genevieve Batoche.[692] Norwest's father lived for a time with the band led by Kiskaquin (Bobtail). The senior Norwest accepted scrip and was subsequently enfranchised.[693]

In all likelihood, Norwest sharpened his marksmanship and patience while hunting as a child in the woodland areas of Alberta. These skills would serve him well as soldier and helped him gain an edge as a sniper. His patience and stealth were known and feared by the Germans.

Henry Norwest joined the Canadian Expeditionary Force when war broke out in 1914. Norwest went under the alias of Henry Louie and served with the 3rd Canadian Mounted Rifles. Norwest was discharged from the Rifles but re-enlisted as a private on September 8, 1915 in Calgary.[694]

Norwest's 50th Infantry Battalion went to England two months after his enlistment, and headed to France in August 1916.[695] It was in France where Norwest solidified his reputation as one of the greatest snipers in the Canadian and British forces.[696]

Norwest is credited with 115 hits, but it is possible that because of the circumstances this tally could be higher.[697] (A sniper would only be credited with a "hit" when another person was there to observe the shot.)

Norwest was known for waiting for days across from enemy lines until his target made himself vulnerable. He would fire on his target only if he knew he could not be seen. Norwest's reputation among German's inspired fear and respect, according to German POWs in British camps.[698]

On August 18, Norwest was shot by a German marksman. Norwest was in the process of trying to eliminate advance snipers who were threatening the Canadian advance posts. On Norwest's temporary grave, fellow soldiers inscribed "It must have been a damn good sniper that got Norwest."[699]

Norwest was buried in Warvillers Churchyard Extension near Amiens, France. One of his rifles now hangs in exhibit at Calgary's Museum of Regiments.[700] Norwest was awarded a Military Medal in 1917, and then in 1918 posthumously awarded a military medal for "gallantry in the Field."[701]

Profile by: David Christiansen

Omeniho, Melanie

1958 -
Metis
Community
Development
Consultant and
Advocate

"Don't wait for others to do what needs to be done" is the credo at the heart of this hard-working community advocate.[723] Melanie Omeniho is one of the first people called when "things go crazy" in Edmonton's Metis community. She is a self-starter and she gets things done.

Melanie Friedel was born in Edmonton, Alberta on May 22, 1958.[702] She was one of five children born to Marge (Cunningham) and Clifford Friedel.[703] After high school, Melanie attended Westerra College in Stony Plain and earned certificates in Business Administration and Communication and another in Computer Engineering Technology.[704]

She is the mother of three daughters: Janice, Megan and Emily. As a single parent she is aware of the struggles of others in the same situation. An incident with her daughter Megan caused her to initiate a hot lunch program at Prince Charles School in the mid-1990s. Megan's lunch was going missing with great regularity. Melanie surmised that someone was taking Megan's lunch because they did not have their own. As a result of this incident, she contacted the school, wrote a proposal and the hot lunch program was born. The program still runs.[705]

Her involvement with Prince Charles School heightened her interest and her commitment to Aboriginal children. She served as the chair of the Edmonton Aboriginal Coalition for Children Services, is the past chairperson of the Awasis (Child) Society, and is a board member of the Oskaya (Youth) Family Society. She was also a found-

187

ing member of the Aboriginal Human Rights Commission and was a board member for the Canadian Native Friendship Centre.[706]

Her expertise was sought by Alberta Learning when it was restructuring the Social Studies 10, 20 and 30 high school curriculum. The department wanted to ensure that Metis and Aboriginal historical and contemporary issues were accurately depicted in school programming.[707] She believes that Aboriginal people must be part of school curriculum and that this inclusion helps to promote understanding and tolerance of others.

In the late 1980s Melanie became heavily involved with Women of the Metis Nation, an advocacy group with the mandate to improve the social, economic, and political situation of Metis women.[708] She would later serve as its president. The Women of the Metis Nation took on social issues that other agencies shied away from, such as family violence and sexual abuse. They were involved in social justice issues on a national level and were involved in justice consultations which lead to the closing of the women's prison in Kingston, Ontario.

Melanie is currently employed with the Zone IV office of the Metis Nation of Alberta. She is the administrator and contract manager of Metis Opportunity Corporation. The Metis Opportunity Corporation identifies and develops employment and business opportunities for Metis in the vast Metis Zone IV region (which encompasses the area from the British Columbia border to Camrose and from Westlock to Red Deer). She is responsible for negotiating sole source and competitive contracts. She also manages a staff of between forty and fifty people.[709]

Melanie remains active in the Metis community and she lives in Edmonton.

Profile by: Cora Voyageur

Ominayak, Bernard

1950 -
Cree
Community
Leader

Bernard Ominayak is the personification of persistence. He has fought a battle that began in the early 1970s and still fights it to this day. The fight is over land and the right to a way of life.

Bernard Ominayak was born in 1950 in an area of Alberta that was rarely travelled by non-Aboriginal people. He was born the son of a trapper and spent his first eight years living on the shores of Lubicon Lake.[710] Bernard was sent to residential school at Grouard at eight years of age.[711] He married Louise and they would have five children.[712]

His people, the Lubicon Cree, tell stories of the area that go back to the 1700s.[713] The Lubicon people lived a traditional lifestyle and were virtually unknown to the outside world. In fact, they were so remote that they were missed when the commissioner's party for Treaty 8 were meeting with Indians in the region. Land negotiations continue and this dedicated chief continues to fight for a sixty-year-old land claim. Oil companies were producing revenues of $1.2 million per day while the Lubicon Crees' traditional economy was destroyed.[714]

He was elected to band council upon his return to Little Buffalo and was elected to the position of chief at the age of twenty-eight.[7315]Chief Ominayak speaks of a time in the not too distant past where the only transportation to the nearest town (Peace River) was a one hundred kilometre trip on horseback or by cart.[716] This would all change when exploration companies moved into the area. Oil and gas developments destroyed much of the land, sending moose off to other areas, thus removing a key source of country food.[717] He became embroiled in a battle with the federal government over a land-claim settlement and compensation.

The Lubicon Cree have built up international support over the years, and an active national support group called the Friends of the Lubicon.[718] Many commissions have noted injustices and human rights violations in government and corporation dealings with the Lubicon. The World Council of churches declared the situation as having "genocidal consequences."[719]

In 1991, the federal government decided to establish a new band called the Woodland Cree and sought Lubicon members to join it and receive new houses with running water. This pitted some families against each other and some of these rifts have yet to heal.

Bernard is regarded by many people, both native and non-native, as a man of principle and great integrity. He has always been clear in his goals and endeavors and has always had strong community support.

The Lubicon Crees' story is the story of an Indian band's fight to maintain a traditional lifestyle on resource-rich land. Although he has been up against insurmountable odds, he has never abandoned his vision and his demand that the land claim issue be settled with the Lubicon Cree.

Profile by: Joan Ryan and Cora Voyageur

Parenteau, Lillian

1950 -
Metis
Administrator,
Children's
Advocate

In the area of social and cultural services for the Metis Nation in Alberta, Lillian Parenteau has been able to overcome barriers and accomplish deeds that some people thought could never be done.[720] Born in Elk Lake, Alberta, in 1950, Lillian is one of nine children in her family. She has two children, Shannon Souray and Sheldon Souray (who plays in the National Hockey League).

In 1993, the Alberta Government gave the Metis settlements the opportunity to form their own Child and Family Services Authority. Lillian organized the community consultations.[721] After the Metis Settlements All Council voted unanimously to form their own Child and Family Services Authority, Lillian guided the steering committee to develop the service plan.[722] Due to the development of the Metis Settlements Child and Family Services Authority, twenty-four full time jobs were created with the province. In 1998, Lillian became the chief executive officer for the Metis Settlements Child and Family Services Authority.

One of Lillian's first accomplishments as CEO was to lead the negotiations for the development of a justice protocol with the Canada Justice Directorate, Alberta Justice, the Metis Settlements General Council and Region 18.[723] This protocol allowed for the development of justice committees on each of the Metis Settlements in Alberta. The groundbreaking protocol was signed in November 1999.

Lillian has been given special awards and honors including an Esquao Award for Community Involvement in 2000. Other awards include an Appreciation Award in recognition of her contribution to the Aboriginal people of Alberta in 2001, and recognition from the Nechi Institute in 2001. Nominator Sonya Kobelsky stated that, "Lillian not only holds a strong sense of values and morals but she practices them on a day-to-day basis. Her love for her people has been a driving force and motivation to do what she has to do to ensure that children and families in our settlements have a future they can look forward to."[724] Lillian is also the team leader for the Metis Settlements Transition Commission, Community Development Unit.

As the CEO for the Metis Child and Family Services Authority, Lillian continues to advocate on behalf of the Metis settlements so that they will receive community-based, culturally appropriate services in areas such as justice, mental health, health and education.[725]

Profile by: Casie McGonegal

Poitras, Audrey

1950-
Metis
President,
Metis Nation
of Alberta

When people of Alberta think about a well-known and influential Metis woman, one of the first persons that comes to mind is Audrey Poitras. Audrey is the president of the Metis Nation of Alberta.

Audrey was born in Elk Lake, Alberta on May 5, 1950. She traces her lineage to the famous Metis activist and strategist, Gabriel Dumont.[726] Audrey has one son, Robert, and two grandchildren, Cody and Kaitlin.[727] Audrey moved to Red Deer, Alberta and began a dry cleaning business with her husband Gordon. They ran the business from 1979 to 1990.[728]

In 1991, Audrey was offered a position as director of finance with the Metis Nation of Alberta. She also serves as the vice-president for the Metis National Council, the national political body representing Metis people, and holds the economic development portfolio.[729] However, in 1996 Audrey's focus shifted and she made history by becoming the first female president of the Metis Nation of Alberta. Her career in politics was borne out of the desire to contribute to a better world for Metis people.[730]

Audrey has been instrumental in several projects within the Metis community, such as the inclusion of the "Metis child" in the Child Welfare Act in Alberta, and negotiating an Aboriginal Human Resource Development Agreement. Audrey was also involved in signing the first Metis Nation of Alberta Government Framework Agreement. The Agreement was renewed in April 1999.[731] As George Vass, General Manager, Apeetogosan (Metis) Development Inc.

states, "Audrey is an inspiration, not only to all Metis women, but also to all Metis who strive to build a Nation within a Nation."[732]

Audrey has been given many awards for her contributions to Alberta and the Metis community in Canada. These include the Metis Nation of Alberta Region 2 Recognition Award (1999), the Metis National Council – Youth – Appreciation Award (1999). Other awards include Native Counselling Services of Alberta Appreciation Award (2001); Esquao Lifetime Achievement Award from the Institute for the Advancement if Aboriginal Women (2002); Louis Dorion Award for Outstanding Commitment – Batoche (2002); and the 2002 Aboriginal Role Model of Alberta – Politics Award (2002).[733]

As a role model to Metis women, Audrey has shattered the glass ceiling in the political realm and initiated the development of a more vibrant and purposeful direction of the Metis people of Alberta.[734] Audrey contributes to her community by sitting on various boards such as the Aboriginal Program Council at the Banff Centre and she is member for the Aboriginal Human Resource Development Council of Canada.

Audrey lives in Edmonton with her husband, Gordon.

Nominated by: Helen Calahasen

Profile by: Casie McGonegal

Poitras, Jane Ash

1951 -
Chipewyan/Cree
Artist

Jane Ash Poitras has earned an international reputation as an innovative and avant-garde artist. Her artwork carries messages of the Aboriginal experience in Canada. She has overcome the uncertainty of early life to become a vibrant and confident artist whose work includes symbols and iconography associated with the Plains and the Cree.

Jane Ash Poitras was born in Fort Chipewyan, Alberta. Her mother passed away of tuberculosis when she was only four years old.[735] Little is known about how she got from the isolated community of Fort Chipewyan to the streets of Edmonton. A mix-up at the child welfare office left Jane, the then five-year-old Cree-speaking child, on the streets of Edmonton. Marguerite Runck found her. Runck tried to find an adult to take charge of Jane. Unsuccessful in her attempts, Runck took Jane home and three weeks later she became her foster mother.[736] The German widow provided a strong and stable foundation for Jane, although she was denied her Aboriginal heritage. She was in her twenties before she found her family in Fort Chipewyan. She began making regular visits to see them.[737]

Jane had plans to become a medical doctor when she completed a bachelor's degree in microbiology at the University of Alberta in 1977. However, she caught the painting bug. Soon she found herself enrolled in a Masters of Fine Arts program at Columbia University in New York.[738] She completed the program in 1983 and the rest is history.[739]

The art world came calling and Jane Ash would become one of the most sought after Aboriginal artists in Canada and the United States. In describing her paintings she says, "I guess I am political to some degree but I'm political about philosophical issues of truth. I am after truth and justice."[740] She held an exhibition with Rick Rivet in 1999 at the Canadian Cultural Centre in Paris, France. A year earlier, the Shamans and Sages exhibit was housed at The Russell Gallery of Fine Art in Peterborough, Ontario.[741] A select list of her displayed work include: Alberta Art Foundation (Edmonton), Art Gallery of Ontario (Toronto), Canada Council Art Bank (Ottawa), Canadian Museum of Civilization (Hull), Leonard and Bina Ellen Art Gallery (Montreal), and the House of Commons (Ottawa).[742]

Jane Ash Poitras has overcome many adversities in life and says she can still go out and whip anybody at a game of pool and outdance anyone.[743] She has a zest for life. She expects her art will continue to evolve for many years to come. She has two sons, Josh and Eli, who live with her in Edmonton.

Profile by: Marlaine Metchewais

Randle, Kenton

1960 - 2003
Metis
Professional
Bareback
Bronc Rider

Rodeo was always a calling for Kenton Randle, and he rode it to success during his two-plus decades on the professional rodeo circuit. The Metis cowboy rode bareback bronc and bulls during his years on the circuit.

Randle was born in October 1960 on the Paddle Prairie Metis settlement in northwestern Alberta.[744] Kenton was the second of five children born to Richard and Mona Randle.[745]

He worked briefly on the oil patch near Devon following high school. Randle worked as a steamer before beginning his career as a professional rider.[746] It was around this time in his life when he began to ride bulls. He noted that he learned to ride the bull primarily through watching others since he was the only member of his family who attempted to ride. Randle would continue to ride bulls for eleven years before choosing to go with strictly bareback broncs. He made the decision with his health in mind. "It's just too hard on my body to ride bulls," said Randle. "My heart was telling me not to."[747]

Randle would win the Indian Rodeo Cowboy Association award in 1982.[748] Following the triumph he would take a five-year hiatus from the professional rodeo circuit before returning in 1987, minus the bulls.

Randle has performed all over western Canada on the pro rodeo circuit and has chalked up a number of victories alongside his IRCA win. He won the bareback bronc competition at the Indian National Finals Rodeo in 1989. Randle would add three more victories at the INFR in 1992, 1995 and 1996.[749] He was a mere half-point out of a top-ten finish at the famous Calgary Stampede in 1994 and took third at Edmonton's Canadian Finals Rodeo in November 1997.[750]

The Paddle Prairie native lived near Fort Vermilion with this wife Audrey and his three boys, Clinton, Chad, and Justin.[751] Randle found time to work in the logging industry during the winter months. He would drive to each of his rodeo events in his half-ton Chevy due to his disdain for flying.

Randle continued to love of the thrill of the rodeo and some of the challenges it presented in the last years of his life. "I think it's the challenge of different stock," says Randle.[752]

Kenton Randle was diagnosed with brain cancer in 2002. Sadly, the disease would take his life on November 23, 2003. He passed away with his wife Audrey at his side.

Profile by: Drew Calliou

Roberts, Jed

1967-
Sioux
Football Player

Growing up the son of an Ottawa Rough Rider legend, it was only natural for Jed Roberts to follow in his father's footsteps into football. Roberts would play thirteen successful years in the Canadian Football League.[753]

Jed Roberts was born in Ottawa on November 10, 1967.[754] Robert's father, Jay, was a tight end with the Ottawa Rough Riders in the 1960s and helped the nation's capital team win back-to-back Grey Cup championships in 1968 and 1969.[755]

Roberts, who has Sioux blood in him, admits he grew up in what he calls a "city culture" and never paid much attention to his native roots.[756] "I had no native awareness," says Roberts, who was actively involved in the "Stay in School" program during his years with the Edmonton Eskimos.[757]

Roberts attended the University of Northern Colorado and gained the interest of the CFL's Winnipeg Blue Bombers when his college career drew to an end.[758] He spent most of the 1990 season on the practice roster of the Blue Bombers before being picked up by the team he would spend the remainder of his career with, the Edmonton Eskimos.[759] Roberts made his CFL debut on October 25, 1990 against the Saskatchewan Roughriders, which produced what he called the most embarrassing moment in the game.

"I got hit by a player and ended up on the wrong bench before getting yelled at," recalls Roberts. Moving from linebacker to defensive line, he became a starter on the Eskimos defence alongside the likes of Larry Wruck, Willie Pless, Trent Brown and Leroy Blugh. 1993 was the pinnacle year for Roberts, as he collected ten sacks on a tough Eskimos defensive line. He even got himself on the front page of the *Edmonton Sun* following his 10th sack of the season, on Calgary Stampeder quarterback Doug Flutie during the final game of the regular season. The Eskimos got hot late in the season and rode it all the way to the Grey Cup game in Calgary, ironically against Roberts's first team, the Winnipeg Blue Bombers.[760] The Eskimos defeated the Bombers 33–23 and the victory is still fresh in his mind. "It was the sweetest feeling I've ever had," recalled Roberts.[761]

Roberts later became one of the CFL's best special-teams players before retiring at the end of the 2000 season. He returned early the following season due to an unusual number of injuries to Eskimo players, and played the final years of his career. Roberts's final game on the active roster was on July 4, 2002.[762] While attempting to block on an extra point attempt, he was pushed back awkwardly and broke his right ankle, signalling the end of his professional career.

He recalls some of the fine people he met during his years in football, and makes special mention of Henry "Gizmo" Williams, the fantastic kick returner who played with the Eskimos from 1986 through 2000.[763]

He currently works as a sales representative for Team Skyline Sports and also works as a councillor for emotionally disturbed boys on weekends. He is involved with many initiates involving Aboriginal youth.[764] Jed recently accepted an offer from the University of Alberta Golden Bears football team to work as a linebacker coach.[765] Roberts continues to live in Edmonton and still follows his Eskimos with a passion.[766]

Profile by: Drew Calliou

Samson, John

1914 – 2000
Cree
Chief and
Politician

John Samson was Chief of the Samson Cree at Hobbema. He was active in the Indian Association of Alberta and involved in a key judicial ruling in 1957 that had consequences for all First Nations people.

Samson was a direct descendent of the first chief of the Samson tribe, Kanatakasu. Samson's mother, Sophie, was told by her father that she would have a son, and she named him Standing Eagle. He was particularly close to his grandparents, especially his grandmother, Sophie.[767] Samson went to residential school in Edmonton from the age of ten to eighteen. He married Nancy Ward on December 12, 1933, in a traditional Cree marriage that was arranged by their parents. Ward was also from Hobbema and had attended the same residential school. The couple had ten children over the years.[768]

The Samsons began farming soon after they were married. They lived in a simple mud-plastered log home, and John made all the furniture himself. Over time, John became involved in the leadership of the Samson Cree. He was elected to Samson band council in 1954, and was elected chief in 1955. He continued as chief until 1961 and was a member of the band council until 1975.

Samson was also involved in the foundation of the Indian Association of Alberta (IAA) in 1942. He was President of the IAA from 1962 to 1967, when it was undergoing the challenge of declining membership.[769]

Samson was also involved in a key judicial ruling in 1957, while he was chief. It stemmed from an argument that began in 1952 over a stolen horse, but it soon escalated. There was a charge brought forward that John Samson's ancestors had accepted scrip for land in the 1880s. Much was at stake, for if the charge was true, Samson and his immediate family would lose their Indian status and be banned from the reserve. More than this, it would provide the government with a precedent for using the revised 1951 Indian Act to "integrate" aboriginal families off reserves and into urban areas.[770]

A young Calgary lawyer, Ruth Gorman, took up the cause and rallied her colleagues to defend the Samsons. A protracted legal battle ensued, with Gorman determined to outmanoeuvre the government. She rallied public support for her Indian friends and even appealed directly to the Queen. The 1957 ruling in favor of the Samsons was considered a victory for all Indian people. Ultimately, John Samson and Ruth Gorman were named advisors to the Joint Committee of the Senate and the House of Commons on Indian Affairs, which submitted a 1961 report on the Indian Act.[771]

His activism continued and in 1966, Samson and Metis president Stan Daniels made headlines when the two hitch-hiked to Ottawa to protest the high cost of food in northern and remote Alberta Aboriginal communities.[772]

John Samson provided leadership at a key time in the Samson Cree's history, which continued throughout his entire life. In his honour, the Johnny Samson Prize in Native Studies is awarded annually at the University of Alberta.[773]

Profile by: Lee Tunstall

Sewepagaham, William Andrew Joseph "Bill"

1944 –
Dene/Cree
Teacher

Bill Sewepagaham is committed to educating youth. He has played a significant role in Aboriginal education in Alberta for more than thirty years. He has taught, been an education administrator, and also been an education director.

Bill Sewepagaham was born in 1944 in High Level. He was one of twelve children born to a Dene mother, Madeline (Boucher) and a Cree father, Pierre Sewepagaham.[774] He is a member of the Little Red River First Nation in northern Alberta. He entered residential school when he was a young child and remained there for eleven years.[775]

Sewepagaham has volunteered throughout his adult life. He helped organize the Slave Lake Winter Games in 1974. He has served on a number of service organization boards, including the board of directors for the Slave Lake Native Friendship Centre and the Little Red River Education Board.[776]

He has worked in a number of education-related positions over the years. He is currently the education director for Little Red River. Prior to this, he worked as a school teacher and school principal. Before entering the education field Bill worked for the Alberta Forest Service as a recreation director for the Treaty 8 political organization.[777]

Bill received a recreation/outdoor education diploma from Mount Royal College in Calgary in 1970. He earned a Bachelor of Education from the University of Calgary in 1983. He was the first member of the Little Red River First Nation to earn a graduate university degree. He continued his education by earning a Master of Educational Administration degree from the University of British Columbia in 1998. His masters thesis was entitled, Local Control and parental Involvement in Native Education.[778]

Bill has been a teacher for more than thirty years in First Nation schools in Alberta and Saskatchewan. His commitment to Aboriginal education caused him to return to his community after completing his education. It was a big change moving from Vancouver to Little Red River. He believes that young people can achieve their goals if they have determination and just a little bit of encouragement. Sewepagaham is always willing to provide that little bit of coaching and support to help people succeed.[779]

In 1993 he received the Ethel Blondin Education Award from the University of British Columbia. The award, named after the Aboriginal Member of Parliament from the Western Arctic constituency, is given to a student who shows determination and commitment to education.[780] In March 2006, Bill journeyed to Kenai, Alaska to serve as cultural coordinator of Team Alberta North at the 2006 Arctic Winter Games.[781]

He has been married to Emily since 1969. They have four children: Weylon, Sheryl, Jennifer and Sheldon. They also have five grandchildren.[782]

Nominated by: Sheldon Sewepagaham

Profile by: Cora Voyageur

Shot On Both Sides (Atso-to-ah)

1873 – 1956
Kainai
Chief

Chief Shot On Both Sides was a warrior in the traditional sense of the word, since he participated in raids on neighboring tribes for horses and women. He chose not to learn to speak English and was an effective leader for forty-three years. He saw the buffalo vanish from the Prairies, and as a child witnessed the signing of Treaty 7.

Shot At From Both Sides (Atso-to-ah) was born on the land that would become the Blood Reserve four years prior to the signing of Treaty 7 in 1877. He was the son of Crop-Eared Wolf (who would be the Blood chief from 1900 to 1913).[783] He was a young child when he and his family travelled to Blackfoot Crossing where his grandfather, Red Crow, signed treaty. As he grew to adulthood his name was modified to Shot on Both Sides.[784]

The robe of head chief was placed on his shoulders in 1913 with the death of his father, Crop Eared Wolf.[785] He had watched his father and his grandfather lead the Kainai during a tremendous change. They had moved from traditional lifestyle of hunting and migrating with the buffalo herds to one of sedentary life on the reserve. They had moved from being hunters to being farmers.[786]

He did not attend school and did not accept western-based religion because he wanted to preserve as much of the traditional ways of life as possible. He pleaded with his people to retain the best of their traditions even in the face of indignities.[787] However, he did not oppose children attending school because he wanted them to get the benefits of education.[788]

He believed his people should do all they could to improve their lives on the reserve and he promoted farming and ranching. The Ksninsi successfully raised cattle, horses, and grains. Under Shot On Both Sides' leadership, the Kainai became the most prosperous Indians in Canada.[789]

He was instrumental in the formation of the Kainai Chieftainship, an honorary tribal fellowship, that was designed to "foster and propagate a policy of future Canadian citizenship" for his people.[790] With Shot on Both Sides as the president, the Kainai Chieftainship would grow to include some of the best-known personalities (mostly non-Aboriginals) in the western hemisphere. The society's induction ceremony included all the traditional pomp and ritual. The first honorary chief of record was the Duke of Windsor, who was named Chief Mountain in 1919. The society is limited to forty living members.[791]

Shot on Both Sides had been healthy for most of his life but he suffered a stroke at the age of eighty. He never fully recovered and passed away on the Blood Reserve on March 15, 1956.[792] He was eighty-two years old.

Profile by: Cora Voyageur

Sinclair, Samuel

1926 – 2005
Metis
Politician,
Community
Worker, and
Veteran

Sam Sinclair has worked on behalf of Aboriginal people for most of his adult life. This work has taken him all over the world, even to Rome to have an audience with Pope John Paul II in 1985.

Sam Sinclair was born in Old Town near Slave Lake, Alberta on November 22, 1926. His mother was Agathe Courtrielle and his father was Alfred Sinclair; he had six brothers and five sisters.[793] He married Edna Pierce in 1946 and the couple went on to have six children: Gordon, Linda, Lorraine (deceased), Jeanette, Rodney, and Rocky.[794]

Sam could not speak English when he started school at the age of six.[795] When the teacher wrote the number one on the blackboard and asked the children what it was, Sam answered in Cree saying it was a fence post. The children started to laugh and the teacher was not amused. She sent Sam home to his mother. His mother hugged the sobbing Sam and she told him that some day things would be different.[796]

Sinclair was working for a company running telephone lines when he when joined the Royal Canadian Army Service Corps in 1942.[797] His mother approached the local priest to help her get her son out of the military because he was underage – but to no avail. He was stationed in Canada in 1942–43. He was sent overseas in 1944 and was stationed in England, France, Belgium, and Holland. He was in Germany when the war ended in 1945.[798] While in the army he began training in track and field and as a boxer. He won a number of track and field medals and the Army's middleweight boxing title in Holland.[799]

After the war Sam worked at a number of jobs. For example, he worked as an assistant forest ranger for the Alberta Forestry Department from 1957 to 1966. He was then seconded to Community Development in 1966 and moved his family to Hinton. There he worked as an Aboriginal employment officer for the towns of Jasper, Grande Cache, Whitecourt, Edson, and Marlboro. He encountered racism with some employers who believed that Aboriginal people were poor and unreliable employees. Sam's persistence paid off and the Aboriginal employees that industry hired turned out to be reliable and highly productive workers.[800]

Sam had been involved in politics since the 1960s. He served as special advisor on Aboriginal issues to Fred Colburn. In 1977, he was elected vice-president of the Metis Association of Alberta and would go on to be its president. As president of the Metis Association of Alberta he attended the First Ministers Conferences that followed the repatriation of the Canadian constitution in 1982. He was also involved with the Aboriginal War Veterans Association and served as its president from 1991 to 1998.[801]

Throughout his life, Sinclair was involved in sports. He was a boxing and baseball coach for many years. He took the Alberta boxing team to Expo 67 in Montreal. Both he and his son Gordon were inducted into the Canadian Boxing Hall of Fame in 1994. He kept himself busy in retirement.[802] Sam and Edna Sinclair lived in Edmonton until his death in November, 2005.

Profile by: Cora Voyageur

Smallboy, Robert

1898 – 1984
Cree
Chief, Spiritual
Leader

Robert Smallboy was a legendary Cree chief who was considered to be one of the major spiritual leaders of his generation. He believed that the social problems of First Nations people were the result of the loss of traditional ways and cultural identity. They were being corrupted by the influence of white man's culture, which replaced the old ways.[803]

Chief Smallboy was a member of the Ermineskin Band of Cree at Hobbema in central Alberta. He served as chief from 1959 to 1968. Robert and Dorothy Smallboy had one son, Joseph and two daughters, Clara and Elizabeth. They had twenty-seven grandchildren and twenty-one great grandchildren.[804]

To Chief Smallboy, the most likely solution was for First Nation people to remove themselves from the negative influences and re-learn their cultural and spiritual practices. He decided to put this idea into action. In 1968, Chief Smallboy left the reserve at Hobbema to lead about 150 members of the band to a remote spot in the foothills of the Rocky Mountains near Nordegg. There he planned to establish a camp where his people could renew themselves. They could return to their traditional ways and live in harmony with the Creator. They would no longer be moving in an unwholesome direction where the evils of gambling, drinking, delinquency, and other vices could no longer ruin their lives.[805]

The wilderness camp that Chief Smallboy set up had strict rules. The chief and council made all decisions. Liquor was forbidden.

Nobody left the camp without permission and duties were delegated.[806]

Living as their forefathers did proved a struggle for some members of the Smallboy camp. After the first winter in tents they built log cabins. The difficulty of being self-sufficient and surviving was not their only problem. Wide publicity for the camp brought an influx of visitors. Oil was discovered on the Ermineskin reserve and many camp members returned to Hobbema.[807]

In spite of these drawbacks, Chief Smallboy persevered with his dream and remained at the camp until his death. The camp became a symbol of the importance of maintaining First Nation culture and values. Smallboy himself was revered for his wisdom and the guidance that he gave in Aboriginal gatherings. Many people visited the camp to benefit from this wise counsel. He helped to set the stage for powerful Aboriginal movements.[808]

In 1980, Smallboy received the Order of Canada for his contributions to the well-being of First Nation people. When he visited Europe in 1982 he met Queen Elizabeth II, Pope John Paul II and other dignitaries.[809] In 1991 a scholarship in his name was established by the Assembly of First Nations for outstanding post-secondary academic achievement by First Nation students.[810]

Chief Smallboy died in 1984 and is buried in the Smallboy camp cemetery. He had dedicated his life to preserving traditions and improving the lives of his people. As a leader, he led by example.

Profile by: Margaret Burgess

Soop, Everett

1943 - 2001
Cartoonist,
Artist, Writer,
and Advocate

Everett Soop's life was not an easy life since he fought many personal and political battles. However, he was a man of conviction, and his opinions caused him to be liked by some and disliked by others. He was blessed with many gifts as cartoonist, artist, writer and community advocate.

Soop, fluent in Blackfoot, was born on the Blood Reserve in southern Alberta on July 7, 1943. His parents, Arthur and Josephine Soop, had five boys and one girl.[811] Everett graduated from high school in Cardston, Alberta in 1964 and went on to study art and drawing at the Alberta College of Art and Design in Calgary. Soop continued his education at Brigham Young University in Provo, Utah where he took additional art courses. He then returned to Mount Royal College in Calgary, where he took journalism.[812]

In 1968, Everett was hired as an editorial cartoonist and columnist for the *Kainai News,* (the Blood Reserve Newspaper).[813] His political views and humor offended some and delighted others. Despite his outlook, his cartoons were picked up by other Aboriginal publications across the continent and appeared in mainstream newspapers. Soop became the country's leading Aboriginal cartoonist, according to long-time friend Hugh Dempsey.[814] His struggles began when he touched on sensitive issues such as tribal corruption, suicide, and family violence.[815] "I brought most of this out because I think it's something we had to face. As long as it was under the carpet nothing was going to be done," he explained in an interview with The *Globe and Mail* writer Sandy Greer.[816]

On a personal level, Soop had a debilitating illness to contend with. He was diagnosed with muscular dystrophy at the age of sixteen and this disease would eventually lead to his death. Everett's humor and political satire helped him to cope with his challenges.

Everett Soop said his greatest accomplishment was being an advocate for native people with disabilities. He served two terms as a band councillor, served on educational committees, wrote articles on disability for newspapers and served on the Premier's Council on the Status of Persons with Disabilities in Alberta.[817] In an interview with Sandy Greer, Soop spoke of how self-determination "requires healing, and healing means no longer pushing unpleasant realities under the carpet."[818]

Everett Soop once said: "Indians have become too materialistic and they try to be Indian in such a phoney way, and capitalize on it materially. But it's not in the spiritual way. You cannot maintain culture. It constantly evolves. What you can maintain is pride."[819]

Profile by: Marlaine Metchewais

Souray, Sheldon

1976-
Métis
Professional
Hockey Player

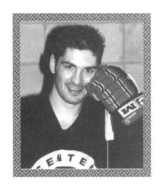

Playing against the likes of Sydney Crosby, Alex Ouechkin and Ryan Getslaf on any given night can be a daunting task, but it is what Edmonton Oilers' Sheldon Souray thrives on. The hulking six-foot-four, 223-pound Canadian has become a top-echelon defenseman in the National Hockey League.

Souray was born on July 13, 1976 in Elk Point, Alberta.[820] The future NHL star spent his early years on the Fishing Lake Metis settlement before spending his early teen years in Edmonton where he played minor hockey.[821]

Souray began his junior hockey career with the Tri-City Americans of the Western Hockey League during the 1992–93 season, playing in two games as a sixteen-year-old. He would hone his craft over the next three seasons with the Americans, Prince George Cougars and the Kelowna Rockets. Following a 54-point season in 1995–96, he was selected to the WHL's second all-star team.[822]

Souray was chosen 71st overall in the 1994 NHL entry draft by the New Jersey Devils.[823] The thirty-three-old would play parts of three seasons in the minor leagues before making his NHL debut during the 1997–98 season.[824] He scored three goals and added seven assists during his first full season in the NHL. Souray struggled during his first couple of seasons in the NHL, before eventually being traded to the Montreal Canadiens during the 1999–00 season.[825] His career began to flourish with the Canadiens. Souray sat out the 2002–03 season while rehabbing an injured wrist, before making a triumphant comeback with an all-star season, scoring fifteen goals and adding another twenty assists.[826] Souray's accomplishments during the season included a first trip to the annual all-star game in St. Paul, Minnesota, as well as scoring six points in a single game, a record with the Montreal Canadiens that he now has the distinction of holding.[827]

Souray's good looks have landed him inside the pages of magazines such as *Maxim and GQ.*[828] He also appeared in an episode of the TV soap opera One Life to Live.[829] Souray has taken an interest in native youth hockey players, participating and speaking in a number of native hockey camps including the Aboriginal Role Model Hockey School.[830]

Sheldon Souray spent the locked-out 2004–05 NHL season playing with Farjestads BK of the Swedish Elite League.[831] He continues to mind the blue line with the Edmonton Oilers after signing a five-year deal in 2007. Souray won a silver medal as a member of Canada's World Hockey Championship team in May 2005.[832]

Nominated by: Lillian Parenteau

Profile by: Drew Calliou

Steinhauer, Ralph G.

1905 – 1987
Cree
Lieutenant
Governor,
Politician and
Farmer

Ralph Garvin Steinhauer was a person who successfully bridged two cultures. While he was a prominent player in Aboriginal affairs, he was also very involved in non-Aboriginal politics, especially agricultural organizations. Steinhauer, the great-grandson of Methodist missionary, Henry Bird Steinhauer, was born June 8, 1905 at Morley, Alberta.[833] His biological father was Josiah Apow and his mother was Amelia Mildred Mumford from the Saddle Lake Reserve.[834] Ralph's biological father died when he was only two-and-a-half years old, and his mother moved the family back to the reserve at Saddle Lake where she married James Arthur Steinhauer, who adopted the children of his new wife. Ralph was given his adopted father's surname.[835]

Ralph went to school at the Doucet Public School followed by the Roseneath School near Ashmont, and the Red Deer Indian Industrial School.[836] He went on to work first as a clerk in a general store, and then on to be an assistant postmaster at Vilna, Alberta.[837] He met and married Isobel Florence Margaret Davidson in 1928; she was the daughter of O.G. Davidson of Buffalo, New York. Ralph and Margaret had five children: Muriel, Doreen, Kathleen, Isabel, and Kenneth.[838] Ralph ran a farm at the Saddle Lake Indian Reserve.[839]

Ralph Steinhauer was very involved in politics. He joined the United Farmers' Association in 1923, was district president of the Farmers' Union, and served as councillor for the Saddle Lake Band for thirty-four years and as chief for three years.[840] In 1963, he ran as a federal Liberal candidate in the Vegreville electoral district, but lost the election.[841] He was a founder and president of the Alberta Federation of Indians, served as president of the Alberta Indian Development Corporation and served on many boards.[842]

Effective July 2, 1974, on the advice of Prime Minister Pierre Trudeau, the Governor General of Canada, Jules Leger, appointed Ralph Steinhauer as Alberta's tenth lieutenant governor.[843] He served in that role until October 18, 1979. Afterward, he returned to Saddle Lake Reserve to his farm. While serving as lieutenant governor, Ralph was made an honorary Kainai chief by the Blood Indians in southern Alberta, receiving the name "Chief Flying Eagle."[844]

Ralph Steinhauer received many awards for his achievements. He was awarded the Canadian Centennial Medal in 1967, a Medal of Service of the Order of Canada in 1967, and was made an Officer of the Order of Canada in 1972. Ralph also received honorary Doctor of Laws degrees from the University of Alberta in 1976 and the University of Calgary in 1979, and an honorary Doctor of Divinity degree from St. Stephens College in Edmonton in 1985. Ralph was inducted into the Agricultural Hall of Fame and an elementary school in Edmonton was named after him.[845]

Ralph Steinhauer died at Edmonton, Alberta on September 19, 1987, at the age of eighty-two. He was buried at Saddle Lake, Alberta in the United Church cemetery. He bridged cultures and made great contributions to both Aboriginal society and to Alberta society.

Nominated by: Muriel Manywounds

Profile by: Brian Calliou

Supernault, Clifford Rodger

1944-
Metis
Public Servant

Clifford Rodger Supernault was born at Fort Vermilion, Alberta on September 5, 1944. He was the third of seven children born to Jonas Supernault and his wife, Margaret (Cardinal). The Supernault family moved to the Paddle Prairie Metis Settlement near High Level, Alberta when Cliff was one year old. He completed Grade 9 at the Paddle Prairie School and completed Grade 12 at Alberta College in Edmonton in 1967. He enrolled in a general arts program at the University of Alberta in the following year. He was one of very few Aboriginal students on post-secondary campuses in Canada.

After leaving university he worked at a variety of jobs including recreation and housing coordinator for the British Columbia Association of Non-Status Indians. His study of Metis recreation and housing needs and conditions earned him a job as national housing officer with the Central Mortgage and Housing Corporation (CMHC). Later Cliff joined the Department of Northern Saskatchewan heading their Housing Department in Prince Albert and was soon promoted to assistant deputy minister with portfolios in municipal services, manpower secretariat, renewable resources and economic development. In 1984, he moved to Edmonton, first as the director of Metis Settlements Branch, Alberta Municipal Affairs, then as executive director of Native Services Unit, then chief executive officer of Aboriginal Affairs. Over the years, Cliff has served on many boards and committees including the Peace Arch Project, Conference Board of Canada/Aboriginal committee, Alberta Chamber of Resources/Boreal Group, Fort McKay – Interface Committee, and the EUB Aboriginal Advisory Committee. He was also instrumental in the development of the Metis Settlements Act, proclaimed by the Alberta Government in November 1990.

Cliff has always been a sports enthusiast. Cliff's fastball playing from his teens onward earned him top pitcher, top hitter and most valuable player awards for several years running in Dawson Creek. He picked up similar awards playing broomball in the winter. Cliff pitched for Hythe's Men Team, winning the Alberta' Senior Men's B League Championship. Cliff went on to pitch for the Vancouver Molson's Senior Men's team the year before they turned professional. While living in Ottawa, he began running and has participated in marathons and the Jasper to Banff relay and the Kananaskis 100-mile relay.

Cliff is also an accomplished carver. His soapstone, alabaster and lava carvings have sold in Canada, Germany, Britain, Japan, Australia and the United States. David Suzuki, Robert Bateman, Buffy Ste. Marie, Ralph Klein, and Don Getty have purchased his carvings.

Cliff's career goal is to give Aboriginal people a voice in what happens in their communities. He believes that native people's economic development starts with themselves and with their local land resources. He strives to establish positive working relationships between the governing bodies and Alberta's Aboriginal communities. Cliff found his niche when he began negotiating with federal and provincial departments on everything from land claims, to forestry, gas and oil development projects, to human resource and economic programs for Aboriginal people. He is respected in both Aboriginal communities and governing departments for his straightforward honesty and knowledge of Aboriginal history and the legal parameters of Treaty rights, his skills in negotiation and mediation and his policy and program strategies.

Cliff has been married to Esther since 1969. They have two children and two granddaughters. The Supernaults live near Spruce Grove, Alberta.

Submitted by: Lawrence Gauthier

Tailfeathers, Gerald

1925 - 1975
Blood
Artist and
Illustrator

Gerald Tailfeathers' pictorial and nostalgic artistic style won him acclaim. He was one of the first Aboriginal artists to pursue a professional artistic career.[846] He often depicted nineteenth century Blood and Plains Indian life in his paintings.[847] He created pictures of wild horses, animals, and hunters pursuing the buffalo herds.[848]

Gerald Tailfeathers was born to Fred Tailfeathers, and his wife Ethel Bamberry on February 14, 1925 at the Blood Reserve in southern Alberta. He was the grandson of Tailfeathers around his Neck, a scout for the Northwest Mounted Police.

At the age of seven, Gerald Tailfeathers attended St. Paul's Anglican Residential School.[849] He was taught to paint by his uncle, Percy Plainwoman, who painted under the name Two Gun.[850] He sold his first painting, a portrait of Big Bull, for five dollars in 1937 at the age of twelve years old. He held his first art exhibit at age thirteen at the Fort McLeod branch of the Canadian Handcrafts Guild.[851]

While on a trip to Glacier National Park in Montana, Tailfeathers' talent was noticed by art-school teacher Winold Reiss. Tailfeathers would attend the annual art school for the next three years. Gerald's work would also win him a scholarship to the Banff School of Fine Arts. Over the years, his artwork would include pen and ink sketches, watercolors, oils and bronze sculpture. He also illustrated a children's book called *The White Calf* (by Cliff Faulkner) in 1965.

He designed the logo for the newly formed Indian Association of Alberta (IAA) in 1944.[852] The IAA was a political representative organization that advocated Indian and treaty rights for Alberta Indians.

His Red Indian head logo is still used today on Indian Association of Alberta correspondence and letterhead.

His art was displayed on the cover of Western Horseman in December 1958. It was the first time a Canadian artist's work had ever graced the cover of that magazine.[853] He displayed his art at Expo 67 in Montreal. He also had art shows in San Francisco, Charlottetown, Ann Arbor, and Calgary.[854] He served a term as band councillor at the Blood reserve but this greatly hampered his art production and he did not seek a second term.[855] He was selected as one of seven Canadian Indians to form an Indian Arts and Crafts Committee who advised the federal government on production and marketing of native craftwork and gave recommendations on art programming, grants and services.[856]

Gerald Tailfeathers was awarded an honorary doctorate from the University of Lethbridge in 1974. Tailfeathers married Irene Goodstriker. They had four daughters: Sherry Lynn, Pamela, Heather Ann, and Laurie Lee. Gerald Tailfeathers passed away on the Blood Reserve in 1975 at the age of fifty years.

Profile by: Cora Voyageur

Three Persons, Tom

1888 - 1949
Blood/Kainai
Rodeo
Champion,
Farmer and
Rancher

Tom Three Persons was one of the first aboriginal rodeo champions in Alberta. He was a member of the Blood Tribe and was also a successful rancher and farmer.

Tom Three Persons was born in 1888 on the Blood Reserve. His mother was Double Talker (Ayakohtseniki), of the Fish Eaters clan while his birth father was a British immigrant, Fred Pace. Pace abandoned Double Talker soon after she became pregnant and she returned to her band. She married Three Persons, a young widower, who doted on her son as his own. Bobtail Chief, Three Persons' brother-in-law, also tutored the young Tom, as was the custom.[857]

Tom's marital life was complicated. He was known to mistreat his wives, but nonetheless, he had five of them over his lifetime. He met his first wife, Eliza Frank or Far Away Women, at St Joseph's Indian Industrial School, which he attended from age fifteen to eighteen. His second wife was Ambush Woman (Issyo'maki), but this only lasted two years. Lily or Wolf Long Face (Makoyi-niski) was his third wife, and while still with her he took another wife, Katie or Trouble Shining Star (Somitsi'kunatsoyi). His last wife was Josephine Eagle Child.[858] He had four children, but only one, Jesse, lived until adulthood and he later died in his twenties. Tom also had four stepsons.

Three Persons is best known for his rodeo career. He began performing in local rodeos in 1908, but his greatest achievement was winning the saddle bronc riding competition at the first Calgary Stampede in 1912. He rode the horse Cyclone, considered unrideable to many. But Three Persons gave a magnificent ride, at a time when cowboys had to ride until the bronc stopped bucking to win. He was the only Canadian to win a top prize at the Stampede that year and became a hero in both his Aboriginal and white communities.[859] His rodeo career after that was patchy, as he was injured various times and never quite attained the acclaim he had in 1912. But even after he had given up bronc riding, his roping skills kept him winning at rodeos until he was fifty years old.

Three Persons was also ambitious and became one of the wealthiest members of the Blood tribe. He also had a brief stint as an RCMP scout. He lost most of his herd in the disastrous winter of 1906–07, but by 1928 had rebuilt his herd and his crops and had become one of the richest men in the reserve.[860] Many believed he was successful because of a pact with the Devil, who appeared to Tom in the guise of a white cowboy named Billy, riding a black horse.[861]

Tom lived a life that straddled both the white and the Aboriginal communities. He acted as a mentor and trainer to generations of Blood Indians who participated in rodeos alongside white cowboys. He died on August 13, 1949 in a Calgary hospital, where he had been transferred after a fall. He was posthumously named to the Cardston Hall of Fame and was inducted into the Canadian Cowboy Hall of Fame on July 11, 1983.[862]

Profile by: Lee Tunstall

Tomkins, Peter Jr.

1899 - 1970
Metis
Politician and
Blacksmith

Peter Tomkins Jr. was best known for the political role he played in the organization and establishment of the Alberta Metis Association and the Alberta Metis Colonies. He assisted in the land selection and development of the regulations that would govern these colonies. He moved on to assist with the marketing of game and the development of cooperatives in Alberta. He eventually moved to Saskatchewan where he worked for the CCF party in northern Saskatchewan to establish cooperatives and government stores. He was fluent in Cree and worked with the CBC to deliver Cree-language programming.

Peter Tomkins Jr. was born on January 21, 1889 in what is now North Battleford, Saskatchewan.[863] Tompkins Sr. passed his views on to his son, and those opinions would figure prominently in Peter Tomkins Jr.'s future. He would later became an organizers of the Metis Association of Alberta. As a child he was sent to Winnipeg to live with his aunt and continue his education. School was very difficult because he could only speak Cree. After completing school education he moved to the Grouard area and opened a blacksmith shop. It was here that he met and married Isabella Andrews, who was also Metis.[864]

Tomkins became involved in the Metis movement in 1933 and was formally elected to the position of third vice-president in 1934.[865] On December 12, 1934, the Ewing Commission was formed to investigate the Metis situation, "[k]eeping particularly in mind the health, education, relief and general welfare of such population."[866] Peter

Tomkins, along with two other members of the Metis Association executive were the main people to testify to the Ewing Commission on behalf of the Metis people of Alberta.[867] As a result of their efforts, the Metis Betterment Act was passed and Metis colonies were established.[868]

In 1938, the Alberta government hired Tomkins as a temporary administrator. Tomkins and another member of the Metis executive selected the locations for the Metis colonies.[869] They also assisted in drafting the regulations that would govern the colonies. In addition, they formed part of a four-person committee whose purpose was to help the government to implement the settlement plan.[870] Tomkins was hired as supervisor of the Metis settlements but was replaced by a non-Aboriginal. This resulted in the Metis settlements being operated with very little input from the Metis people.[871]

In 1950, Jim Brady and Malcolm Norris arranged to have Tomkins move to northern Saskatchewan to work for the CCF government as a special field officer where he helped set up cooperatives and government stores. He assisted in the organization of fish marketing, fur marketing and cooperative movements in northern Alberta and Saskatchewan.[872] In addition to his work as a government official he also worked with CBC to provide Cree-language programming.[873]

Pete Tomkins died in 1970 after suffering a series of strokes.[874]

Profile by: K. Patricia Colosimo

Tuccaro, David Gabriel

1959 –
Cree
Entrepreneur
and Business
Consultant

David Tuccaro's business motto rings true throughout his businesses, "to create opportunities for Aboriginal people at every level of employment."[875] The goal of his companies is to achieve 80 per cent Aboriginal employment.[876] David not only backs the educational and training initiatives to ensure his own staff is fully qualified, but he also encourages other Aboriginal people to become entrepreneurs.[877]

David Tuccaro was born one of nine children to Gabriel and Therese (Mercredi) Tuccaro in Fort Chipewyan, Alberta. He spent his childhood in Fort Chipewyan, Alberta. After completing Grade 9 at Bishop Piche School he attended high school at Grandin College in Fort Smith, NWT and graduated from Grade 12 in 1976. In an interview, Tuccaro admitted that he never excelled at his academics but only attained the minimum to ensure that he could play collegiate sports.[878] In his last year at Grandin College, Mr. Tuccaro won a gold medal in the Arctic Winter Games. After graduating from high school in 1976 David believed that Grade 12 was "good enough" to get a job, hence he did not further his education.[879] At one point David worked in construction and owned and operated a taxi. However careers like this did not satisfy him because he always knew he wanted to be his own boss.[880]

David Tuccaro has become a well-known successful business owner in Fort McMurray and western Canada. David owns and controls Tuccaro Inc., which finances property rentals and commercial development. He is also president of Aboriginal Global Investments,

Aboriginal Technical Services, Tuc's Contracting, and Neegan Development Corporation Ltd., all of whom deal with anything from market investment, environmental engineering or heavy equipment earth moving.[881]

One of David's greatest accomplishments was the creation of the National Aboriginal Business Association (NABA) in 1996. NABA is a not-for-profit business association that recognizes that creating sustainable Aboriginal enterprises is critical to economic growth.[882] As president, David's goal is to oversee and promote members' involvement in bulk purchases as a way of saving on the cost of doing business.[883] Mr. Tuccaro is also very active with his message of self-determination, taking it to regional high schools "Don't listen to those who say you won't succeed . . . a lot of times people quit one day before they [would reach] success."[884] In April 1998, David was included as one of the "Top 40 under 40" by the *Financial Post Magazine*.[885] In March 1999 he was a recipient of the National Aboriginal Achievement Award for his contribution in business and commerce.[886] Mr. Tuccaro's volunteer activities encompass sitting on the board of the Regional Health Authority and the Alberta Chamber of Resources. He spearheaded the formation of the Northeastern Alberta Aboriginal Business Association.[887] Currently Mr. Tuccaro sits as a director of the National Aboriginal Achievement Foundation and co-chaired the 2004 Arctic Winter Games Committee.[888] David was also honored in the July/August 2000 issue of *Venture Magazine* for being one of "Alberta's 50 Most Influential People." David lives in Kelowna.

Profile by: Jocelyn Obreiter

Urion, Dr. Carl

1940 -
Metis
Educator,
Linguist, and
Professor
Emeritus

Metis have made significant contributions to Alberta's Aboriginal and non-Aboriginal society. This man's work as a linguist and university professor is a bold example. Carl Urion has managed to preserve the Cree language through his work with Elders. In the early 1990s Urion was contacted by Cree Elders from the Hobbema area in central Alberta to help them preserve and document their language.[889]

Urion was born in Plains, Montana in 1940. He was the sixth of eight children born to a British mother, Gladys North, and a Metis father, Loren Urion. Urion's Metis roots are closely linked to Canada's Metis community since Louis Riel retreated to that state after the Northwest Rebellion in 1885.[890] Urion has a varied career path having earned a living as a freight weight assessor, labourer, and as a petty officer in the United States Navy. It was as an educator that Carl would make his mark.[891]

In 1963, Carl Urion and Greta Reimchen were married in Jasper Place, Alberta. They would go on to have five children: Anna, Armand, Julie, Jo, and Madeleine. To date, the Urions have six grandchildren.[892]

Carl received a Bachelor of Education degree from the University of Alberta in 1970. He worked briefly as a schoolteacher in an English as a Second Language program and as an instructor at the Alberta Newstart Program in Lac La Biche in central Alberta. He returned to studies at the University of Alberta where he concentrated on systems of language use. He completed a Ph.D. in linguistic anthropology in 1978. In honor of completing his doctoral studies he was named "White Cloud" by Elder George Saddleback of Hobbema at a public ceremony at the annual powwow held at Ben Calf Robe School in Edmonton.

Urion would teach at the University of Alberta for the next twenty years. He would serve as a teacher and mentor to many students. Some of his former students include a member of parliament, Ethel Blondin Andrew; the dean of extension at the University of Saskatchewan; and a former Ontario cabinet minister, just to name a few. During this time he was able to advance the interests of Aboriginal students. He found a need to support the few Aboriginal students there were at the university. Carl was the founder of Native Students Services and served as its first director from 1982 to 1987. The office provided many types of academic and non-academic services to the few Aboriginal students attending one of the largest post secondary institutions in Canada.

His interest in advancing the discipline and his commitment to ensuring factual information about Aboriginal education issues caused him to serve as the editor of the *Canadian Journal of Native Education* (CJNE), one of the primary Aboriginal education journals in Canada, from 1991 to 1994.[893]

Urion's has demonstrated continued commitment to linguistic integrity and the preservation of the Cree language and the recording of traditional knowledge. Some of this work has been reflected in land use studies conducted at the Canadian Circumpolar Institute. He earned a National Aboriginal Achievement Award in 2004 for his work in education.[919] Urion is now retired and lives in Edmonton.

Profile by: Cora Voyageur

Venne, Muriel Stanley

1938 -
Cree
Project
Management,
Consultant

Muriel Stanley Venne has had a varied career, dominated by Aboriginal women's and human rights issues. Her many memberships and awards attest to her long-time dedication to worthwhile causes.[894]

Muriel was born at Lamont, Alberta in 1938. She attended the University of Alberta for three years before leaving to work as department head for Job Opportunities and Placement with the Metis Association of Alberta.[895]

In 1973 Premier Peter Lougheed appointed her to the first Alberta Human Rights Commission. She served as Commissioner for four years. For ten years she was executive director of Native Outreach, an organization that helps Aboriginal people to find employment.[896]

Muriel was appointed to the board of the Native Economic Development Program and to the board of the Canadian Council for Native Business in 1986.[897] After an unsuccessful run for the New Democratic Party in the 1988 federal election, she was hired as the marketing officer for the National Film Board in Edmonton.[898]

On March 8, 1989, Muriel gave the keynote address for International Women's Day in Edmonton. At that time she was president of the Women of the Metis Nation. In her speech she pointed out that Canadian Aboriginal women are discriminated against on two counts, for being Aboriginal and for being women.[899]

Muriel was named Metis Woman of the Year on May 26, 1991. She was one of the founders of the Metis women's group and was a major contributor to its success in improving the lives of Metis women.[900] She was also a driving force behind the Voice of Alberta Native Women Society, a provincial Aboriginal women's advocacy group that had local chapters throughout the province.

As project manager for Western Aboriginal Development Alliance "Stronger Together," she ran one of the most successful human resources programs in Canada.[901] She also chaired the Aboriginal Human Rights Commission and helped produce "The Rights Path – Alberta." This booklet informs Aboriginal people of their human and legal rights.[902]

Muriel was a founding member of the Institute for the Advancement of Aboriginal Women (IAAW). As its president she assists Aboriginal women with the problems confronting them and ensures that the IAAW, as an organization, champions and supports Aboriginal women. She also was founder of the Esquao Awards, which recognizes outstanding achievements of Aboriginal women.[903]

For her lifelong contribution to the advancement of human rights in Alberta, especially the rights of Aboriginal women, Muriel was honored with the prestigious Alberta Human Rights Award in December 1998. In 2002 Muriel received the Queen's Medal. In 2004, she was given the National Aboriginal Achievement Award in the Justice Category.[904]

Muriel is now a consultant and operates her own company, Dynamic Dimensions Consulting, Inc. In 2009 she was elected Vice-President of the Metis Association of Alberta. She lives in Edmonton.

Profile by: Margaret Burgess

Vinson, Laura

1947-
Metis
Singer,
Songwriter,
Teacher

Laura Vinson was told to change her ways when she first started performing country music.[905] Fortunately, she decided to stay with her Aboriginal roots and has boldly had them serve as the basis of many of the songs she writes.

Laura Vinson was born in Edmonton, Alberta on May 23, 1947. She is the eldest of seven children born to parents Tom and Yvette Vinson. She was raised in Brule, a small town nestled in the foothills near Hinton, Alberta. She began writing poetry and making music as a child. She also barrel-raced and helped her father who ran an outfitting business.[906]

Her mother encouraged her to get an education and she received a Bachelor of Education degree from the University of Alberta. She taught school for many years and began performing as a sideline. It then became her vocation.

Vinson has been on the Canadian music scene since the late 1970s. When Laura began in the music business she was told, "Don't wear that buckskin stuff anymore, it looks too country and too Indian," her reaction was "Wait a minute, I am Indian and that's what I wear."[907] Laura and her band began by playing in bars. "I was really good at selling booze and that's what is expected of you when you are on the bar circuit."[908] She decided that she wanted to move in another direction.

The new direction was an exciting journey that was welcomed by the fans as they toured to promote their album. Laura and her band have completed tours of Canada, Europe, played at Expo 86 in

Vancouver, and made television appearances on both sides of the Canada-United States border.[909]

She and her band, Free Spirit, have been nominated many times for Juno Awards and Canadian Country Music Awards. She has won many Alberta Recording Industry Awards, including female artist of the year in 1993 and her album, Rise Like a Phoenix, was voted best album the same year. Laura and her band Free Spirit were named the best roots/traditional/ethnic artist in 1997.[910]

Besides being a musician, Laura was also a schoolteacher and taught at Ben Calf Robe School in Edmonton. She encouraged youth to pursue their education and to follow their cultural background.

She had been able to express herself through her songwriting. Vinson has performed at many benefits including Earth Day celebrations, and those that support the end of family violence and homelessness.[911] She received an Esquao Award from the Institute for the Advancement of Aboriginal Women in 2003. She was also awarded a Queen Elizabeth Golden Jubilee Medal for her community work in 2002.[912]

Laura lives in Edmonton with her husband, David Martineau.

Profile by: Marlaine Metchewais

Voyageur, Alice

1942 - 2005
Dene
Business Woman
Community
Worker

Alice Voyageur was one of twelve surviving children born to Isadore Voyageur and Colombe Marce. She was bornl on December 19, 1942 at Lac Brochet, Alberta. Her mother passed away when Alice was sixteen. She met her husband, Harry Adams, shortly before her mother's death in 1958. They raised five children: Cora, Lillian, Dorothy, Harry Jr. and Mark. They celebrated forty-two years together before Harry passed away in May, 2001. At the time of Harry's death, they had twelve grandchildren and twelve great-grandchildren.

The family moved to Edmonton in 1959. Alice Voyageur was one of a group of First Nations people who migrated to the cities in the late 1950s. She had only a Grade 8 education – an education level that was standard for First Nations people at that time. She was so proud when she went back to school at Ben Calf Robe's Adult Education Program and completed Grade 10. She had great leadership qualities and she was voted the class president. She was tickled pink when she was presented with a paper headdress and was named "Chief Alice" by her classmates.

She had five children and spent many years as a single parent. She worked very hard to provide for her family, including jobs as a cook and a house cleaner. In 1978, she started a trucking company called Pocahontas Enterprises and ran it for twenty-five years. This business took her all over North America. After retiring, she opened a restaurant and catering business in Fort Chipewyan. She ran that business until her husband was stricken with cancer. She took care of him until he died in 2001.

Years of experience as a camp cook served her well as the owner of Alice's Place. Her meals were legendary and her banquet attendees would take home "doggie bags" to enjoy later. She used to laugh when she would receive take-out orders from Fort McMurray — a forty-five minute plane ride away. She would prepare meals and take them to the airport to have them flown to hungry customers who would pick them up at the airport. She even received a thank-you letter from the Premier of Alberta's wife, Colleen Klein, who praised the excellent meal that she cooked for her on her trip to Fort Chipewyan.

Alice ran a food booth at the Lac Ste. Anne pilgrimage for a number of years. Word got around that she made great bannock and people lined up for it. Some customers would buy her bannock a dozen at a time. At one point she was so tired from cooking that she took an afternoon nap. People waited for her to wake up so they could buy her food.

Alice instilled a strong work ethic in her children. She was an active community member and was always the first to lend a hand when a job needed to be done.

In spite of what seem insurmountable odds, she managed to raise a healthy and productive family. All but one of her children has a post-secondary education — a rarity in the First Nations community. They all have good jobs. She was very proud of that fact.

Alice passed away in June 14, 2005 of a heart attack.

Profile by: Cora Voyageur

Walking Buffalo aka George McLean

1871 – 1967
Stoney
Leader and
Statesman

Walking Buffalo or Tatanga Mani was born in a teepee on the banks of the Bow River near Morley, Alberta on March 20, 1871.[913] His parents were Wolf Ear and Leah Wolf Ear.[914] Within days of Walking Buffalo's birth, his mother passed away and his grandmother cared for him.[915] He was six years old when he witnessed the signing of Treaty 7 at Blackfoot Crossing in 1877.[916] Methodist missionary John McLean, who renamed him George McLean, later adopted him.[917]

Walking Buffalo attended school at the McDougall orphanage at Morley and later attended the Red Deer Industrial School and St. John's College in Winnipeg, Manitoba.[918] He had aspirations of becoming a medical doctor but confusion erupted when it came time for his grandfather, also named Walking Buffalo, to sign the papers for him to leave. It seems that the junior Walking Buffalo was the only Indian on the Morley reserve who could translate, read, and write the English language. He was deemed too important to the community to be allowed to leave.[919] He married the daughter of Hector Crawler.[920]

He worked at a variety of jobs including reserve schoolteacher and RCMP scout and interpreter. He did not hold the job with the RCMP for very long because he was repulsed by the idea of one Indian being used to pursue another.[921] He first attended the Calgary Exhibition in 1900. Trained as a carpenter and a blacksmith, he spent six months making "democrats," a form of light horse-drawn wagon that sat two or more people.[922] He learned his own traditional ways and became a traditional healer. He was also a chief for fifteen years and voluntarily retired from the position.[923]

He travelled widely and was viewed as the most travelled Indian of his time, with trips to Europe, Asia, Africa, and Australia.[924] He was involved in several "reconciliation" meetings with members of different tribal groups to help them to forgive non-Aboriginals for the treatment they have received over the years.

In an interview with the *Calgary Herald*, he remarked, "I had a better chance than most of them and now, in the autumn of my life, I do not feel that it has been wasted. I feel that I have brought health and comfort to many of my people. I have tried to make the white people understand the ways of the Indian, and I believe I have succeeded to some extent."[925]

He was revered as an elder statesman by the community and known worldwide. He was acclaimed as a messenger of goodwill and brotherhood among people of all races and colors. Walking Buffalo passed away at the Banff hospital on December 26, 1967.[926] He was ninety-seven years old.

Profile by: Joan Ryan and Cora Voyageur

Ward, Ken

1958 –
Cree
HIV/AIDS
Educator and
Motivational
speaker

Ken Ward is known to many for his inspiration and for the hope he gives to other individuals who have been diagnosed with HIV/AIDS. After being diagnosed with HIV in 1989, he was the first Aboriginal person in Canada to publicly acknowledge his disease.[927] Ken has made numerous appearances promoting awareness and attempting to break down the social stigma attached to HIV/AIDS. Throughout his courageous journey, Ken has brought a keen sense of understanding of HIV/AIDS to communities with a sense of humor that leaves a lasting impression.

Ken is a Cree from Enoch Cree Nation, located on the western outskirts of Edmonton. Ward has never married and has no children. He says this is his biggest regret[928]

Ken Ward's life has not been a pleasant one. He was taken from his parents at age five and sent to a residential school. He later lived in a series of foster homes. He was hit hard by his father's suicide and he turned to drugs. Ward blames nobody but himself for his tough lifestyle.[929] Throughout his struggles, Ken has forgiven himself and dealt with the circumstances.

Ward has been an aspiring educator on this issue and has also brought awareness through the media. He has worked in television, radio, and in print as a columnist and contributor for *Windspeaker*, a national Aboriginal newspaper.[930]

He has many accomplishments. For example, he helped form the Feather of Hope Aboriginal AIDS Prevention Society in 1990 in Edmonton and CAAN (Canadian Aboriginal AIDS Network) in 1991.

Ward has been given a Lifetime Advisor of All Nations Hope in Saskatchewan in 1992 and has been the coordinator for Treaty 6 HIV/AIDS Assembly in 1996. He also initiated the first Aboriginal Men's Wellness Conference in Alberta. Ken has contributed to the Alberta Aboriginal HIV/AIDS Conference I & II in 1997. He developed a training program and worked with high risk youth at the Enoch Cree Nation in 1999 and together they produced the "Be Aware" rap video in 1998. Ken Ward received the Alberta Aboriginal Role Model Award for the health category in 2000.

In 1995, Ken Ward's immune system began to deteriorate. His life expenctancy is not known but he continues to break down the barriers associated with HIV/AIDS. His dedication to educating Aboriginals about prevention shows in his determination even though his condition is a constant struggle. As his energy level is waning he still visits jails and talks to inmates about the reality of HIV/AIDS in the Aboriginal communities.[931] Ken Ward gives new meaning to the word "hope."

Profile by: Marlaine Metchewais

Willier, Billy

1936 –
Cree
Musician

Billy Willier was born on the Driftpile First Nation, near Slave Lake in central Alberta, on July 4, 1936.[932] He was one of eight children born to William (Okimaw) Willier and his wife, Marie (Sowan).[960] He, along with his brother and sisters, attended the Joussard Indian Residental School until he was fifteen years old.

Music has always been a part of Billy's life. When he was seven years old, his uncle James Walker custom-made a fiddle for him. He taught himself to play the fiddle, guitar, bass and other musical instruments. Although music was his first love, Billy worked as a logger and slasher over the years to support his wife, Mageurite and their four children.[933]

Billy Willier became a professional musician in 1956. Over the years he has played everything from rock and roll to traditional country and cross-over music. He is both a musician and a singer. He has played with such notable musicians as Reg Bouvette, the Metis fiddler from Manitoba (now deceased) and other artists such as Alfie Mynre (the North American fiddling champion), Jimmy Arthur Ordge, Frankie Rodgers (champion fiddler), and Rich Chernesky from Sun Country TV. He served as sideman and backup singer for Harry Davies (a Sunshine Recods recording artist) for a decade.[934] He was part of the pioneering group of musicians who played in bars when dance floors were introduced in the 1970s.

Along the way, Billy formed a band mixed with Aboriginal and non-Aboriginal musicians and he taught most of his band members how to play on stage. He was, and still is, a promoter for Aboriginal talent.[935] Billy has been promoting talent since he first came into the music business. Even today, people interested in the music business ask his advice on how to a better performer. He has thirty years of promoting and booking talent under his belt.

Billy was blessed with tremendous musical talent as both a musician and a singer. However, he is humble about his gifts and regards himself a an "average musician." Billy still performs in a classic ountry hand, even though he is past the retirement age. He has no plans to quit playing music and singing any time soon.

Nominated by: Darren Brule

Profile by: Cora Voyageur

Notes

[1] Hugh A. Dempsey. "Aatsista-Mahkan (Running Rabbit)" *Dictionary of Canadian Biography,* Vol.14, 1911 to 1920. (Toronto: University of Toronto Press, 1998), 3.

[2] *Ibid.*

[3] *Ibid.*

[4] *Ibid.*

[5] *Ibid.*

[6] Hugh A. Dempsey. "Running Rabbit (Aatsista-Mahkan)" *Tribal Honors: A history of the Kainai Chieftainship.* (Calgary: Kainai Chieftainship, 1997). 129.

[7] *Ibid.*

[8] *Ibid.*

[9] Government of Canada. Copy of Treaty and Supplementary Treaty No. 7. Ottawa: Supply and Services. 6

[10] Dempsey, 1998, 3

[11] *Ibid.*

[12] Dempsey, 1998, 3

[13] *Ibid.*

[14] *Ibid.*

[15] *Ibid.*

[16] *Ibid.*

[17] *Ibid.*

[18] *Ibid.*

[19] Judy Shuttleworth, "Metis historian and teacher retires at 85," *Windspeaker 9* (January 31, 1992), 7.

[20] Carol Berger, "Savior of the Cree language; Mother's deathbed plea inspired Anne Anderson," *Edmonton Journal*, October 31, 1994, B3.

[21] "Dr. Anderson profiled," *Windspeaker 4* (May 23, 1986), 14.

[22] Shuttleworth.

[23] "Indians push for language revival New life breathed into Cree," *Calgary Herald,* January 4, 1990, E6.

[24] Kenneth Williams, "Educator set out to preserve Cree language," *Windspeaker* (May 1997), 26.

[25] *Ibid.*

[26] Berger.

[27] Terri Mason, "Dale Auger: On Art, Blood And Kindred Spirits"; <http://www.cana-diancowboy.ca/artistprofile/dale_auger.html> (accessed May 31, 2005).

[28] Ibid.

[29] Ibid.

[30] Personal Interview with Dale Auger at Redwood Meadows, Alberta conducted January, 2005.

[31] *Medicine Walker*, directed by Gregory Coyes with Dale Auger, Good Medicine Media Ltd., produced with APTN.

[32] Roland Bellerose, "Margaret Bad Boy," *Aboriginal Times 5* (2001), 48.

[33] David Bly, "Margaret 'mother' to Siksika: Custodian of Native Ways dies at age 101," *Calgary Herald,* May 29, 2001, A3.

[34] *Ibid.*

[35] *Ibid.*

[36] Bellerose, "Margaret Bad Boy."

[37] Bly, "Margaret 'mother' to Siksika: Custodian of Native Ways dies at age 101."

[38] *Ibid.*

[39] <http.//www.goodminds.com.books/Sissika%20Old%20Stories-Level%20Thre.html> (accessed July 7, 2003).

[40] Bly, "Margaret 'mother' to Siksika: Custodian of Native Ways dies at age 101."

[41] Joe Bachmier, "Elder's Shield Protects Shelter," *Calgary Herald*, May 25, 2000, B2.

[42] *Ibid.*

[43] Quote from Leroy Good Eagle in Bellerose, "Margaret Bad Boy."

[44] Biography of Mel E. Benson provided by nominator, Margaret Benson, June 2003.

[45] Ibid.

[46] Ibid.

[47] NAAF-2003 recipients; <http://www.naaf.ca/rec2003.html> (accessed June 19, 2003).

[48] Benson biography, 1

[49] Inna Dansereau, *Alberta Sweetgrass* (February 2003), 4.

[50] Dansereau, 4.

[51] Benson biography, 2

[52] Government of Alberta. Seekers & Storytellers: Aboriginal role models share their career journeys (Calgary: Human Resources and Employment, 2002). 22.

[53] Zander Hollander. "Craig Berube" *The Complete Encyclopedia of Hockey.* (Detroit: Gale Research Inc., 1993), 410

[54] "Getting a cup of coffee" refers to playing for a team for a short time.

[55] "Craig Berube" Legends of Hockey: NHL Player Search. Retrieved from http//:www.legendsofhockey.net:8080legends of Hockey/sjp/SearchPlayer.jsp?player=10107

[56] Sam Lakaris. "Veteran continues to contribute in NHL" *Windspeaker.* March 1997. Vol. 14(11), 22

[57] Legends of Hockey, 2006

[58] *Ibid.*

[59] Hollander, 410

[60] Hollander, 410

[61] Hollander, 410

[62] Michael Ulmer. "Capitals Todd Krygier is a bit player" *CanWest News.* June 1, 1998. (Don Mills: Southam Newspapers, 1998), 1

[63] Scher, Jon. "Swapped by the Calgary Flames to the Toronto Maple Leafs in an unprecendented 10-man deal, playmaking centre and would be actor Doug Gilmour. *Sports Illustrated.* Volume 76(1), 82

[64] Craig Berube Player Page. "NHL Playoffs" retrieved from http//:wwwsportsillustrated.cnn.com/hockey/nhl/players/106/

[65] Sam Lakaris. "NHL bad boy is changing his ways to coach." *Sports – Alberta Sweetgrass*, October, 2004. 7

[66] Lakaris, October, 2004, 7

[67] Lakaris, October, 2004, 7

[68] Profile based on newspaper article written by the author and there are no other citations as a result. Terry Lusty. "Pool Tourney recognizes Canadian living legend". *Windspeaker.* August 2002, 23

[69] Meili, Dianne. 1991. *Those Who Know: Profiles of Alberta's native Elders.* Edmonton: NeWest Press, 91.

[70] *Ibid.*

[71] Sherri Zickefoose. "School Plants Deep Cultural Roots: Aboriginal Languages, Timeless Traditions Passed Down". *Calgary Herald,* December 4, 2002. Arts 16

[72] *Ibid.*

[73] *Ibid.*

[74] Meili, 1991

[75] *Ibid.*

[76] *bid.*

[77] Ethel Winnipeg. People and Places, November 11, 1996. *Sweetgrass.* November 11, 1996. 15

[78] "Maggie Black Kettle". Actress – Filmography. Retrieved from http://www.imdb.com/name/nm/0085708

[79] 1899 scrip application of John Bourassa. National Archives of Canada, RG 15, Series D-II-8-c, Volume 1337, Reel C14951. His mother's name is given as Nisandeway in John's scrip application, as Lafleur in other scrip applications; and as Otaikijik in her marriage record. Since Lafleur was her mother's, Josephte Page's, second husband, Marguerite was probably a Lafleur by adoption.

[80] For example, see 1899 scrip applications for Maggie Bourassa and Francoise Courteoreille Bourassa. RG 15, Series D-II-8-c, Volume 1337, Reel C14951.

[81] Fort Vermilion RC Marriages, 1876. On the same day, his sister, Sophie Bourassa, married Lucia's brother, Francis St. Cyr and they moved to the Lesser Slave Lake by the end of the century.

[82] Hudson's Bay Company Archives, B.224/e/3, Fort Vermilion Post Report.

[83] Provincial Archives of Alberta, 70.387 A.281, Item 104, Letter, March 27, 1888, Alfred C. Garrioch to Bishop Young; Treaty No. 8 made June 21, 1899 and Adhesions, Reports, etc. p. 15, reprinted 1966, Queen's Printer: Roger Duhamel; Goddard, Earle Pliny. 1913. "Beaver Texts, Beaver Dialect" *Anthropological Papers of the American Museum of Natural History.* Volume X, Parts V and VI, p. 299.

[84] Fort Vermilion and District Association, *Fort Vermilion: People in Our Vast Trading North, 1788-1988* (Alton, MB: Friesen, 1992), 23.

[85] Provincial Archives of Alberta, 85.34, Item 590, plan showing the connection between the three settlements at Fort Vermilion, Peace River, 1906, J. B. St. Cyr, DLS.

[86] Canada. 1906 Census. NW Province, District 21, Fort Vermilion, T-18363.

[87] Marilee Toews, Coordinator, Fort Vermilion Heritage Centre, personal comment., April 2005.

[88] Telephone interview with Sharon Bourque was conducted by the author in May, 2005.

[89] *Ibid.*

[90] *Ibid.*

[91] Grant McEwen Community College. *Dreamcatcher: Start the Fire Conference Program.* (Edmonton: Grant McEwen Community College, 2004). Retrieved May 2005. http://www.dreamcatcher.macewan.ca/2004/steering.cfm

[92] Interview, May 2005.

[93] Wayne Newbert. "Dare Program keeps children off drugs" Alberta Teachers Association – In the News. Retrieved May 2005 from http://www.teachers.ab.ca/Quick+Links/Publications/ATA+News/Volume+30/Number+12

[94] Interview, May 2005.

[95] *Ibid.*

[96] *Ibid.*

[97] Anne Anderson, *The First Metis: A New Nation* (Edmonton: UVISCO Press, 1985), 132.

[98] Laurie Meijer-Drees, *The Indian Association of Alberta: A History of Political Action,* (Vancouver: University of British Columbia Press, 2002), 19.

[99] Murray Dobbin, The One-and-a-half men; the story of Jim Brady and Malcolm Norris, Metis patriots of the twentieth century. (Vancouver: New Star Books, 1981), 48.

[100] Anderson, 132.

[101] Dobbin, 64.

[102] Alberta Order in Council No. 1095, 12 December 1934, Commission Evidence, p. 323, as cited in Dobbin, p. 88.

[103] Dobbin, 88–105.

[104] Punch, Donald, *The Metis,* (Toronto: James Lorimer & Company, 1988), p. 142.

[105] Fred Gaffen, Forgotten Soldiers, (Penticton: Theytus Books, 1985) 57.

[106] Dobbin, 164.

[107] Gaffen, 64.

[108] Dobbin, 166–181.

[109] *Ibid., 191–200.*

[110] *Ibid., 243–252.*

[111] Deanna Cardinal. "Pearl Calahasen Nomination Form." (Calgary: Great Aboriginal Albertans Project. 2003) 1

[112] Cardinal, 2

[113] Government of Alberta. "The Honourable Pearl Calahasen." Edmonton: Government of Alberta, 2003). 1.

[114] Rocky Woodward. "Metis Politician Rebounded from Dashed Dream" *Windspeaker.* (Edmonton: AMMSA, 1991) 19

[115] Government of Alberta, 1

[116] *Ibid.*

[117] Woodward, 19

[118] Government of Alberta, 1

[119] *Ibid.*

[120] Cardinal, 4

[121] Government of Alberta, 1

[122] *Ibid.*

[122] *Ibid.*

[123]Cardinal, 4

[124]"Johnny Callihoo Passing Great Loss," *The Native Voice*, September 1957, 2.

[125]J. Laurie, "One of the Greatest Indians Ever Born In Alberta", Sketch of the Indians of Alberta. (sn:1955), 9.

[126]L. Meijer Drees, *The Indian Association of Alberta: A History of Political Action* (Vancouver: University of British Columbia Press, 2002), 22.

[127]J.G. MacEwan, *Portraits From The Plains* (Toronto: McGraw-Hill, 1971). Pp.241-6

[128]Meijer Drees, The Indian Association of Alberta, 22.

[129]*Ibid., 176.*

[130]*Ibid., 177.*

[131]*Ibid., 22.*

[132]Veterans Affairs Canada, Medals Page, "Queen Elizabeth II Coronation Medal"; <http://www.constable.ca/qe2cm.htm> (accessed May 2005).

[133]Meijer Drees, The Indian Association of Alberta, 24.

[134]"Johnny Callihoo Passing Great Loss," 2.

[135]Brian Brennan, *Building a Province: 60 Alberta Lives* (Calgary: Fifth House Ltd., 2000), 25–26.

[136]Grant MacEwan, *And Mighty Women Too, Stories of Notable Western Canadian Women* (Saskatoon: Western Producer Prairie Books, 1975), 195.

[137]Brennan, *Building a Province,* 27.

[138]Grant MacEwan, *Metis Makers of History* (Saskatoon: Western Producer Prairie Books, 1981), 146.

[140]Brennan, Building a Province, 27.

[141]MacEwan, And mighty women too, 197.

[142]Ibid., 198.

[143]MacEwan, *Metis Makers of History*, 146.

[144]Indigenous Bar Association, "IBA Objectives"; <http://www.indigenousbar.ca/home/board_members.html> (accessed May 2005).

[145]The Banff Centre, "The Banff Centre Biography: Brian Calliou"; <http://www.banffcentre.ca/faculty/faculty_member.aspx?facId=80> (accessed May 2005).

[146]*Ibid.*

[147]*Ibid.*

[148]*Ibid.*

[149]An earlier version of this profile appears in *Hidden in Plain Sight: Contributions of Aboriginal people to Canadian Culture and Society,* ed. David Newhouse, Cora J. Voyageur and Daniel Beavon (Toronto: University of Toronto Press, 2005). Paul Melting Tallow, "Activist by Design: Douglas Cardinal," in *Aboriginal Times* (Calgary: Cree-ative Media, 2001), 22.

[150]http://www.djcarchitect.com

[151]Trevor Boddy, *The Architecture of Douglas Cardinal* (Edmonton: NeWest Press, 1989), 11.

[152]Melting Tallow, "Activist by Design," 24.

[153]Boddy, The Architecture of Douglas Cardinal, 7.

[154]Ibid., 11.

[155]Ibid., 13.

[156] Ruth Rosenburg, "Douglas Cardinal," *Notable Native Americans,* ed. Sharon Malinowski (New York: Gale Research, 1995), 69.

[157] *Ibid.,* 22.

[158] http://www.djcarchitect.com.>

[159] *Ibid.*

[160] *Ibid.*

[161] Melting Tallow, "Activist by Design."

[162] Rosenburg, "Douglas Cardinal," 69.

[163] An earlier version of this profile appears in *Hidden in Plain Sight: Contributions of Aboriginal people to Canadian Culture and Society,* ed. David Newhouse, Cora J. Voyageur and Daniel Beavon (Toronto: University of Toronto Press, 2005). Gil Cardinal, Foster Child, National Film Board of Canada, 1987.

[164] "Gil Cardinal: Alberta director gets film and television award," *Windspeaker,* Aboriginal Multi-Media Society Web site; <http://www.ammsa.com> (accessed June 14, 2003).

[165] Gil Cardinal, "Film and Television," National Aboriginal Achievement Awards Web site; <http:// www.naaf.ca/rec97.html> (accessed May 7, 2003).

[166] Gil Cardinal, Foster Child, National Film Board of Canada, 1987.

[167] National Film Board of Canada Web site; <http://www.cmm.onf.ca> (accessed May 7, 2003).

[168] Gil Cardinal, "Film and Television," National Aboriginal Achievement Awards Web site; <http:// www.naaf.ca/rec97.html> (accessed May 7, 2003).

[169] *Ibid.*

[170] Northern Alberta Institute of Technology Web site; <http://www.nait.ab.ca/about/honorarydiploma2001.pdf> (accessed May 7, 2003).

[171] "Harold Cardinal," in *Biographical Dictionary of Indians of the Americans* (Newport Beach: American Indian Publisher, Inc., 1991), 114.

[172] Harold Cardinal," in *Contemporary Canadian Biographies,* University of Alberta, 1997, CPI.Q Database; <http:/web4.infotrac.galegroup. com/itw/i_L9746468&dyn= 16_ar_fmt?sw_aep =edmo698. Accessed March 2002

[173] Ruth Rosenburg, "Harold Cardinal," in *Notable Native Americans,* ed. Sharon Malinowski (New York: Gale Research, 1995), 6.

[174] Bob Bettson, "Cardinal again cast in leading role," *Calgary Herald,* November 10, 1983, D1.

[175] "Harold Cardinal," in *Contemporary Canadian Biographies.*

[176] Rosenburg, "Harold Cardinal," 70.

[177] "Harold Cardinal," in *Who's Who in Canada,* Vol. XXXV, ed. Elizabeth Lumley (Toronto: University of Toronto Press, 2000), 77.

[178] "Harold Cardinal" Folio, University of Alberta, 1999; <http://www.ualberta. ca/ FOLIO/9899/06.18/04.htm>. [needs access date]

[179] Tina Kennedy, "'Liberal loss not all bad' Cardinal," *South Peace News,* 2000. http://www.southpeacenews.com/electon2000/story3.html.

[180] Aboriginal Achievement Foundation, 2001 Recipients, National Aboriginal Achievement Foundation, November 25, 2001; <http://www.naaf.ca/rec2001.html#4>. Accessed March 2002

[181] *Ibid.*

[182] John Copley, "Politicians on the Move," *Native Network News,* July 1988, 3.

[183] "Mike Cardinal," in *Who's Who in Alberta: A Biographical Record of the men and Women if Our Time* (Vancouver: B&C List, 1998), 125–6.

[184] Personal interview with Connie Johnson at Calling Lake, Alberta. June 2003.

[185] Who's Who, 125.

[186] "Mike Cardinal," in *Who's Who in Alberta: A Biographical Record of the men and Women In Our Time* (Vancouver: B&C List, 1998), 125–6.

[187] *Ibid.*

[188] "Biography for Mike Cardinal," Alberta Legislative Assembly; <http//:www.assembly.ab.ca/adr/adr_ template.aspx?type=mal_bio&number=44>. Accessed June 2005

[189] *Ibid.*

[190] An earlier version of this profile appears in *Hidden in Plain Sight: Contributions of Aboriginal people to Canadian Culture and Society*, ed. David Newhouse, Cora J. Voyageur and Daniel Beavon (Toronto: University of Toronto Press, 2005).

[191] P. Kunesh, "Tantoo Cardinal," in *Notable Native Americans,* ed. Sharon Malinowski (New York: Gale Research, 1995), 70.

[192] Tantoo is a brand of insect repellent.

[193] "Tantoo Cardinal," in Who's Who of American Women (New Jersey: Reed Publishing Company, 1993), 80.

[194] Bernelda Wheeler, "Tantoo Cardinal," *Eagle Feather News*, 2000; <http://www.sicc.sk.ca/faces/wcardta.htm> (accessed 1 November 2001).

[195] *Ibid.*

[196] *Who's Who of American Women,* 80.

[197] "Tantoo Cardinal," in *Canadian Who's Who, 2000,* ed. Elizabeth Lumley (Toronto: University of Toronto Press, 2000), 205.

[198] Brian D. Johnson, "Masks of a Metis Star," *Maclean's Magazine,* October 20, 1986, 63.

[199] James Defelice, "Tantoo Cardinal," *Canadian Encyclopedia,* 2000 World Edition (Toronto: McClelland and Stewart Inc., 2000).

[200] *Canadian Who's Who, 2000,* 205.

[201] Bruce Weir, "Actress wants to tell stories that make people feel good," *Windspeaker,* April 1998, 5.

[202] *Ibid.*

[203] *Ibid.*

[204] Trevor Boddy, *The Architecture of Douglas Cardinal* (Edmonton: NeWest Press, 1989), 11.

[205] "Honorary Degree Recipient: Joane Margeurite Cardinal" University of Calgary Spring Convocation Program.

[206] *Ibid.*

[207] "Joane Cardinal-Schubert," *Contributors* (Banff: The Banff Centre Press., 2002).

[208] *Ibid.*

[209] "Honorary Degree Recipient: Joane Margeurite Cardinal."

[210] "About Joane Cardinal-Schubert";
<http://www.mastersgalleryltd.com/website/artists1/cfm?ArtistID=39>
(accessed April 25, 2005).

[211] "Joan Cardinal-Schubert," Contributors.

[212] "Honorary Degree Recipient: Joane Margeurite Cardinal."

[213] Personal interview with Nellie Carlson, May 2005, Edmonton

[217] Nellie Mildred Carlson personal biography. Author: nd., 1

[218] *Ibid.*

[219] *Ibid.*

[220] Personal interview with Nellie Carlson, May 2005, Edmonton.

[221] City of Edmonton Names Advisory Committee. "Carlson Close". (Edmonton: City of Edmonton, nd)., 1

[222] Personal interview.

[223] *Ibid.*

[224] *Ibid.*

[225] Personal biography, 1

[226] Ibid.

[227] An earlier version of this profile appears in Hidden in *Plain Sight: Contributions of Aboriginal people to Canadian Culture and Society*, ed. David Newhouse, Cora J. Voyageur and Daniel Beavon (Toronto: University of Toronto Press, 2005). Anna Hoang, "From Single Mom to Senator," *Western Catholic Reporter,* Edmonton, Alberta, 1999; <http://www.wcr.ab.ca/news/1999/0621/thelmachal-ifoux062199.shtml> accessed June 2004

[228] *Ibid*

[229] Thelma Chalifoux profile, Liberal Party of Canada Web site;
<http://www.ipc.ab.ca/en/team/sen/chalifoux> (accessed 2003).

[230] *Ibid.*

[231] "Senator Thelma Chalifoux," Leadership Pages Web site;
<http://www.ualberta.ca/~walld/chalifoux.htm> (accessed 1999).

[232] *The Windsor Star,* December 10, 2001. accessed June 2004

[233] *Edmonton Journal*, April 11, 2003. accessed June 2004

[234] *Calgary Herald,* January 9, 2003. accessed June 2004

[235] "Chief Harry Chonkolay," 1994. Personal documents on loan to the author from Harry Chonkolay's daughter, Rosemarie Willier.

[236] Alana Mitchell. "Grand Chief Harry Chonkolay's Passing Marks End of an Era". Globe and Mail: Lives Lived. September 17, 1998.

[237] Interview with Rosemarie Willier, May 8, 2005.

[238] Mitchell,

[239] *Ibid.*

[240] *Ibid.*

[241] "Ex-Judge named to Order of Canada," *Edmonton Journal*, June 30, 1989, H6.

[242] *Ibid.*

[243] Willier interview, May 8, 2005

[244] *Ibid.*

[245] Mitchell,

246 Ginny Belcourt Todd, "Corporal Bertha Houle: A Woman of Substance" in *Our Women in Uniform,* ed. Muriel Stanley Venne (Calgary: Bunker to Bunker Publishing, 2003), 11–19.

247 *Ibid.*

248 Marilyn Adsit. "Our Women in Uniform." *Esqauo.* Vol. 5(1). (Edmonton: Institute for the Advancement of Aboriginal Women, 1999). 3

249 Todd, 12

250 *Ibid.*

251 "Bertha Clark Jones," Esquao Awards Program, 1996.

252 Government of Alberta. "Board Members announced for 10 new Child and Family Services Authorities". (Edmonton: Children's Services, 2000.), 12

253 Metis National Council. "Metis Veterans Honoured with Golden Jubilee Medals"

254 Personal interview with Joan Collins, May 2005, Edmonton

255 *Ibid.*

256 *Ibid.*

257 Alberta Solicitor General and Public Security. "Youth Justice Committees Around the Province" (Edmonton: Alberta Solicitor General and Public Security, 2001) 1

258 *Ibid*

259 Allyson Jeffs. "Justice Counsellor provides vital link" *Edmonton Journal.* May 10, 2004. B1

260 *Ibid.*

261 *Ibid.*

262 Collins interview, May 2005

263 YWCA. "Joan Collins" Women of Distinction Awards Program, 2001. (Edmonton: YWCA, 2001). Retreived from
http://www.ywcaofedmonton.org/events/tribute.php

264 Collins interview, May 2005

265 M. Burke, "Oldest living Cree Elder delivers land claim," *Windspeaker;*
<http://www.mcaonline.ca/rara/raphael_cree.htm> (accessed May 2005).

266 Burke, "Oldest living Cree Elder delivers land claim."

267 "Raphael Cree" *The Report Magazine*
http://www.findarticles.com/p/articles/mi_hb3543/is_200202/ai_n8359914(accessed May 2005).

268 Burke, "Oldest living Cree Elder delivers land claim."

269 "Raphael Cree" *The Report Magazine*
http://www.findarticles.com/p/articles/mi_hb3543/is_200202/ai_n8359914(accessed May 2005).

270 Burke, "Oldest living Cree Elder delivers land claim."

271 Adapted from Hugh Dempsey, "Makaoyi-Opistoki (Crop Eared Wolf) ," *Dictionary of Canadian Biography,* Vol. 14, (Toronto: University of Toronto Press, 1998), 737–738.

272 Hugh Dempsey, *Tribal Honours: A History of Kainai Chieftainship* (Calgary: The Chieftainship, 1997), 119–120

273 Dempsey, "Makaoyi-Opistoki (Crop Eared Wolf)," 738

274 *Ibid., 738.*

[275]Public Safety and Emergency Preparedness Canada, "1995-09-22/ABO: Historical Artifact – Blood Tribe/Kainawa," August 10, 2002; <http://www.psepc-sppcc.gc.ca/publications/news/19950922_e.asp> (accessed May 5, 2005).

[276]Hugh Dempsey, "Crowfoot, Bearspaw, Deerfoot, and Crowchild: Indians Behind the Place Names," in *Citymakers: Calgarians After the Frontier,* ed. Max Foran and Sheilagh Jameson (Calgary: Historical Society of Alberta, 1987), 55–58.

[277]Laurie Meijer-Drees, *The Indian Association of Alberta: A History of Political Action* (Vancouver: University of British Columbia Press, 2002).

[278]*Ibid.*

[279]Hugh Dempsey, "David Crowchild," in *Calgary: A Living Heritage,* ed. Susie Sparks (Calgary: Junior League of Calgary, 1984), 49–50.

[280]*Ibid.*

[281]*Ibid.*

[282]J. W. Grant MacEwen, "David Crowchild," in *Portraits from the Plains* (Toronto: McGraw-Hill, 1971).

[283]Meijer-Drees, The Indian Association of Alberta.

[284]Heather Andrews, "Chief Crowchild award given to Millican," *Windspeaker,* June 7, 1991, 14.

[285]MacEwen, "David Crowchild."

[286]Meijer-Drees, The Indian Association of Alberta.

[287]Hugh Dempsey, "David Crowchild," 49–50.

[288]Hugh Dempsey, "David Crowchild," 49–50.

[289]*Ibid.*

[290]Chris Reading, "Something Big," Alberta Views (May/June 2001), 39.

[291]*Ibid., 40.*

[292]*Ibid., 40.*

[293]*Ibid., 37.*

[294]*Ibid., 37.*

[295]*Ibid., 40.*

[296]Annette Bourdeau, "Survive and Conquer," *Ryerson Review of Journalism* (Summer 2004), 2.

[297]*Ibid.*

[298]Trina Gobert, "Going Where No One Has Gone Before," *Grassroots* (Spring 2001), 3.

[299]McKinley, Rob. "Elders spend a lifetime preserving traditions and religion". *Windspeaker Special Focus.* (Edmonton, AMMSA, April 1998). 3

[300]*Ibid.*

[301]Sybille Manneschmidt. "Lives Lived: Joe Crowshoe" *Globe and Mail.* January 6, 2000, 1

[302]Meili, Dianne. "Joe and Josephine Crowshoe" *Those Who Know: Profiles of Alberta's Native Elders.* (Edmonton: Newest Publishers, 1991). 97-106

[303]McKinley, 1998

[304]Tribal Chiefs Institute. "Joseph Crowshoe" *In Their Footsteps: Contributions of First Nations of Alberta.* (Edmonton: Duval House, 2001), 15

[305]*Ibid.*

[306]McKinley, 1998.

[307] *Ibid.*

[308] Manneschmidt, 2000

[309] Carla Higheagle. "Joe Crowshoe Sr. 92" Nimiipu News of the Nez Perce Tribe. (Idaho: Nez Perce Tribe, 1999), 15

[310] Manneschmidt, 2000

[311] *Ibid.*

[312] National Aboriginal Achievement Foundation. "Joe Crowshoe: Heritage and Spirituality" National Aboriginal Achievement Foundation Awards Program. (Toronto: National Aboriginal Achievement Foundation, 1998.) 1

[313] Meili, 1991

[314] Indian Affairs and Northern Development. "Joseph and Josephine Crowshoe - Elders" retrieved from Http://www.ainc-inac.gc.ca/ks/english/6063_e.html

[315] Meili, 1991

[316] Canadian Honours. "Josephine Crowshoe, CM" retrieved from http://wwww.gg.ca/cgi-bin/oc_details.pl?lang=e&rec_id=98

[317] McKinley, 1998

[318] Manneschmidt, 2000

[319] Alberta Centre for Child, Family & Community Research, <http://www.research4children.org/admin/contentx/default.cfm?PageId=352> accessed June 1, 2005).

[320] Aboriginal Framework News, Spring 2003; <http://www.aand.gove.ab.ca/PDFs/afn_spring2003.pdf> (accessed June 1, 2005).

[321] Gail Anne Corbett, "Understanding beyond facts," Your Faculty, Spring 2005; <http://files.myweb.med.ucalgary.ca/files/68/files/unprotected/April_2005_issue.pdf> (accessed June 1, 2005).

[322] Lindsay Crowshoe, Julia Bickford, Michele Decottignies, "Interactive drama teaching aboriginal health medical education," *Medical Education 29* (May 2005), 521-522.

[323] Stage Left Productions; <http://www.stageleft.orgpast_adult.htm. (accessed June 1, 2005).

[324] Dave Lowery, "Aboriginal Program Aims to Reverse Alarming Statistice," Vital Signs (April 2003); <http://www.crhahealth.ab.ca/nav/VS19.pdf> (accessed June 1, 2005).

[325] Aboriginal Capacity and Development Research Environment; <http://www.acadre.ualberta.ca/about_us/co_investigator/crowshoe.htm> (accessed June 1, 2005).

[326] Shahzeer Karmali, Kevin Laupland, A. Robert Harrop, Christi Findlay, Andrew W. Hameed, "Epidemology of severe trauma among status Aboriginal Canadians: a population-based study," CMAJ 172 (April 12, 2005); <http://www.cmaj.ca/cg/content/full/172/8/1007> (accessed June 1, 2005).

[327] First Nations Drum; <http://firsnationsdrum.com/Sum2001/NAAA-Crowshoe.htm> (accessed June 1, 2005).

[328] "Shawna Cunningham, personal conversation, June 24, 2003.

[329] "Chester Cunningham" *Who's Who in Alberta: A biographical Record of the Men and Women of Our Time,* 1st ed., 1994–98 (Vancouver: B&C List, 1994), 179.

[330] Alberta Order of Excellence, October 17, 2000, Government of Alberta, Office of the Lieutenant Governor; <http://www.lieutenantgovernor.ab.ca/aoe/bio/cunningham/htm>.Accessed May 2003

[331] *Who's Who in Alberta,* 179.

[332] *Ibid.*

[333] Cited in Cheryl Petten, "Order of Excellence recognizes public service," *Alberta Sweetgrass 7* (November 2000), 9.

[334] "Willingness to help lead to Order of Canada," Windspeaker 10 (March 1, 1993), 12.

[335] *Ibid.*

[336] *Ibid.*

[337] Alberta Order of Excellence.

[338] *Who's Who in Alberta,* 179.

[339] *Ibid.*

[334] *Ibid.*

[341] Anne Anderson, *The First Metis . . . A New Nation* (Edmonton: Uvisco Press, 1985), 186.

[342] *Ibid.*

[343] Personal communication with Shawna Cunningham and Geoff Burtonshaw. May 2005

[344] Anderson, *The First Metis,* 186.

[345] Cunningham conversation

[346] Anderson, *The First Metis,* 186.

[347] Cunningham conversation

[348] Joe Sawchuk et. al. *Metis Land Rights in Alberta: A Political History.* (Edmonton: The Metis Association of Alberta, 1981)

[349] Murray Dobbin. *One and a half men.* (Vancouver: New Star Books, 1981)[347] T.C. Pocklington. *The Government and Politics of the Alberta Metis Settlements.* Regina: Canadian Plains Research Centre.

[350] Cunningham conversation.

[352] Telphone interview with Theresa Daniels (Christine Daniels' daughter). May 2005

[353] *Ibid.*

[354] *Native Journal,* February 2001, 15.

[355] *Ibid.*

[356] *Ibid.*

[357] *Ibid.*

[358] Telephone interview with Theresa Daniels (Christine Daniels' daughter). May 2005

[359] *Ibid.*

[360] Revised from: Heritage Community Foundation, Alex Decoteau Edukit, 2003; <http://www.edukits.ca/decoteau> (accessed May 2, 2005).

[361] *Ibid.*

[362] *Ibid.*

[363] Grant MacEwan, "Alex Decoteau," in *Portraits from the Plains* (Toronto: McGraw-Hill, 1971), 238–39.

[364] Heritage Community Foundation, Alex Decoteau Edukit.

[365] MacEwan, "Alex Decoteau," 240.

[366] Alberta Sports Hall of Fame and Museum, Pioneer Award, 2002; <http://www.albertasportshalloffame.com/pages/awards3.html> (accessed May 2, 2005).

[367] An earlier version of this profile appeared in *Hidden in Plain Sight: Contributions of Aboriginal People to Canadian Society and Culture,* ed. David Newhouse, Cora Voyageur and Daniel Beavon (Toronto: University of Toronto Press, 2005). "Olive Dickason: Woman who Changed History wins Lifetime Achievement Award," *Windspeaker,* 1997; <http://www.ammsa.com/achieve/AA97-O.Dickason.htm>. March 2002

[368] Christopher B Tower, "Olive Patricia Dickason," in *Notable Native Americans,* ed. Sharon Malinowski (New York: Gale Research, 1995), 124.

[369] Fred Favel, "Success by Degree: Olive Patricia Dickason, CM , Ph.D., D.Litt. Professor Emeritus," in *Transition* (Portrait) 8 (April/May 1996); <http://www.inac.gc.ca/pubs/transition/apr96/port.html> (accessed May 10, 2002).

[370] Tower, "Olive Patricia Dickason."

[371] Favel, "Success by Degree."

[372] Tower, "Olive Patricia Dickason."

[373] Christopher Moore, "The First People of America," *The Beaver: Exploring Canada's History 72* (1992), 53.

[374] *Ibid.*

[375] *Ibid.*

[376] "Dickason, Olive Patricia," in *Canadian Who's Who,* Volume XXXV, ed. Elizabeth Lumley (Toronto: University of Toronto Press, 2000).

[377] "Olive Dickason: Woman who Changed History wins Lifetime Achievement Award," *Windspeaker.*

[378] Murray Dobbin, *The One-And-A-Half Men* (Vancouver: New Star Books, 1981), 57.

[380] Anne Anderson, *The First Metis: A New Nation,* (Edmonton: UVISCO Press, 1985), 192.

[381] *Ibid., 190.*

[382] Joseph Dion Fonds, Glenbow Archives Main Catalogue, Calgary; <http://www.glenbow.org/lasearch/basic.htm> (accessed May 21, 2003).

[383] Dobbin, The One-And-A-Half Men, 57.

[384] Anderson, The First Metis, 190.

[385] Joseph Dion Fonds.

[386] Dobbin, *The One-And-A-Half Men,* 57.

[387] Dobbin, *The One-And-A-Half Men,* 64.

[388] *Ibid., 88–120.*

[389] *Ibid., 118–120.*

[390] Anderson, *The First Metis*, 191.

[391] Laurie Meijer Drees, *The Indian Association of Alberta* (Vancouver: University of British Columbia Press, 2002), 25.

[392] *Ibid., 32.*

[393] Anderson, *The First Metis,* 191.

[394] "Cree Historian," *Alberta Historical Review 9* (Summer 1961), 31.

[395] Joseph Dion Fonds.

[396] Anderson, The First Metis, 191.

[397] *Ibid.*

[398] Personal Interview conducted by the author on May 2005 in Edmonton, Alberta.

[399] Georgina Donald Biography.

[400] *Ibid.*

[401] Donald interview, May 2005

[402] *Ibid.*

[403] *Ibid.*

[404] *Ibid.*

[405] Donald biography

[406] This profile is based on an interview conducted by the author. May 2005

[407] *Ibid.*

[408] *Ibid.*

[409] *Ibid.*

[410] *Ibid.*

[411] *Ibid.*

[412] *bid.*

[413] *Ibid.*

[414] *Ibid.*

[415] *Ibid.*

[416] *Ibid.*

[417] Peter Erasmus, *Buffalo Days and Nights*, as told to Henry Thompson (Calgary: Glenbow Institute and Fifth House Publishers, 1999), vi.

[418] Name <http://www.gov.edmonton.ab.ca/comm_..._attractions/fort/1885/erasmus> June 2005

[419] Grant McEwan, *Metis Makers of History* (Saskatoon: Western Producers Prairie Books, 1981), 68.

[420] *Ibid., 68–69.*

[421] "Peter Erasmus" www.peakfinder.com/people.asp?PersonsName=Erasmus,+Peter> Accessed May 23, 2003

[422] Erasmus, Buffalo Days and Nights, viii.

[423] James Ernest Nix, "Erasmus, Peter (1833-1931), Canadian Methodist lay assistant to Indian missionaries," The Alberta Conference of the United Church of Canada, 1964-1965. Edmonton: United Church of Canada, 1965

[424] McEwan, Metis Makers of History, 70.

[425] "Peter Erasmus" <http://www.gov.edmonton.ab.ca/comm_..._attractions/fort/1885/erasmus.html. Accessed May 2003

[426] Nix, "Erasmus, Peter."

[427] Erasmus, *Buffalo Days and Nights.* vi

[428] Office of the Treaty Commissioner, "Peter Erasmus"; <http://www.otc.ca/modules.php?name=Sections&op= viewarticle&artid=31>. May 2003

[429]"Mount Erasmus" http://www.ourheritage.net/hector_pages/erasmus_mtn> Accessed May 2003

[430]Nix, "Erasmus, Peter"; <http://www.gov.edmonton.ab.ca/comm_..._attractions/fort/1885/erasmus.htm l. Accessed May 2003

[431]Lee Ann Shank, Nomination for Cora Fedyk's Esquao Aboriginal Achievement Awards, Institute for the Advancement of Aboriginal Women. 2002

[432]Eric E. Nystrom, Esquao Awards, 2002 Nomination.

[433]Telephone interview with Cora Fedyk in May 2005

[434]Shank, 2002

[435]Nystrom, 2002

[436]Institute for the Advancement of Aboriginal Women. Retrieved from http://www.iaaw.org

[437]Shank, 2002

[438]Tribal Chiefs Institute, *In Their Footsteps: Contributions of First Nations Peoples of Alberta* (Edmonton: Duval House, 2001) 17.

[439]Terry Lusty, "Sports advocate, gentle warrior leaves us," *Alberta Sweetgrass*, September, 1995, 10.

[440]Tribal Chiefs Institute, *In Their Footsteps,* 17.

[441]Lusty, "Sports advocate, gentle warrior leaves us," 10.

[442]*Ibid.*

[443]Tribal Chiefs Institute, *In Their Footsteps: Contributions of First Nations Peoples of Alberta* (Edmonton: Duval House, 2001) 17.

[444]Tribal Chiefs Institute, *In Their Footsteps: Contributions of First Nations Peoples of Alberta* (Edmonton: Duval House, 2001) 17.

[445]Speaking notes, Terry Lusty, John Thomas Fletcher, Athlete, Builder, War Veteran

[446]Speaking notes, Terry Lusty, John Thomas Fletcher, Athlete, Builder, War Veteran

[447]Terry Lusty, "Sports advocate, gentle warrior leaves us," *Alberta Sweet*grass, September, 1995, 10.

[448]Terry Fortin Curriculum Vitae, Quality Learning Solutions Inc.

[449]Terry Fortin, "Teachers Made the Difference," *ATA Magazine 82* (June 2002); <http://www.teachers.Ab.ca/archive/magazine/teachers.ab.ca/index.cfm290.ht m> (accessed March 23, 2005).

[450]*Ibid.*

[451]David Bell, ed., *Sharing Our Success: Ten Case Studies in Aboriginal Schooling* (Kelowna: Society for the Advancement of Excellence in Education, 2004) 9.

[452]Terry Fortin Curriculum Vitae.

[453]Terry Fortin Curriculum Vitae.

[454]Lella Blumer, "Superintendent Steps Down: Fortin Happy With Growth of Catholic Faith Community," *Western Catholic Reporter,* March 22, 1999; <http://www.wcr..ab.ca/news/1999/0322/terryfortin032299.shtml> (accessed June 30, 2005).

[455]Terry Fortin, "Teachers Made the Difference."

[456]National Archives of Canada. Canada Census, 1901, T-6551, Lac la Biche, 4. Note that a different date is given in Louison's 1886 scrip application, but many of the dates in the latter are inaccurate: RG 15, Series D-II-8-c, Volume 1384.

[457] Gregory A. Johnson, Lac la Biche Chronicle: The Early Years (Portage College and the Town of Lac la Biche, 1999), 179.

[458] National Archives of Canada. 1886 scrip application of Louison Fosseneuve: RG 15, Series D-II-8-c, Volume 1384.

[459] Johnson, Lac la Biche Chronicle, 177.

[460] Letter of Christophe Tissier, Dunvegan, to Henri Faraud, September 19, 1867. Provincial Archives of Alberta, 91.345, Box 5, Item 56.

[461] National Archives of Canada.Lac la Biche RC Marriages, 1867.

[462] Provincial Archives of Manitoba. Hudson's Bay Company Archives. B.224/a/15, entry of January, 13, 1869.

[463] Provincial Archives of Manitoba. Hudson's Bay Company Archives, B.224/a/15 , winter establishment, 1870-71.

[464] Lac la Biche RC Marriages, 1872.

[465] Provincial Archives of Manitoba. Hudson's Bay Company Archives, B.60/e/18, Reel IM1255, *Edmonton Post Report,* 1889, 5.

[466] Quoted in Johnson, Lac la Biche Chronicle. 176–189.

[467] Gabriel Breynat, *Cinquante Ans au pays de neiges* (Montreal: Editions fides, 1947), 89–90.

[468] Johnson, *Lac la Biche Chronicle,* 178.

[469] Johnson, *Lac la Biche Chronicle,* 179–180. Janey Canuck [Emily Ferguson Murphy], *Seeds of Pine* (Toronto: Musson Book Co., 1992), 92–94.

[470] Personal interview with Marge Freidel, May 8, 2005, conducted by Cora Voyageur May 2005

[471] *Ibid.*

[472] Inna Dansereau, "Nursing Assistants in High Demand" *Alberta Sweetgrass* (October 2001), 13.

[473] Personal interview with Marge Freidel.

[474] *Ibid.*

[475] *Ibid.*

[476] Alfred Garrioch, *A Hatchet Mark in Duplicate* (Toronto: Ryerson Press, 1929).

[477] Scrip applications of Garrioch children, RG 15, Series D-ii-8-a, Vol. 1321, Reel C14928. Garrioch, *A Hatchet Mark in Duplicate.*

[478] Letter to Bishop Young, October 13, 1884, Provincial Archives of Alberta, 70.387, A.281, item 104.

[479] Garrioch, *A Hatchet Mark in Duplicate,* 59.

[480] Garrioch, *A Hatchet Mark in Duplicate,* 247–8.

[481] Alfred Garrioch, *First Furrows* (Winnipeg, 1923) and The Correction Line (Winnipeg, 1932).

[482] Provincial Archives of Alberta: Correspondence to Bishop Young, 70.387, A. 281, Item 104-106; Correspondence to Archbishop Reeve, A. 380, Item 7; Correspondence to Bishop Bompas, A.429, Items 1, 2, 6; Translations. Some of Garrioch's correspondence is held at the Anglican Church of England Archives in Toronto, Ontario

[483] Bill Mah, "Metis leader wins national award," Edmonton Journal, October 21, 1997; Terrie Petz-Welwood, "Genaille receives medal," The Russell Banner, October 28, 1997. The Governor General's Award in Commemoration of the Person's Case, 1997, was awarded in commemoration of a case that involved the British Privy Council decision in 1929 to declare Canadian women to be persons and thus eligible for the Senate.

[484] Letter from the YES Canada Committee (Harry Near, Les Campbell, and Gordon Ashworth) to Sheila Genaille, October 27, 1992.

[485] Interview with Pauline M. Vaugeois. February 2005

[486] Statement by Sheila Genaille to the 37th Parliament, 2nd Session, Standing Committee on Finance, Evidence Contents, November 8, 2002; <http://www.parl.gc.ca/committee/CommitteePublication.aspx?SourceId=11931> (accessed June 1, 2005).

[487] Petz-Welwood, "Genaille receives medal."

[488] Ibid.

[489] "Sheila Genaille", Indian and Northern Affairs Canada; <http://www.ainc-inac.gc.ca/ch/dec/genail_e.html> (accessed June 20, 2003).

[490] "Aboriginal women in leadership," Aboriginal Times, 3 (June, 1999).

[491] Metis National Council of Women, President Bio; <http://www.metiswomen.ca/home/president_bio.htm> (accessed June 1, 2005).

[492] Indian and Northern Affairs Canada.

[493] Ibid.

[494] "I'll Never be Too Old to Learn," The Native Voice (March 1958), 3.

[495] Duane Champagne, "James Gladstone," in The Native North American Almanac (Detroit: Gale Research, 1994), 1064.

[496] "Senator James Gladstone, 1887-1971," Saskatchewan Indian 2 (September 1971), 1.

[497] Ibid.

[498] Champagne, "James Gladstone," 1064.

[499] Ken Bolton, Sharon A. Fogerty, Donalee Saul and Sheenaid Ursan, "James Gladstone," in The Albertans (Edmonton: Lone Pine Publishing, 1981), 130.

[500] "I'll Never be Too Old to Learn," 3.

[501] Phyllis Cardinal, In their Footsteps: Contributions of First Nations People in Alberta (Edmonton: Duval House, 2001), 20.

[502] Personal communication with Heather Poitras, In Loving Memory of Late Joey Wayne Gladue.

[503] Letter from Kipohtakaw Wheelers Dance Group, Alexander Reserve, May 4, 2000.

[504] Poitras.

[505] Letter from Kipohtakaw Wheelers.

[506] Yvonne Irene Gladue, "Accident Claims Life of Dancer," Alberta Sweetgrass (September 13, 1999); <http://www.ammsa.com/sweetgrass/SEPT99.html> (accessed May 5, 2005).

[507] Edmonton Metis Cultural Dance Society, Community Scholarship Program; <http://www.metisdance.com/scholarships.asp> (accessed May 5, 2005).

[508] Poitras.

[509] Norris Reta, Nomination Form, 1997 Esquao Awards

[510] January 3, 2000 vol. 26 No. 45 p. 55

[511] *Ibid*

[512] *Ibid*

[513] Metis Cultural Dance Society Publication

[514] *Ibid*

[515] Canadian Council for the Arts, Press Release, Ottawa, July 10, 2003. http://www.canadacouncil.ca/news/releases /2003/qg127245397155625000.htm accessed May 2005

[516] "Louise Bernice Halfe" Who's Who. Poet in the School, Saskatchewan, http://www.poets.ca/linktext/direct/halfe/htm. accessed April 2005

[517] "Louise Bernice Halfe" Banff Centre, Aboriginal Arts Faculty http://www.banff-centre.ca/aboriginal_ arts/faculty/halfe_louise.htm accessed, accessed April 2005

[518] CBC News, CBC Saskatchewan, Arts Report, July 17, 2003.

[519] Banff Centre, Aboriginal Arts Program, July 23, 2003.

[520] CBC News, CBC Saskatchewan, Arts Report, July 17, 2003.

[521] Banff Centre, Aboriginal Arts Program, July 23, 2003.

[522] Adrian Hope - Kikino Metis Settlement - 1978 at the Alberta Vocational College in Grouardhttp://www.ualberta.ca/~walld/hope.html> Accessed April 2005

[523] Terry Lusty, "Adrian Hope," *Alberta Pioneers* (1980), 15–16. Toronto, OISE Press,

[524] "Adrian Hope dies," *Windspeaker, 4* (January 2, 1986), 10.

[525] *Ibid.*

[526] "Adrian Hope great champion of Alberta's Metis," *Calgary Herald*, February 22, 1986, D10.

[527] *Ibid.*

[528] Lusty, Alberta Pioneers.

[529] "Adrian Hope dies," Windspeaker, 4 (January 2, 1986), 10.

[530] An earlier version of this profile appears in *Hidden in Plain Sight: Contributions of Aboriginal Peoples to Canadian Identity and Culture,* ed. David Newhouse, Cora J. Voyageur and Dan Beavon (Toronto: University of Toronto Press, in press). Cheryl Petten, "Gala Salutes Achievement [National Aboriginal Achievement Awards]," *Windspeaker 20* (2002).

[531] *Contemporary Native Art in Canada: Alex Janvier* (Toronto: Royal Ontario Museum, 1978), 2.

[532] "Alberta Artist recognized with Lifetime Aboriginal Achievement Award," Canadian Press Newswire, January 2002, 23.

[533] Royal Ontario Museum, 3.

[534] *Ibid.*

[535] *Ibid.*

[536] *Ibid.,* 4.

[537] *Ibid.*

[538] Ibid.

[539] *Ibid.*

[540] *Ibid.,* 6

[541] Elizabeth Lumley, ed., "Alex Janvier," in *Canadian Who's Who 2003*, (Toronto: University of Toronto Press, 2003), 671–72.

[542] The completed profile was submitted by the author and no citations are available as a result.

[543] Exovedate was a term used by Louis Riel to describe his provisional government. It derives from Latin "ex" for out of, and "ovile" for fold. According to Maggie Siggins, many of his "flock" had difficulty getting their tongues around the term and called themselves la petit provisoire. Maggie Siggins, Riel: a Life of Revolution (Toronto: Harper Collins Publishers, 1994), 376.

[544] Profile based on an interview with Connie Johnson in June 2005

[545] *Ibid.*

[546] *Ibid.*

[547] *Ibid.*

[548] *Ibid.*

[549] Walter Bigbeel, *This Path We Travel,* (Washington, DC: Smithsonian Institute, 1994).

[550] *First Nations Drum,* Biography, Margo Kane, Fall 2000.

[551] *Ibid.*

[552] *Ibid.*

[553] *Ibid.*

[554] *Ibid.*

[555] Sandy Greer, "Margo Kane," *Turtle Quarterly* (Spring/Summer 1991), 30.

[556] *Ibid.*

[557] *First Nations Drum,* Biography, Margo Kane, Fall 2000.

[558] Grouard RC Baptisms, 1864.

[559] Provincial Archives of Manitoba, Hudson's Bay Company Archives, F21, Journal of Athabasca, 1786.

[560] Fort Des Prairies, Marriages, 1846, notes on file with author.

[561] Fort Vermilion and District Historical Association, *Fort Vermilion: People in Our Vast Trading North.*

[562] Fort Chipewyan Marriages, 1885.

[563] Hudson's Bay Company Archives, B.39/e/16, Fort Smith Post Report, 1889 (included with Fort Chipewyan Post Report).

[564] Hudson's Bay Company Archives, B.39/e/22, Fort Chipewyan Post Report, December 12, 1892, by J. MacDougall, 27.

[565] RG 15, Series D-II-8-c, Volume 1353, C14979, 1899 scrip application of Joseph Lafleur.

[566] Canada, 1906 Census, North West Province, District 21, T-18363.

[567] John Lafleur, personal comment, 1982.

[568] Hudson's Bay Company Archives, B.348/e/2, Fort Smith Post Report, June 25–July 1, 1892.

[569] Provincial Archives of Alberta, Oblate Correspondence, 91.345, Box 6, Item 56, Letter from St. Henri mission, Father Christophe Tissier to Msgr. Faraud, 17 June 1868.

[570] Fort Vermilion and District Historical Association, *Fort Vermilion: People in Our Vast Trading North.*

[571] Terry Lusty, "Willard Lewis on a tear for a title," *Windspeaker*: the top Aboriginal News for April 1998; < http://www.ammsa.com/windspeaker/WINDNEWS-APR98.html> (accessed July 7, 2003).

[572] Tribal Chief Institute, *In Their Footsteps: Contributions of First Nations Peoples of Alberta* (Edmonton: Duval House, 2001) 54.

[573] Tribal Chief Institute, *In Their Footsteps,* 54.

[574] D. Maria Cheechoo, "Local boxer a knock-out," *Alberta Sweetgrass,* December 1994, 12.

[575] Tribal Chief Institute, *In Their Footsteps,* 54.

[576] Terry Lusty, "Willard Lewis on a tear for a title."

[577] BoxRec, Willard Lewis; < http://www.boxrec.com/boxer_display.php?boxer_id=007933> (accessed June 2, 2005).

[578] Bob Oliver, "Red Thunder Rock rolls into Kahnasake; Cruiserweight boxing champ unwinds before Montreal fight," *Eastern Door 9* (23); < http://eastern-door.com/9-23/9-23-5.htm> (accessed July 20, 2003).

[579] Terry Lusty, "Bruisers bust out at fundraiser," *Alberta Sweetgrass,* February 1995, 12.

[580] Terry Lusty, "Fighters 3-0 on Edmonton card," *Alberta Sweetgrass,* September 1995, 9.

[581] Canadian Professional Boxing Federation, Official Ratings, April 2003; < http://www.boxeo boxing.com/ranking/canada0403.pdf > (accessed June 3, 2005).

[582] Terry Lusty, "Fighters 3-0 on Edmonton card."

[583] Louis Maurice L'Hirondelle biography supplied by the L'Hirondelle family, May 2005

[584] *Ibid.*

[585] A. McEachern" The Maurice L'Hirondelle Story" *The History of Local Government, Lac Ste Anne Area.* Stony Plain: The Reporter, 1970) np

[586] "Maurice L'Hirondelle" *East Prairie Metis: 1939-1979.* Edmonton: Federation of Metis Settlements, 1979). 31

[587] One and a Half Million for Metis Settlements. Press Release. Federation of Metis Settlements. 1973.

[588] *Ibid.*

[589] Martin Thompson. "Maurice L'Hirondelle A Fighter that Retires' *Edmonton Journal.* 1980. 1

[590] *Ibid.*

[591] *Ibid.*

[592] Mark McCallum. "Elder L'Hirondelle recalls first official Metis Assembly" *Native Network News,* August 1990. 14

[593] *East Prairie Metis,* 1979.

[594] "Elder's dedication crucial to founding settlements" Alberta Sweetgrass. November, 1994. 5

[596] Dianne Meili, "Albert Lightning," in *Those Who Know: Profiles of Alberta's Native Elders* (Edmonton: NeWest Press, 1991), 85.

[597] *Ibid., 86.*

[598] Heather Andrews, "Buffalo Child laid to rest," *Windspeaker,* April 26, 1991, 17.

[599] Laurie Meijer Drees, *The Indian Association of Alberta: A History of Political Action* (UBC Press: Vancouver, BC, 2002), 148–49.

[600] Meili, "Albert Lightning," 81, 86.

[601] Andrews, "Buffalo Child laid to rest," 17.

[602] Meili, "Albert Lightning," 81–82.

[603] Roland Bellerose, "Leroy Little Bear," Aboriginal Times 3 (1999), 10.

[604] "Native American Studies Professor Leroy Little Bear to Receive National Aboriginal Achievement Award," University of Lethbridge Press Release, January 15, 2003.

[605] National Aboriginal Achievement Foundation, "Leroy Little Bear," NAAF Awards Program, 2003.

[606] Bellerose, "Leroy Little Bear," 10.

[607] "Leroy Little Bear," Faculty Profile, The Banff Centre.

[608] "University of Lethbridge Senate Announces 2004 Honorary Degree Recipients" retrieved from http://www.uleth.ca/notice/display.html?b=4&s=978

[609] Willock & Sax Ltd. Gallery, George Littlechild; <http://www.willockandsax-gallery.com/twillock/littlec1.htm> (accessed June 26, 2003).

[610] Artists for Kids - George Littlechild - "Plains Cree Chiefs"; <http://www.artists4kids.com/product9.php> (accessed June 30, 2003).

[611] George Littlechild resume; <http://www.georgelittlechild.com/resume.html>

[612] Artists for Kids - George Littlechild.

[613] Artists For Kids Gallery, George Littlechild; <http://www.artists4kids.com/prod-uct9.php> (accessed July 7, 2003).

[614] *Ibid.*

[615] George Littlechild; <http://www.tandanya.com.au/touring_exhib/4circles/lit-tlechild.html> (accessed June 1, 2005).

[616] Artists For Kids Gallery, George Littlechild.

[617] First Nations Art: An Introduction to Contemporary Native Artists in Canada, George Littlechild; <http://collections.ic.gc.ca/artists/littlechild.html> (accessed June 19, 2003).

[618] George Littlechild Biography; <http://sd71.bc.ca/Sd71/Edulinks/BCATA/files/georgebio.htm> (accessed June 30, 2003).

[619] Willie Littlechild, Curriculum Vitae supplied to author with nomination form.

[620] Duane Champagne, "J. Wilton Littlechild," *The Native North American Almanac* (Detroit: Gale Research, 1994) 1092.

[621] Champagne, "J. Wilton Littlechild," 1092.

[622] Littlechild, Curriculum Vitae.

[623] *Ibid.*

[624] Terry Lusty, "Origin of the North American Indigenous Games: The How, Why, Where and When," unpublished paper provided to editor by the author.

[625] Terry Lusty, "Former MP active Internationally," *Alberta Sweetgrass,* August 1994, 2.

[626] Heather Andrews Miller, "Willie Littlechild headlines student club activities," *Alberta Sweetgrass,* December 1994, 6.

[627] Terry Lusty, "Former MP active Internationally," 2.

[628] Littlechild, Curriculum Vitae.

[629] Champagne, "J. Wilton Littlechild," 1092.

[630] Littlechild, Curriculum Vitae.

[631] Linda Goyette. History Lives through Lusty's lens. *Edmonton Journal*. August 2, 1998. B1

[632] *Ibid.*

[633] Personal interview with Terry Lusty, Edmonton. May 2005

[634] *Ibid.*

[635] *Ibid.*

[636] Terry Lusty biography provided by subject. May 2005

[637] Lusty interview, May 2005

[638] John W. Friesen and Terry Lusty. *The Metis of Canada: An Annotated Bibliography.* (Toronto: OISE Press,1980).

[639] Terry Lusty. *Louis Riel, Humanitarian.* (Edmonton: Northwest Publishing and Lithographing Ltd, 1973).

[640] Lusty biography, May 2005

[641] *Ibid.*

[642] Lusty interview, May 2005

[643] Lusty biography, May 2005

[644] *Ibid.*

[645] Norma Large, "Healing Justice," *Alberta Views,* May/June 2001, 20–25.

[646] Alan Chambers, "First Judge of an Aboriginal Court in Canada," *The Edmonton Journal,* February 6, 2001, B4.

[647] Cam Cole papersMandamin%20Bio.html (accessed June 23, 2005).

[648] *Ibid.*

[649] *Ibid.*

[650] Large, "Healing Justice."

[651] Chambers, "First Judge of an Aboriginal Court in Canada."

[652] Large, "Healing Justice."

[653] Chambers, "First Judge of an Aboriginal Court in Canada."

[654] Chambers, "First Judge of an Aboriginal Court in Canada."

[655] Personal interview with Gordon Margetts, Edmonton, Alberta, May 27, 2005.

[656] *Ibid.*

[657] City of Edmonton. Edmontonians of the Century. (Edmonton: Corporate Identity Consulting Inc, 2004)

[658] Gordon Margetts interview, May 2005

[659] *Ibid.*

[660] *Ibid.*

[661] *Ibid.*

[662] *Ibid.*

[663] Personal interview with Nellie Carlson, Edmonton, May 2005

[664] *Ibid.*

[665] Awasis means "child" in the Cree language.

[666] Gordon Margetts interview, May 2005

[667] City of Edmonton. *Edmontonians of the Century.* (Edmonton: Corporate Identity Consulting Inc, 2004)

[668]Richard T. Prince and Cora Voyageur, Moostoos. *Dictionary of Canadian Biography,* vol. 14, 1911–1920 (Toronto: University of Toronto Press, 1998).

[669]*Ibid.*

[670]*Ibid.*

[671]*Ibid.*

[672]*Ibid.*

[673]*Ibid.*

[674]*Ibid.*

[675]*Ibid.*

[676]Donald Punch, *The Metis* (Toronto: James Lorimer & Company, 1988), 134.

[677]Murray Dobbin, *The One-And-A -Half Men* (Vancouver: New Star Books, 1981), 34–36.

[678]Punch, *The Metis,* 134.

[679]Dobbin, *The One-And-A -Half Men,* 37.

[680]*Ibid., 37–38.*

[681]*Ibid., 38–40.*

[682]*Ibid., 38–42.*

[683]Punch, *The Metis*, 134–135.

[684]Dobbin, *The One-And-A -Half Men,* 64.

[685]Alberta Order in Council No. 1095, 12 December 1934, Commission Evidence, as cited in Dobbin, *The One-And-A -Half Men,* 88.

[686]Dobbin, *The One-And-A -Half Men,* 88–105.

[687]*Ibid., 88–142.*

[688]Laurie Meijer Drees, *The Indian Association of Alberta* (Vancouver: University of British Columbia Press, 2002) 26.

[689]Dobbin, *The One-And-A -Half Men,* 145.

[690]*Ibid., 160.*

[691]James Dempsey, "Henry Norwest," in *Warriors of the King: Prairie Indians in World War I* (Regina: Canadian Plains Research Centre, 1999), 52.

[692]James Dempsey, "Henry Norwest," in *Dictionary of Canadian Biography 1911-1920* (Toronto: University of Toronto Press, 1998), 786.

[693]*Ibid.*

[694]Dempsey, "Henry Norwest," in *Warriors of the King*, 52.

[695]*Ibid.*

[696]Dempsey, "Henry Norwest," *Dictionary of Canadian Biography*, 786.

[697]Dempsey, "Henry Norwest," in *Warriors of the King,* 52.

[698]Dempsey, "Henry Norwest," *Dictionary of Canadian Biography*, 786.

[699]*Ibid.*

[700]Dempsey, "Henry Norwest," in *Warriors of the King,* 52.

[701]*Ibid.*

[702]This profile is based on an interview conducted by the author in Edmonton on May 12, 2005.

[703]*Ibid.*

[704]Melanie Omeniho resume provided by subject. May 2005

[705]Omeniho interview, May 2005

[706]Omeniho resume, May 2005

[707]Omeniho interview, May 2005

[708]*Ibid.*

[709]*Ibid.*

[710]Duane Champagne, "Bernard Ominayak," in *The Native North American Almanac* (Detroit: Gale Research, 1994) 1122.

[711]*Ibid.*

[712]*Ibid.*

[713]"Chief Ominayak – This is Where We are From," *Friends of the Lubicon Court Update,* Toronto, November 25, 1997.

[714]John Godard, *Last Stand of the Lubicon Cree* (Vancouver: Douglas and McIntyre Ltd., 1991).

[715]Duane Champagne, "Bernard Ominayak," 1122.

[716]"Chief Ominayak – This is Where We are From."

[717]Godard, *Last Stand of the Lubicon Cree.*

[718]*Ibid.*

[719]*Ibid.*

[720]Debbie Ben Mahjoub, reference letter for Lillian's Esquao Award 2000 nomination. Institute for the advancement of Aboriginal Women. Edmonton, 2000.

[721]Taken from Lillian's submission for the Great Aboriginal Albertan's Project.

[722]*Ibid.*

[723]Nomination submission for the 2000 Esquao Awards.

[724]Sonya Kobelsky, reference letter for Lillian's Esquao Award 2000 nomination.

[725]Nomination submission for the 2000 Esquao Awards.

[726]"Women of Distinction: Politics," *Aboriginal Times, 2* (July/August 1998), 13.

[727]*Ibid.*

[728]*Ibid.*

[729]"Aboriginal Women in Leadership," *Aboriginal Times, 3* (June 1999), 7.

[730]Metis Nation of Alberta. Minister of Economic Development. April 19, 2002. retrieved from http://www.Metisnation.ca/MNC/CABINET/MIN_economic.html

[731]George Vass, reference letter for Audrey's Esquao Award 2002 nomination.

[732]*Ibid.*

[733]Audrey Poitras. Esquao Awards, 2002. Edmonton: Institute for the Advancement of Aboriginal Women, 2002)

[734]*Ibid.*

[735]Barbara Hager, *Honour Song* (Vancouver: Raincoast Book Distribution, 1996), 52.

[736]*Ibid.*

[737]*Ibid.*

[738]Paul Gessell, "Don't call me mellow: Hold on to your socks, warns rebel artist Jane Poitras," *Ottawa Citizen,* November 7, 2002, E1.

[739]Clint Beuhler, "Poitras wins $5,000 Scholarship," *Windspeaker 2* (July 13, 1984), 8.

[740]Hager, *Honour Song,* 55.

[741]First Nations Art Web site; <http://collections.ic.gc.ca/artists/poitras_janeash.html> (accessed June 16, 2003).

[742] Phyliss Cardinal, *In their Footsteps: Contributions of First Nations People in Alberta* (Edmonton: Duval House, 2001), 9.

[743] Gessell, "Don't call me mellow."

[744] *Ibid.*

[745] *Ibid.*

[746] *Ibid.*

[747] *Ibid.*

[748] *Ibid.*

[749] *Ibid.*

[750] *Ibid.*

[751] *Ibid.*

[752] *Ibid.*

[753] Rob McKinley. "CFL father and some tackle Native issues". *Windspeaker.* October 1998. Vol. 16(6). 27

[754] "Jed Roberts" retrieved from http://www.brainyistory.com/events/1967/November _10_1967_133954.html

[755] McKinley, 1998

[756] *Ibid.*

[757] John R. Hayes. "Lineman establishing himself as role model" Windspeaker. October 1995. Vol. 13(6). 20

[758] *Ibid.*

[759] "Eskimos defence ready to copy Grey Cup (against Toronto Argonauts)" Canadian Press NewsWire (Toronto: November 22, 1996) na

[760] *Ibid.*

[761] *Ibid.*

[762] Gerry Prince. "Roberts Ride is Over" retrieved from <http://www.canoe.ca/Slam03031/cfl_edm-sun.html>

[763] Dan Barnes. "Gizmo heads for Hall of fame" *CanWest News.* January 27, 2006. 1

[764] Hayes, 1995

[765] Home of the Golden Bears and Pandas. "Golden Bears Football" .retrieved from http://www.bears. ualberta.ca? Football/Men/?pt=news&ID-1457

[766] Prince Dianne Meili, "Samson's long life shows him changes in Cree culture over the years," *Windspeaker, 25* (March 1988), 13.

[767] Rona Simonson, Nancy (Ward) Samson (1914-1998), 2002; <http://www.albertasource.ca/aspenland/eng/women/popwomen_samson.html> (accessed May 29, 2005).

[768] 50th Wedding Anniversary program, 2002; <http://www.albertasource.ca/aspenland/images/bannerPics.gif> (accessed May 29, 2005).

[769] Heritage Community Foundation, "The Righteous Anger of Queen Mother Morningstar: The Sequence of Events," 2002; <http://www.albertasource.ca/lawcases/constitutional/morningstar/trial_sequence_of_events.htm> (accessed May 6, 2005).

[770] *Ibid.*

[771] Terry Lusty, "Elder leaves behind a lasting legacy," *Alberta Sweetgrass,* June 10, 2000; <http://wwwammsa.com/sweetgrass/JUNE2000.html> (accessed May 30, 2005).

[772] Office of the Registrar and Student Awards, University of Alberta, "Native Studies," 2005; <http://www.registrar.ualberta.ca/ro.cfm?id=561> (accessed May 29, 2005).

[773] *Ibid.*

[774] Information for this profile was provided through an interview with Sheldon Sewepagaham. July, 2005

[775] *Ibid.*

[776] *Ibid.*

[777] University of British Columbia. Department of Educational Studies – 1998 Theses and Dissertations. (Vancouver, University of British Columbia, Department of Educational, 1998). Retrieved from http://www.educ.ubc.ca/downloads/Library/Thesis%20&%20Dissertations%201988.pdf

[779] Sewepagaham interview, July 2005

[780] *Ibid.*

[781] Peace River School Division. "FNMI coordinator to play role in 2006 Arctic Winter Games" (Peace River: Peace River School Division News Release, 2006). 1

[782] Sewepagaham interview, July 2005

[783] "Chief of Blood Tribe Shot Both Sides Dies," The Camsell Arrow 9 (April 1956), 9.

[784] J.W. Grant MacEwan, "Shot on Both Sides," in *Portraits of the Plains* (Toronto: McGraw-Hill, 1971), 214.

[785] "Chief of Blood Tribe Shot Both Sides Dies."

[786] Ibid.

[787] MacEwan, "Shot on Both Sides," 215.

[788] Ibid.

[789] MacEwan, "Shot on Both Sides," 214.

[790] "Chief of Blood Tribe Shot Both Sides Dies."

[791] MacEwan, "Shot on Both Sides," 216.

[792] Ibid.

[793] This profile is based on an interview conducted by the author in Edmonton on May 12, 2005.

[794] *Ibid.*

[795] *Ibid.*

[796] *Ibid.*

[797] *Ibid.*

[798] *Ibid.*

[799] *Ibid.*

[800] *Ibid.*

[801] *Ibid.*

[802] *Ibid.*

[803] Clint Beuhler, "Cree Spiritual Leader Dies," Windspeaker, July 1984, 4.

[804] *Ibid.*

[805] *Ibid.*

[806] *Ibid.*

[807] Joe Rosenthal, "Chief Smallboy," in *Indians: A Sketching Odyssey* (Toronto: Clarke, Irwin & Company, 1971), 65–74.

[808] Beuhler, "Cree Spiritual Leader Dies," 4.

[809] Heather Andrews, "Scholarship established in chief's name," *Windspeaker,* April 1991, 14.

[810] *Ibid.*

[811] Everett Soop, I see my tribe is still behind me! (Calgary: Glenbow-Alberta Institute, 1990), 8.

[812] David Bly, "Native Cartoonist used humour to fight injustice," The Calgary Herald, August 17, 2001, B4.

[813] Sandy Greer, "The Pitbull of Native journalism," *The Globe and Mail,* August 29, 2001, R7.

[814] Bly,"Native Cartoonist used humour to fight injustice," B4.

[815] Harmony Rice, "Humourist tells it like it is," *First Nations Messenger,* January/February, 2001.

[816] *Ibid.*

[817] Greer, "The Pitbull of Native journalism," R7.

[818] Bly,"Native Cartoonist used humour to fight injustice," B4.

[819] *Ibid.*

[820] "Sheldon Souray" Legends of Hockey: NHL Player Search. Retrieved from http//:www.legendsofhockey.net:8080legends of Hockey/sjp/SearchPlayer.jsp?player=10...

[821] R. John Hayes. Devils' draft anchors contending defense" *Alberta Sweetgrass,* February 1996. 11

[822] David Winchar. "Aboriginal NHL'ers shine in Montreal." *Winspeaker.* February 2001 Vol. 18(10) 18

[823] Hayes, 1996

[824] *Ibid.*

[825] Winchar, 2001

[826] David Stubbs. "Souray exists slump just when habs need him most" CanWest News March 27, 2006. 1

[827] Hayes, 1996"

[828] "Sheldon Souray" New Jersey's Hunk A handsome Devil. *Sports Illustrated.* December 2001. 86

[829] Legends of Hockey

[830] *Ibid.*

[831] *Ibid.*

[832] *Ibid.*

[833] Legislative Assembly of Alberta, "The Honourable Ralph G. Steinhauer, 1974-79"; http://www.assembly.ab.ca/lao/library/lt-gov/steinhau.htm>. May 2005

[834] *Ibid.*

[835] Duane Champagne, ed., The Native American Almanac (Detroit: Gale Research, 1994), 1170.

[836] Legislative Assembly of Alberta, May 2005

[837] *Ibid.*

[838] Tribal Chiefs Institute, In *Their Footsteps: Contributions of First Nations People of Alberta* (Edmonton: Duval House, 2001), 55.

[839] *Ibid.*

[840] Tribal Chiefs Institute, 2001

[841] Champagne, 1994

[842] Ken Bolton et. al., The Albertans (Edmonton: Lone Pine Publishing, 1981), 164.

[843] *Ibid.*

[844] Tribal Chiefs Institute, 2001

[845] Bolton, 1981

[846] Duane Champagne, "Gerald Tailfeathers," in *The Native North American Almanac* (Detroit: Gale Research, 1994), 1172.

[847] *Ibid.*

[848] J. W. Grant MacEwen, "Gerald Tailfeathers," in *Portrait from the Plains* (Toronto: McGraw Hill, 1971), 273–278.

[849] "Alberta Artist recognized with Lifetime Aboriginal Achievement Award," Canadian Press Newswire, January 2002, 23.

[850] Hugh Dempsey, *Tailfeathers: Indian Artist* (Calgary: Glenbow Alberta Institute, 1970).

[851] *Ibid.*

[852] *Ibid.*

[853] MacEwen, "Gerald Tailfeathers," 273–278.

[854] *Ibid.*

[855] Dempsey, *Tailfeathers: Indian Artist.*

[856] *Ibid.*

[857] Adapted from Hugh Dempsey, *Tom Three Persons: Legend of an Indian Cowboy* (Saskatoon: Purich Publishing, 1997) 13–16.

[858] *Ibid.*, 21, 61, 64, 117.

[859] *Ibid.*, 42–44.

[860] *Ibid.*, 87.

[861] *Ibid.*, 11–12, 21–22.

[862] Marie Barr, "Tom Three Persons," Cardston Chronicle, 8 August 1989, cited in Mary Tollstrup, "Tom Three Persons," 2000; <http://www.telusplanet.net/public/mtoll/threet2.htm> (accessed May 23, 2005).

[863] Letter written by James L. Tomkins, grandson of Peter Tomkins Jr., to Geoff Burtonshaw, November 25, 2002.

[864] *Ibid.*

[865] "Key Figures – Peter Tomkins Jr.," Alberta Metis Historical Society, 2001; <http://collections.ic.gc.calalbertametis/history/petertimkins.htm> (accessed June 19, 2003).

[866] Murray Dobbin, The One-And-A -Half Men, (Vancouver: New Star Books, 1981), 64.

[867] Alberta Order in Council No. 1095, December 12, 1934, Commission Evidence, p. 323, cited in Dobbin, The One-And-A -Half Men, 88.

[868] Dobbin, *The One-And-A -Half Men,* 88–105.

[869] Donald Punch, The Métis (Toronto: James Lorimer & Company, 1988), 142.

[870] Dobbin, *The One-And-A -Half Men,* 118–120.

[871] Punch, The Métis, 143.

[872] "Key Figures – Peter Tomkins Jr."

[873] *Ibid.*

[874] *Ibid.*

[875] An earlier version of this profile appears in Hidden in Plain Sight: Contributions of Aboriginal Peoples to Canadian Identity and Culture, vol. 1, ed. David Newhouse, Cora J. Voyageur and Dan Beavon (Toronto: University of Toronto Press, in press).

[876] <http://www.aptn.ca/en/press/19990831_html>

[877] <http://www.nabacanada.com/About-Naba.htm>
<http://www.ammsa.com/achieve/AA99-D.Tuccaro.html>

[878] *Ibid.*

[879] *Ibid.*

[880] *Ibid.*

[881] <http://www.nabacanada.com/About-Naba.htm>

[882] <http://www.aptn.ca/en/press/19990831_html>

[883] <http://www.ammsa.com/achieve/AA99-D.Tuccaro.html>

[884] "Top 40 under 40: reflections on the quality of leadership," *Financial Post Magazine,* April 1998, 18–36.

[885] "Neegan president wins aboriginal business award," Edmonton Journal, March 1999, 1.

[886] <http://www.nabacanada.com/About-Naba.htm>

[887] *Ibid.*

[888] *Ibid.*

[889] Information for this profile was obtained through personal and telephone interviews with the subject.

[890] *Ibid.*

[891] *Ibid.*

[892] *Ibid.*

[893] *Ibid.*

[894] Heather Andrews, "Stanley-Venne named Metis Woman of the Year," *Windspeaker,* June 1991, 14.

[895] Muriel Stanley-Venne biography; http://www.iaaw.ca/MSV_biography.htm> (accessed April 27, 2005).

[896] *Ibid.*

[897] Clint Buelher, "Past Year's Highlights Reviewed," *Windspeaker,* January 1986, 10.

[898] Mark McCallum, "NDP's Muriel Stanley-Venne calls it Quits," *Native Network News,* December 1988, 6.

[899] Laura Langstaff, "March Against Racism," *Native Network News,* April 1989, 18.

[900] Andrews, "Stanley-Venne named Metis Woman of the Year," 14.

[901] Muriel Stanley-Venne biography.

[902] *Ibid.*

[903] *Ibid.*

[904] *Ibid.*

[905] James Muretich, "Native Roots have Vinson Singing her 'red' blues Songs Again," *Vancouver Sun,* August 31, 1995, C8.

[906] "Metis Singer Gains Long Due Acclaim: Laura Vinson Wins at Alberta Recording Industry Awards," *Windspeaker,* March 1993, 13.

[907] Muretich, "Native Roots have Vinson Singing her 'red' blues Songs Again," C8.

[908] Gordon Atkinson, "Singer-Songwriter takes music in different direction," Native Network News 8 (1995), 13.

[909] Atkinson "Singer-Songwriter takes music in different direction," 13.

[910] Laura Vinson Promotional Materials, Spirit Song Productions, Edmonton, 2003.

[911] *Ibid.*

[912] *Ibid.*

[913] Ian A.L. Getty, "Walking Buffalo," in *Historica: The Canadian Encyclopedia* (2002).

[914] J.W. Grant MacEwan, "Walking Buffalo," in *Portrait from the Plains* (Toronto: McGraw Hill, 1971), 220–232.

[915] MacEwan, "Walking Buffalo," 220–232.

[916] Getty, "Walking Buffalo."

[917] *Ibid.*

[918] MacEwan, "Walking Buffalo," 220–232.

[919] "Medicine Man of Stonys [sic] Might Have Been A Doctor," Camsell Arrow 10 (May/August 1956), 41–43.

[920] MacEwan, "Walking Buffalo," 220–232.

[921] Ibid.

[922] "Democrat Wagon," in *The Canadian Oxford Dictionary,* ed. Katherine Barber (Toronto: Oxford University Press, 1998), 373.

[923] "Medicine Man of Stonys [sic] Might Have Been A Doctor," 41–43.

[924] MacEwan, "Walking Buffalo," 220–232.

[925] "Medicine Man of Stonys [sic] Might Have Been A Doctor," 41–43.

[926] MacEwan, "Walking Buffalo," 220–232.

[927] Phyllis Cardinal, In their footsteps: Contributions of First Nations People of Alberta (Edmonton: Duval House, 2001) 57.

[928] Sabrina Whyatt, "Still searching for peace," *Windspeaker,* June 1998, 20.

[929] Mary Jo Laforest, "Blond Cree brings message of hope for those with AIDS," Expositor, Brantford, Ontario, January 9, 1999, D6.

[930] "Ken Ward" http://www.fullcircleentertainment.biz/artists/pages/kward.shtml> (accessed May 5, 2003).

[931] Whyatt, "Still searching for peace," 20.

[932] Information for this profile was provided in a interview with Darren Brule, July 2005

[933] *Ibid.*

[934] *Ibid.*

[935] *Ibid.*

Appendix A: Questionnaire

The information provided below will serve as the basis for a book I want to publish tentatively called, Great Aboriginal Albertans, will highlight select Aboriginal Albertans and bring their many and diverse contributions to Alberta society to light.

Please note that this information may be used for research beyond this project. If this were to happen any information identifying the subject or the contact person will be removed.

By completing and returning this form you are giving your informed consent to participate in this project.

1. Contact Person (If different than Subject Person)
   Name:
   Address:
   Phone:
   Fax:
   Email:
   Relationship to Subject:

2. Subject Person
   Name
   Address
   Phone
   Fax
   Email

3. Vital Statistics
   Date of Birth
   Date of Death (if applicable)
   Birth Place
   Death Place
   Site of internment/inurnment (if applicable)

4. Occupation (s)

5. Aboriginal Affiliation:

Metis	Community
First Nation	Band Affiliation
Other	
Born into community?	Yes No
Married into community?	Yes No

6. Family:

Parents	Mother	Date of Birth
Father		Date of Birth
Siblings	Name(s)	Date(s) of Birth

Spouse(s)   Date(s) of Marriage

Children   Name(s)   Date(s) of Birth

7. Photo(s) Sent:
   Yes   No
   Number sent
   Subject   Description

   Other   Descriptions

8. Community Service:

9. Special Honors/Awards (if applicable)
   Name: Purpose Date   Place Awarded   Given by whom

10. Story/Contribution (50-75 words)

If you have any questions or enquiries about this project you can contact me:
   Dr. Cora Voyageur
   906 Social Sciences Tower
   University of Calgary
   2500 University Drive NW
   Calgary, Alberta   T2N 1N4

   Phone: (403) 220-6507
   Fax: (403) 282-9298
   Email: voyageur@ucalgary.ca

   Please photocopy this form and distribute it to others who might be interested
   in submitting information to profile an individual.

Appendix B: Introductory Letter to Aboriginal Community

Great Aboriginal Albertans Project

I am collecting information for a book called Great Aboriginal Albertans. This publication highlights select Aboriginal Albertans to bring to light their many and diverse contributions to Alberta society.

These profiles will highlight two groups of Aboriginal Albertans. The first is individuals who have been recognized or who have received national, provincial, municipal, or local awards. Official recognition can include the Order of Canada, Military, Citizenship, Community Service or Volunteerism Awards. The second group will profile individuals who have contributed greatly to our Alberta society but have not been formally recognized -- our unsung heroes. We all know of people who work tirelessly in our communities and have yet to receive acknowledgment. I want to draw attention to these people to show how they contribute in positive ways to Alberta society.

This book is a Who's Who of Alberta's Aboriginal community. Community members or community organizations can submit names, information, photos, and short biographies for individuals you feel have made a great contribution to Alberta society and should be included in this book.

All submissions will be reviewed by an editorial board who will decide the entries. However, remaining submissions will be held for future publication or be placed on a website. Please note that this information may be used for research beyond this project. If this were to happen any information that identifies the subject or the contact person will be removed.

Please contact:
Dr. Cora Voyageur
906 Social Sciences Tower
University of Calgary
2500 University Drive NW
Calgary, Alberta   T2N 1N4

Phone: (403) 220-6507
Fax: (403) 282-9298
Email: voyageur@ucalgary.ca

Appendix C: Newspaper Advertisement

Do you know a Great Aboriginal Albertan?

Great Aboriginal Albertans will highlight the many and diverse contributions of Alberta's celebrated and unsung Aboriginal people from 1905 to 2005. Deadline for submissions is February 28, 2003. For more information call:
Dr. Cora Voyageur
906 Social Sciences Tower
University of Calgary
2500 University Drive NW
Calgary, Alberta   T2N 1N4

Phone (403) 220-6507
Fax (403) 282-9298

Appendix D: Scrip Certificate

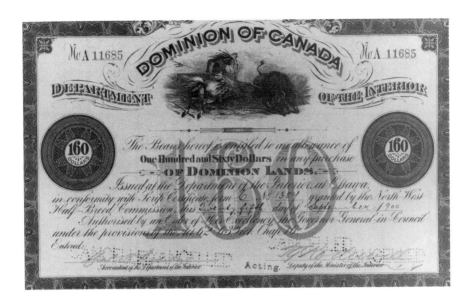

Apprendix E: Metis Settlements in Alberta

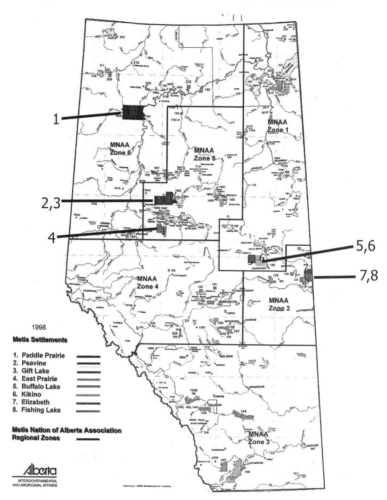

1998

Metis Settlements

1. Paddle Prairie
2. Peavine
3. Gift Lake
4. East Prairie
5. Buffalo Lake
6. Kikino
7. Elizabeth
8. Fishing Lake

Metis Nation of Alberta Association Regional Zones

Alberta
INTERGOVERNMENTAL
AND ABORIGINAL AFFAIRS

Appendix F: List of Indian Reserves inAlberta

Alexander
Alexis
Allison Bay
Amber Lake
Assineau River
Beaver Lake
Beaver Ranch
Big HornRiver Indian Cemetery
Jackfish Point
Janvier
Jean Baptiste Gambler
John D'or Prairie
Kehewin
Louis Bull
Makaoo
Montana
Namur Lake
Namur River
O'Chiese
O'Cheise Cemetery
Old Fort
Pakashan
Peace Point
Peigan
Peigan (Timber Limit)
Pigeon Lake
Puskiakiwenin
Sand Point
Saddle Lake
Samson
Sarce
Sawridge
Siksika
Stoney
Stony Plain
Sturgeon Lake
Sucker Creek
Sunchild Cree
Swan River
Tallcree
Unipouheos
Upper Hay River
Utikoomak Lake

Wabamun
Wabasca
Wadlin Lake
Whitecourt
Whitefish Lake
William McKenzie
Bistcho Lake
Blood
Blue Quills
Boyer River
Buck Lake
Bushe River
Carcajou Settlement
Cardinal River
Charles Lake
Child Lake
Chipewyan
Clear Hills
Clearwater
Cold Lake
Cornwall Lake
Cowper Lake
Coin Lake
Cornwall Lake
Devil's Gate
Dog Head
Driftpile River
Duncan's
Eden Valley
Elk River
Ermineskin
Fort McKay
Fort Vermilion
Fox Lake
Freeman
Gregoire Lake
Grouard
Halcro
Hay Lakes
Heart Lake
Horse Lake
Winefred Lake
Woodland Cree
Zama Lake

Huron County Library

Library name: Exeter Branch Library
User ID: 06492001315483

Title: My heroes have always been
Indians
Date due: 11 June 2011 23:59

Title: William & Kate : celebrating a royal
engagement
Date due: 11 June 2011 23:59

Visit us at
www.huroncounty.ca/library